The
Reference Shelf®

Marijuana Reform

The Reference Shelf
Volume 86 • Number 5
H. W. Wilson
A Division of EBSCO Information Services
Ipswich, Massachusetts
2014

GREY HOUSE PUBLISHING

The Reference Shelf

The books in this series contain reprints of articles, excerpts from books, addresses on current issues, and studies of social trends in the United States and other countries. There are six separately bound numbers in each volume, all of which are usually published in the same calendar year. Numbers one through five are each devoted to a single subject, providing background information and discussion from various points of view and concluding with an index and comprehensive bibliography that lists books, pamphlets, and articles on the subject. The final number of each volume is a collection of recent speeches. Books in the series may be purchased individually or on subscription.

Library of Congress Cataloging-in-Publication Data

Marijuana reform / [compiled by H. W. Wilson]. -- [First edition].
    pages : illustrations ; cm. -- (The reference shelf ; volume 86, number 5)
  Edition statement supplied by publisher.
  Includes bibliographical references and index.
  ISBN: 978-1-61925-436-7 (v. 86, no. 5)
  ISBN: 978-1-61925-261-5 (volume set)
    1. Marijuana--Law and legislation--United States.   2. Drug legalization--United States.
3. Marijuana--Therapeutic use--United States.   4. Marijuana--Economic aspects--United States. I. H.W. Wilson Company. II. Series: Reference shelf ; v. 86, no. 5.
HV5822.M3 M37 2014
362.295

Cover: © Jupiter Images/The Image Bank/Getty Images

The Reference Shelf, 2014, published by Grey House Publishing, Inc., Amenia, NY, under exclusive license from EBSCO Information Services, Inc.

Printed in Canada

Contents

2

Marijuana: Legalization versus Decriminalization

3

Seeking Relief: Medicinal Marijuana

4

Marijuana Reclassification: The Next Debate

5

Taxing Marijuana: Boon or Blunder?

Preface

The State of Marijuana Reform

Marijuana is the Spanish name for *Cannabis sativa* L., an herbaceous plant originally native to Asia. Cultivated for more than five thousand years, marijuana has spread around the world and has had tremendous influence on the evolution of human culture. From the hundreds of industrial uses of marijuana, to the plant's ancient role as a healing herb, to the intoxicating effects that have made marijuana one of the most widely used recreational and spiritual drugs, marijuana sits alongside wheat, rice, and potatoes as one of the most influential species in our shared socio-botanical history.

During the twentieth century, marijuana became a target in the global drive to eliminate drug use and addiction. Decades of prohibition failed to reduce interest in marijuana's healing and intoxicating effects but did help to create and support the existence of a global black market drug industry. In the late twentieth and early twenty-first centuries, laws and attitudes began to change, as countries around the world decided to decriminalize marijuana for both medical and recreational consumption. The United States has been one of the epicenters of this ideological evolution, as politicians, medical professionals, and activists debate the past, present, and future of marijuana in American society.

From Prized Crop to Maligned Weed

Originally native to parts of Asia including China and Pakistan, early botanical explorers discovered that marijuana could be ground into a fiber used to make paper, clothing, rope, and a variety of other textile goods. The term *hemp*, originally another name for the plant itself, is now often used to describe the nonconsumptive, industrial uses of marijuana. Ancient human societies also discovered that consumption of marijuana produced an intoxicating effect due to the presence of psychotropic chemicals called cannabinoids in the plant. Because of the myriad physiological effects of cannabinoid consumption, by 3000 BCE, Chinese physicians were prescribing marijuana to reduce pain and inflammation and to treat maladies that included asthma, epilepsy, and insomnia. As a medicinal herb, marijuana spread from Asia through India and Africa, and eventually to ancient Greece and Rome.

Marijuana was a highly valued agricultural crop in the early American settlements and some of the Founding Fathers, including Thomas Jefferson, grew hemp for industrial use. In the mid-1800s, the medicinal use of marijuana was introduced to Europe and the United States and the herb became a valuable addition to the American pharmacological arsenal into the early 1900s. Marijuana's reclassification as a potentially dangerous drug was tied to a wave of opium addiction that spread through America in the early twentieth century and resulted in a movement to control drug abuse and addiction. Early supporters of marijuana prohibition also believed that marijuana use had been introduced to America through Mexican immigrants who came to the United States following the Mexican Revolution in 1910, and this led to a confluence between the antimarijuana and anti-immigration movements.

Marijuana prohibition was part of the broader attempt to enhance public welfare by eliminating drug use, the same movement that resulted in the disastrous attempt to prohibit alcohol consumption between 1920 and 1933. The antimarijuana propaganda campaign that emerged in the 1930s lacked scientific data (as research on the effects of marijuana was scarce at the time) and was based largely on anecdotal, racially and socioeconomically biased, and highly inflammatory claims about the dangers of marijuana. The 1936 film *Reefer Madness* represents the culmination of marijuana misinformation and panic, equating marijuana with rising levels of violent crime. While states across the nation had been introducing laws to regulate or ban the growth and consumption of marijuana since 1911, it was not until 1937 that the federal government passed the Marijuana Tax Act, officially making marijuana use illegal across the United States.

The Road to Legalization

In 1938, New York Mayor Fiorello La Guardia directed the New York Academy of Medicine to study the effects of marijuana use. The committee found no evidence that marijuana increased crime rates or the use of other drugs like morphine and heroin. The committee's official position was that public concern about the effects of marijuana seemed to be largely unfounded or exaggerated. The LaGuardia study was the first of numerous studies to refute the belief that marijuana functioned as a "gateway drug," leading to the use of other drugs, which is one of the most common justifications for marijuana prohibition.

Over the decades, the public perception of marijuana shifted in consort with other social movements. Marijuana use was high among the youth culture of the 1960s, while legal penalties were reduced. Then, in 1970, Congress voted to classify marijuana as a "Schedule I" substance, a category designated for substances that have a high potential for abuse, no current or accepted medical use, and no accepted standards for safe use. Drugs listed on the Schedule I list are the only substances that cannot be prescribed by a physician. Despite a 1972 report from the National Commission on Marihuana and Drug Abuse that recommended marijuana be taken off the Schedule I list and decriminalized, the administration of President Richard Nixon bowed to the pressure of the conservative lobby that favored a hard line on the substance, equating it with morphine and opium in terms of health and safety concerns.

From the 1970s to the end of the Reagan Era in the 1980s, America's War on Drugs led to increasingly severe penalties for marijuana production and possession. According to a PEW Research study released in 2013, the War on Drugs resulted in increased public support for marijuana prohibition, with more than 78 percent of Americans agreeing that marijuana should be illegal in the late 1980s.

During the 1990s, a growing body of evidence suggested that marijuana was effective in treating a number of serious medical issues, including the side effects from HIV and cancer treatment, glaucoma, multiple sclerosis, and chronic pain.

Bolstered by these studies, the lobby to legalize medical marijuana gained prominence. In 1996, California voters passed Proposition 215, becoming the first state to legalize medical marijuana. By 2014, twenty-three states and the District of Columbia had legalized medical marijuana with increasing support from the medical community. A 2013 poll of doctors published in the *New England Journal of Medicine*, for instance, indicated that 76 percent of physicians polled supported medical marijuana legalization.

Studies released in 2013 and 2014 suggested that marijuana is effective in treating epileptic seizures. This led to the passage of a 2014 bill in Illinois to legalize non-smokable marijuana treatment for children suffering from epilepsy. In July 2014, Pennsylvania Representative Scott Perry introduced H.R. 5226: Charlotte's Web Medical Hemp Act of 2014 to legalize non-smokable marijuana oil for the treatment of seizures and epilepsy to the US House. This was the first attempt to legalize marijuana use at the federal level, with significant potential reverberations for marijuana laws across the nation.

The legalization of medical marijuana was a major factor in changing public opinions regarding marijuana use on a broader level. Coupled with generational changes in political power, polls began to show growing support for the legalization of marijuana for recreation. A 2013 PEW research study found that 52 percent of Americans polled in 2012 and 2013 supported the complete legalization of marijuana, both for medical and recreational use.

In 2013, Washington and Colorado became the first states to legalize marijuana for recreational use. The status of state legalization remains in question, however, as the substance is still illegal on the federal level. In August 2013, the US Department of Justice released a statement claiming that it would challenge any state-level legalization efforts at the current time, though the government reserved its right to intervene in the future. Though many states continue to oppose complete legalization, a number of states passed addendums to state laws in 2013 and 2014 to reduce fines and penalties for marijuana use. Maryland, Missouri, and the District of Columbia, for instance, instituted reforms that replaced incarceration with fines for marijuana possession. By the end of 2014, Alaska and Oregon will become the next states to vote on legalizing recreational marijuana at the state level.

In May 2014, the *New York Times* reported on statistics from the first five months of legal marijuana sales and use in Colorado. According to police numbers, marijuana intoxication accounted for about 12.5 percent of DUI (driving under the influence) incidents reported in that period. Supporters of the law have pointed to reduced crime rates across Colorado as a sign that the law is having positive benefits. Analysts warn that definitive conclusions about the effect of legalization will not be clear for several years, and thus Colorado's experiment in legalization remains the subject of intense scrutiny for those on both sides of the issue.

Reclassification and Taxation

In addition to the national debate regarding marijuana legalization, a more limited and nuanced lobby has been working to have marijuana removed from the Schedule

I list of controlled substances, thus allowing doctors to prescribe marijuana and opening the door to additional research. The reclassification lobby has been working toward this goal since 1972, though the issue has gained new life in light of the broader legalization debate. In April 2014, President Barack Obama made national news when he stated his intention to support a congressional effort to remove marijuana from the Schedule I list.

Another facet of the marijuana debate is the issue of whether marijuana should be decriminalized—which means removing the legal penalties for possession, production, and use—or fully legalized, which means passing laws that grant the right to use marijuana, but might also restrict and regulate use and production.

One of the primary differences between decriminalization and legalization concerns the financial status of marijuana as a crop. If marijuana is legalized, governments can collect sales tax on marijuana sales and can potentially develop specific tax laws to regulate marijuana production and distribution.

In Colorado and Washington, where marijuana has been officially legalized for recreational use, politicians have begun debating instituting specialized taxes, similar to taxes levied on alcohol. Reports in May and June 2014 on the effect of legal marijuana sales in Colorado indicated that the state had seen more than $50 million in legal recreational marijuana sales, translating to $7.3 million in tax revenues, with an additional $12.6 million in state earnings from medical marijuana. Issues related to the taxation of marijuana include the potential to use marijuana taxes to fund addiction and drug abuse education and research, and the potential to use taxation to reduce or discourage the use of marijuana, similar to the "sin taxes" levied on alcohol or tobacco.

Legal Intoxication

A 2014 *New England Journal of Medicine* article describing the known medical risks of marijuana included increased risk of bronchitis and pulmonary disorders as one of the chief medical concerns of marijuana use. The authors noted that these risks do not apply to nonsmokable forms of consumption. In addition, the report cited reduced motor coordination and altered judgment as potential risks, which could lead to increased automobile accidents and other safety concerns. Despite these risks, the authors supported medical marijuana legalization and argued that more research was needed to estimate the risk of marijuana use effectively.

Marijuana is not the only intoxicant legally used in the United States, and the decriminalization of marijuana would place the plant on par with nicotine and alcohol. Toward this end, there has been interest in how marijuana compares with these other substances. A 2007 research study in *The Lancet*, indicated that marijuana was the least dangerous of the three most common social drugs—marijuana, tobacco, and alcohol—both in terms of physical risks and the potential for addiction and dependence. In an interview with the *New Yorker* in January 2014, President Obama stated his belief that marijuana is not more dangerous than alcohol, an opinion supported by decades of research and echoed by the vast majority of physicians in the United States.

While marijuana may be safer than the other legal intoxicants, marijuana use carries physical risks and poses a potential safety hazard that must be addressed as the legalization debate continues. From an ancient medicinal and industrial crop, to the subject of a modern American revolution, marijuana has been an influential part of human culture for millennia. Those participating in the modern public debate are therefore players in a far more ancient pattern of social evolution regarding the right and ethics of intoxication, the use and abuse of natural resources, and the always-evolving relationship between public safety and personal freedom.

—Micah Issitt

Editor's Note: Due to the quickly changing nature of this topic, we encourage you to visit the sites listed in our Websites listing at the end of this book for the most current information regarding state legislation and related topics.

Bibliography

Adler, Jonathan N., and James A. Colbert. "Medical Use of Marijuana—Polling Results." *New England Journ. of Medicine*. Massachusetts Medical Soc., 30 May 2013. Web. 15 Aug. 2014.

Brown, David T., ed. *Cannabis: The Genus Cannabis*. New York: Taylor, 1998. Print.

Buckley, Bruce, and Joan Buckley. "NIDA Study Cites Dangers of Marijuana Use in Teens." *Pharmacy Practice News*. McMahon, July 2014. Web. 15 Aug. 2014.

Clarke, Robert, and Mark Merlin. *Cannabis: Evolution and Ethnobotany*. Los Angeles: U of California P, 2013. Print.

Clarke, Robert Connell. *Marijuana Botany*. Berkeley: Ronin, 1981. Print.

Ferner, Matt. "House Bill Would Legalize 'Charlotte's Web' Medical Marijuana." *Huffington Post*. TheHuffingtonPost.com, 29 July 2014. Web. 15 Aug. 2014.

Healy, Jack. "After 5 Months of Sales, Colorado Sees the Downside of a Legal High." *New York Times*. New York Times, 31 May 2014. Web. 15 Aug. 2014.

"Justice Department Announces Update to Marijuana Enforcement Policy." *Justice. gov*. US Dept. of Justice, 29 Aug. 2013. Web. July 29, 2014.

"Majority Now Supports Legalizing Marijuana." *People-press.org*. Pew Research Center, 4 Apr. 2013. Web. 15 Aug. 2014.

Rosica, James L. "Poll Finds Only Token Opposition to Medical Pot in Florida." *Naples Daily News*. E. W. Scripps, 28 July 2014. Web. 15 Aug. 2014.

1

Marijuana Policy Reform:
The "Tipping Point"

Co-owner Troy Moore weighs marijuana at the Oregon's Finest medical marijuana dispensary in Portland, Oregon, in April 2014.

Reform—The Marijuana Legalization Debate

As more US states legalize the medical and recreational use of marijuana, advocates turn their attention toward federal drug policy. As of 2014, it remains a federal crime to possess, grow, or sell marijuana for any purpose, regardless of any state laws to the contrary. Individuals who use marijuana in states where it is legal can still be subject to federal prosecution, which creates a confusing and politically charged legal landscape. In order to achieve true marijuana policy reform, federal law must change.

This leads to an important question: should the federal government legalize or decriminalize marijuana possession and sale? Numerous arguments exist on both sides. Those who argue against reform believe that legalizing marijuana would encourage its use and lead to increased public health and safety issues. Those who favor reform believe that legalizing marijuana would decrease crime by removing black market demand, and would free up public resources to assist people with substance abuse problems more effectively.

Public opinion on marijuana legalization has changed significantly in the past few decades, and more mainstream public figures now advocate in favor of legalization. With medical use permitted in nearly half of US states (as of August 2014)—plus several states decriminalizing recreational use—the weight of economic and health research combined with public opinion may soon reach a tipping point favoring federal reform. Experts still disagree on many important issues, however, including economic impact, public health concerns, and safety implications.

Economic Impact

Experts disagree on the economic impact of marijuana legalization in the United States. One argument favoring legalization is that the government could raise revenue by regulating and taxing marijuana sales, similar to alcohol and tobacco. However, it is unclear what economic benefit could actually be realized through taxation. A 2006 report stated that marijuana was the largest cash crop in the United States, with an estimated value of $35.8 billion per year—greater than the combined value of corn ($23.3 billion) and wheat ($7.5 billion). This figure was calculated by Jon Gettman, the director of the Coalition for Rescheduling Cannabis, by multiplying the approximately 10,000 metric tons of marijuana produced annually in the United States, with an estimated production value of $1,600 per pound.

This number was criticized on several grounds. Because of the high (and highly variable) price per pound, the relative cash value of marijuana says little about the actual quantity bought and sold. The amount of marijuana produced in the United

States was actually closer to that of beans—a much smaller crop by weight than corn or wheat. Additionally, the cash value of marijuana is likely to drop significantly if no black market exists to drive up the price. For comparison, the production value of tobacco was approximately two dollars per pound in 2007. Because of these factors, the relatively small volume of marijuana bought and sold in the United States might not generate nearly as much tax revenue as hoped. With this amount of uncertainty, some analysts worry that any potential financial benefit would be too small to outweigh the cost of additional public harm caused by increased usage.

Black Market Drug Trade

Critics of the long-running War on Drugs—the US government's campaign of more than four decades to curtail the production and sale of illegal drugs—suspect that criminalization of minor drug offenses actually increases crime, especially organized crime, and contributes to dangerous black markets. The lack of legal availability drives up prices, and, as of 2014, United Nations experts valued the worldwide black market drug trade at more than $300 billion. However, experts disagree whether legalizing marijuana alone would seriously impact the organized crime system supported by the black market drug trade, and whether it would have a significant effect on public safety and global stability.

This issue grows in importance as enforcement efforts in many Latin American countries lead to casualties, police and government corruption, and economic problems. Because marijuana is the most popular recreational drug in the United States, some believe that legalizing its use and sale would keep the increasingly deadly trafficking activities away from the US border. At a recent Organization of American States (OAS) summit, Latin American leaders discussed the future evolution of drug enforcement policy. Marijuana legalization was among the approaches suggested to encourage political and economic stability in the region.

There is disagreement, however, about whether legalizing marijuana alone would significantly impact the revenue of drug cartels. For example, the US Office of National Drug Control Policy (ONDCP) estimated that 61 percent of Mexican drug cartel revenue comes from marijuana; by contrast, the independent research organization RAND Corporation determined that only about 16 percent of cartel income comes from marijuana. The balance, according to RAND, comes from other illegal activities, including the manufacture and sale of harder drugs such as cocaine, heroin, and methamphetamine; trafficking undocumented immigrants and sex workers; ransoming kidnap victims; extorting small businesses; and bribing politicians. Experts debate whether legalizing marijuana would decrease cartel-related violence by lowering the cash flow needed to fund other illicit activity, or simply push the cartels to engage in more illegal activities of a different kind to maintain their revenue.

Curbing Drug Abuse

Similar levels of disagreement exist on the domestic front, with experts weighing in on the potential public health impacts of marijuana legalization. Some argue that punishing users as criminals is ineffective in reducing abuse, and instead wastes public money on searching out, arresting, prosecuting, and incarcerating even the most casual users. Others argue that the potential harm caused by marijuana is not yet fully understood, and it would be imprudent to pursue legalization before being fully prepared for the consequences.

Regardless, many question whether criminalizing drug use really achieves its alleged purpose—namely, curbing drug abuse. According to the Federal Bureau of Prisons, in 2014 almost exactly half of all federal inmates are incarcerated for drug-related offenses. Some economists suggest that the money spent on enforcing criminal penalties would be better spent improving public health infrastructure to provide more effective treatment for individuals with drug abuse problems.

Similarly, pro-legalization activists such as Ethan Nadelmann, executive director of the Drug Policy Alliance, argue that, in their zeal to enforce existing laws, prosecutors and district attorneys ignore the harmful effects of practices like mandatory minimum sentencing and criminal penalties for pregnant women who test positive for drugs. Ultimately, he believes that decriminalization will do more to reduce the harms caused by drug use and abuse, because it will shift the focus from incarceration to rehabilitation.

Public Health

While most marijuana users are unlikely to become drug addicts, questions remain regarding the safety of marijuana for regular or occasional use. Many people consider marijuana to be safe—possibly even more so than alcohol and tobacco—but some studies show potential long-term consequences among young, heavy marijuana users. National Institutes of Health director Francis Collins highlighted studies showing that prolonged marijuana use among teenagers may cause a permanent decrease in cognitive abilities. The potential of marijuana smoke to cause lung cancer is still unknown, and other studies suggest a possible connection between marijuana use and elevated risks of testicular cancer.

Nora Volkow, director of the National Institute on Drug Abuse (NIDA), has noted that one must consider the differing impacts of tobacco, alcohol, and marijuana, rather than grouping them together for discussion purposes. For example, unlike tobacco, alcohol and marijuana impair the brain's cognitive abilities. Numerous studies show that alcohol impairs one's ability to operate a motor vehicle safely, and drivers with even a slightly elevated blood alcohol level have an increased risk of accident. Few studies have evaluated the effects of marijuana on driving, but so far results show similar increases in accident rates because of levels of cognitive decline.

Studies also show increased rates of schizophrenia among marijuana smokers, but they have not proven that marijuana use actually causes schizophrenia. Marijuana use may accelerate the development of symptoms in those who are predisposed to schizophrenia, as the active ingredients in marijuana, including delta-9 tetrahydrocannabinol (9-THC) and cannabidiol (CBD), can trigger paranoia even in a person without predisposition if consumed in sufficiently high doses. These effects are usually temporary, but it could trigger a permanent change for individuals prone to schizophrenia.

Medical Exceptions

Despite these health concerns, marijuana shows potential for a variety of medical applications. Patients report that using marijuana helps alleviate pain, reduce nausea, and stimulate appetite without the side-effects of traditional medication. This makes marijuana a potentially useful treatment for several illnesses, including chronic pain, cancer, HIV/AIDS, glaucoma, epilepsy, and multiple sclerosis. As of July 2014, nearly half of US states have legalized marijuana for medical use, provided that it is administered under the supervision of a doctor or approved caregiver.

However, many states' approval processes are widely criticized, as people question who qualifies as a "caregiver" and under what circumstances an individual can receive a license to use. Additionally, the ailments most likely to benefit from medical marijuana use—such as chronic pain—cannot be tested objectively. Critics observe that recreational users can easily obtain a medical license to use: for example, public health experts in Colorado estimate that only about 20 percent of sales under the state's medical marijuana laws are to individuals with a legitimate medical condition. To combat this, some places like Washington, DC, removed chronic pain from the list of ailments that qualify for medical marijuana use. Unfortunately, this rules out a potentially valuable treatment option for individuals who really do suffer from chronic pain. This leads to an ideological split between those who support legalizing marijuana for medical purposes only and those who support full legalization.

Increased Access

A common argument against legalization is that easier access will lead to increased use, and therefore increased harm. Once again, experts disagree on how much use would increase if marijuana were legal and more widely available. Multiple surveys conducted in the United States show that young people (under twenty-one) report that it is easier to purchase marijuana than alcohol. This suggests that prohibition laws are ineffective at preventing people from accessing drugs. And indeed, experts such as Dr. Benedikt Fischer of Simon Fraser University in British Columbia, Canada, point out that people who want to use drugs are largely already using, despite their illegality.

By contrast, Nora Volkow of NIDA is concerned that legalizing marijuana sale means that corporations will profit from increased sales. This creates an incentive for corporations to develop and market marijuana products to increase sales and enlarge their customer base. Thus, she expects legalization will result in more public health and safety issues, simply because easier access means that more people will be using it, and more frequently.

Aside from access to marijuana itself, many worry about its alleged role as a "gateway" to harder drug use. NIDA suggests that marijuana users are much more likely to use other drugs as well, but this does not necessarily mean that marijuana *causes* other drug use: it simply means the two occur together. Other correlating behaviors exist with hard drug users, such as underage drinking and smoking, so it is equally likely that any of these—or none of these—could be the cause. Interestingly, research suggests that when marijuana is legal, such as in the Netherlands, its market is separate from that of other drugs: marijuana dealers rarely carry other kinds of drugs, and users rarely seek out other drugs. By contrast, in the United States, marijuana dealers may carry other kinds of drugs because they are all equally illegal, which might provide marijuana users with easier access to other drugs.

Conclusion

The public's perception of the dangers of marijuana use has changed over time, and the percentage of Americans who believe it should be legalized has changed as well: when the Gallup polling organization surveyed Americans in 1969, only 12 percent of respondents favored legalizing marijuana. By October 2011, 50 percent of respondents favored legalization.

Similarly, opinion polls show that the public considers marijuana separately from other drugs, particularly when it comes to questions of legalization. While public support for marijuana legalization has increased over the past few decades, support with regard to other drugs remains around 10 to 15 percent favoring legality. This holds true even in the Netherlands, where marijuana is legal, and where there is similarly little public support for legalizing other drugs.

As states continue to pass their own laws with respect to medical and recreational marijuana use, the debate over federal law and policy grows more significant. The confusion created when a federal offense is legalized by a state must be resolved; the question remains whether it will lead to federal legalization, or revocation of state marijuana laws.

—Tracey M. DiLascio

Bibliography

Barcott, Bruce. "NIDA's Director Tells Us What We Know—and Need to Know—about Marijuana." *National Geographic*. Natl. Geographic Soc., 4 Mar 2014. Web. 15 Aug. 2014.

Christensen, Jen, and Jacque Wilson. "Is Marijuana as Safe as—or Safer Than—Alcohol?" *CNN*. Cable News Network, 22 Jan. 2014. Web. 15 Aug. 2014.

Godfrey, Will. "How Far Can Ethan Nadelmann Push America's Drug Laws?" *The Fix*. Fix, 30 June 2013. Web. 15 Aug. 2014.

Jordan, Janelle. "War on Drugs a Global Failure, London School of Economics Says." *CBC News*. CBC, 9 May 2014. Web. 15 Aug. 2014.

Kleiman, Mark. "How Not to Make a Hash out of Cannabis Legalization." *Washington Monthly*. Washington Monthly, Mar./Apr./May 2014. Web. 15 Aug. 2014.

McKay, Tom. "Eight Lies We Have to Stop Telling Ourselves about Marijuana in America." *PolicyMic*. Mic Network, 12 May 2014. Web. 15 Aug. 2014.

Riggs, Mike. "The Three Worst Arguments for Legalizing Marijuana." *Reason*. Reason Foundation, 23 Mar. 2012. Web. 15 Aug. 2014.

Legalization of Marijuana: An Overview

By Alex K. Rich and Alexander Stingl
Points of View Reference Center, 2013

Before 1937, marijuana was freely bought, sold, grown, and smoked in the United States. Since that time, all of these activities have been illegal, but many groups and individuals have fought to decriminalize marijuana. The congressional decision to classify marijuana as a Schedule I drug in 1970 has made the legalization campaign more difficult, since it officially established marijuana as a dangerous, addictive drug with no medicinal benefits.

Much of the opposition to legalizing marijuana has to do with the perceived immorality of marijuana use. One popular argument in favor of legalization takes an economic view of the problem, claiming that the taxes collected on legally sold marijuana would be a boon to the economy.

Those in favor of legalizing marijuana have often based their arguments on the medicinal value of the drug, citing the fact that cancer patients often smoke marijuana to battle the nausea caused by chemotherapy. People on both sides have criticized this argument, claiming that it clouds the debate by making an ancillary issue the main focus of the pro-legalization argument. Anti-legalization activists, as well as the United States Supreme Court, have argued that the federal government should have the power to supplant state and local laws, since people in states with permissive drug laws could conceivably trade with people in states with restrictive laws.

The debate over rescheduling and decriminalizing marijuana has ensued for years, with one side claiming that the drug does not meet all the requirements necessary for classification as a Schedule I drug, and the other side claiming that the drug does not meet all the requirements necessary for classification as a medically applicable substance. Evidence for both arguments tends to be shaky, since very little data on the matter is available. Comparisons are almost inevitably drawn to alcohol and tobacco, both of which are potentially dangerous, yet legal. Much of the debate on the issue of legalization centers on either establishing or debunking the claim that marijuana is no more dangerous than either of these substances, and thus no legal distinction should be made between them.

Understanding the Discussion

Decriminalization: Originally proposed by the Nixon-appointed Shafer Commission, decriminalization is the process of removing criminal penalties for possession, use, and non-profit transfers of marijuana.

Marijuana: As defined by federal and state laws, marijuana is any part of the plant *Cannabis sativa L.,* including viable seeds, resin, and derivatives of the plant, but not the stalk of the plant, or fiber, such as hemp, created from the stalk. Since there are subspecies within the genus Cannabis that are virtually indistinguishable from Cannabis sativa, some states have amended their definition of marijuana to include all plants in the Cannabis genus. Though the intoxicating element of marijuana is THC, the THC levels in a particular plant do not affect the legality of possessing or producing a Cannabis plant. Cannabis is very easy to grow, and can be grown in relatively large quantities in small spaces, such as apartments or garages. Colloquially, marijuana has many synonyms and nicknames, including reefer, weed, pot, and herb.

NORML (National Organization for the Reform of Marijuana Laws): A not-for-profit organization that has lobbied for the rescheduling and decriminalizing of marijuana since the 1970s.

Possession: As it relates to marijuana, legal possession requires physical possession of a "usable amount" of the substance, as well as knowledge of that possession. In order to prosecute someone for marijuana possession, one must prove that they knowingly possessed enough of the substance to use it as a drug.

Prohibition: When capitalized, this term refers to the period from 1920 to 1933 when the sale, possession, or production of alcohol was illegal in the United States. Prohibition was intended to reduce crime and social problems and to improve the health of the nation. Instead, it saw the creation of organized crime, an overall increase in alcohol consumption, and, since the substance was no longer regulated, more potent and dangerous alcohol. Prohibition is generally regarded as a failure of American policy, and is often cited by marijuana legalization activists as justification for repealing marijuana prohibition.

Schedule I: Refers to the most strictly regulated class of drugs. Schedule I drugs are the only controlled substances that may not be legally prescribed by doctors, and must meet three criteria in order to be so classified: the substance must have a high potential for abuse, have no recognized legitimate medical application, and be deemed unsafe when used without medical supervision. Marijuana is currently a Schedule I drug. Most of the lobbying to downgrade the substance to Schedule II or III is concentrated on the second criterion. Activists claim the drug has many recognized medical benefits. The relative safety of the drug compared to other, differently scheduled, substances is also a major issue in the debate.

History

The first American law regarding marijuana was enacted in 1619 in Virginia. It required farmers to grow hemp, because the fiber made from its stalks were essential for making sails, ropes, food, and fuel in the developing nation. As early as 1840, doctors recognized the medicinal applications of marijuana, and the drug was freely sold in pharmacies for over a century.

The origins of marijuana prohibition in the United States stem from fears of a criminal element sneaking into the country, in the form of Mexican immigrants. Mexican people were accused of being addicted to marijuana, and the substance itself was credited with making people become violent and insane, a condition that was labeled "reefer madness."

In 1937, following the United States' unsuccessful experiment with alcohol prohibition, Congress enacted the Marijuana Tax Act. Although twenty-four states already had similar laws, the Marijuana Tax Act made it a federal crime to possess, distribute, or produce marijuana. Henry J. Anslinger, then head of the Federal Bureau of Narcotics, made many claims about the dangers of marijuana, including that it caused users to murder, steal, and generally become insane. Despite claims made by doctors from the American Medical Association, the Division of Mental Health, and other authorities contradicting Anslinger's claims, the act was passed by a unanimous vote.

The Controlled Substances act of 1970 entered the above-mentioned categorization of marijuana as a Schedule I drug, defining it as a substance that a) had no medical value and b) is considered having a high potential of abuse.

The National Commission on Marijuana recognized the renaissance that marijuana was enjoying in the United States and began calling for its legalization in the early 1970s. It was estimated that about twenty-five million Americans were using marijuana in 1972; a 1977 survey indicated that the number of young adults who had tried marijuana was only slightly lower than the number of young adults who had tried tobacco. The number of deaths caused by marijuana during the period from May 1976 to April 1977 was estimated at 10 (and those were caused by hashish oil, which is dangerous because of compounds used to derive it); in the same period, 2,530 deaths were attributed to alcohol, 880 to Valium, and 390 to aspirin.

Nevertheless, even the most liberal politicians of the day sought to decriminalize the drug, rather than fully legalize it in all forms and all uses. In California, the substance achieved almost complete legal status; by 1976, even with the recent rescheduling of the drug, marijuana possession was no longer a crime in the state, and hemp began to be cultivated without restriction. The group NORML even sued the Drug Enforcement Agency (DEA) for allegedly contaminating Mexican cannabis crops in order to make the drug seem more dangerous than it was. By the 1980s, marijuana was either officially or functionally legal in Canada, Spain, Denmark, and Holland, as well as some areas of the United States.

Recognizing that different preparations of the plant had vastly different effects on users, the United States redefined sentencing guidelines in 1995, differentiating among "marijuana," "hashish," and "hashish oil." Hashish oil (or hash oil), according to the DEA, is "a dark viscous liquid" created from extracting the THC from several marijuana flowers, which is, consequently, much more potent than marijuana.

Hashish (or hash) is defined as "a resinous substance" that contains THC, two or more related compounds, and plant fragments.

Criminalization of the use or possession of marijuana is regulated by federal laws on the effect of interstate commerce. Under the Supremacy Clause, federal law supersedes state laws that are in violation of federal law. In 2005, the United States Supreme Court was concerned with these issues in *Gonzales vs. Raich*. Following several states ruling to decriminalize marijuana the case of two women—Angel Raich and Diane Monson—was debated in court. Both had used marijuana for medical purposes, which was admissible by California regulation, and saw their personal crops destroyed by police forces. The Supreme Court voted 6–3 to uphold the 1987 Controlled Substances Act and its Commerce Clause, leaving the right to ban marijuana with Congress.

Legalization of Marijuana Today

An organization called LEAP (Law Enforcement Against Prohibition), consisting of current and former law enforcement agents, takes the position that regulation, rather than criminalization, is the only way to deal with drug use in the United States. Regulation, in turn, necessitates legalization, since the government cannot tax that which it does not allow in the first place.

Several states have enacted policies that deemphasize the enforcement of marijuana laws. Since 1975, Alaska has treated federal anti-drug policies as an unconstitutional invasion of privacy. The state continues to allow simple possession of small amounts of the drug. Cities such as Denver, Colorado and West Hollywood, California have adopted similar policies.

A 2006 public policy report suggested that marijuana is the United States' largest cash crop by a significant margin. A similar study carried out by a prominent Canadian economist in 2004 estimated an average markup of $6.90 for each unit (0.5 grams) of marijuana sold on the street, resulting in $2 billion in revenue for the government (in the form of taxes on marijuana cigarettes) if the drug were legalized. Legalization of the drug in Spain saw a sharp decrease in the number of frequent users, ostensibly because doing so ceased to be seen as a dangerous, rebellious activity. In Holland, where marijuana has been legal for decades, about 5 percent of the population smokes it regularly.

In January 2011, US President Barack Obama stated that he opposed the legalization of marijuana. Meanwhile, medical marijuana programs continue to operate in numerous states.

Bibliography

Books

Boire, Richard Glen. *Marijuana Law*. Oakland: Ronin Publishing, Inc., 1996.

Conrad, Chris. *Hemp for Health: The Medicinal and Nutritional Uses of Cannabis Sativa*. Rochester: Healing Arts Press, 1997.

Escohotado, Antonio. *A Brief History of Drugs: From the Stone Age to the Stoned Age*. Rochester: Park Street Press, 1999.

Gerber, Rudolph J. *Legalizing Marijuana: Drug Policy Reform and Prohibition Politics*. Westport: Praeger Publishers, 2004.

Goode, Erich. *Between Politics and Reason: The Drug Legalization Debate*. New York: St. Martin's Press, Inc., 1997.

Inciardi, James A. *The Drug Legalization Debate*. Newbury Park: Sage Publications, Inc., 1991.

Parks, Peggy. *Drug Legalization: Current Issues*. San Diego, CA: Referencepoint Press, 2008.

Rosenthal, Ed, Steve Kubby and S. Newhart. *Why Marijuana Should Be Legal*. New York: Thunder's Mouth Press, 2003.

Schaler, Jeffrey A. *Drugs: Should We Legalize, Decriminalize or Deregulate?* Amherst: Prometheus Books, 1998.

Periodicals

Cloud, John. "IS POT GOOD FOR YOU? (Cover story)" *Time* 160.19 (04 Nov. 2002): 62. *Academic Search Complete*. EBSCO. 28 July 2008 http://search.ebscohost.com/login.aspx?direct=true&db=a9h&AN=7689338&site=ehost-live.

Fergusson, David M., and Joseph M. Boden. "Cannabis use and later life outcomes." *Addiction* 103.6 (June 2008): 969-976. *Academic Search Complete*. EBSCO. 28 July 2008 http://search.ebscohost.com/login.aspx?direct=true&db=a9h&AN=32006327&site=ehost-live.

Hitchens, Christopher. "Legalize It. (cover story)" *Foreign Policy* 41. *Points of View Reference Center*. EBSCO. 28 July 2008 http://search.ebscohost.com/login.aspx?direct=true&db=pwh&AN=24868544&site=pov-live.

MacCoun, Robert, and Peter Reuter. "Interpreting Dutch cannabis policy: Reasoning by analogy in the legalization debate (Cover story)." *Science* 278.5335 (03 Oct. 1997): 47. *Academic Search Complete*. EBSCO. 28 July 2008 http://search.ebscohost.com/login.aspx?direct=true&db=a9h&AN=9710173672&site=ehost-live.

Mart, AlysonRashidian, Nushin. "Rocky Mountain High." *Nation* 295.18 (2012): 6. *Points of View Reference Center*. Web. 28 Nov. 2012. http://search.ebscohost.com/login.aspx?direct=true&db=pwh&AN=82713880&site=pov-live.

"Mercury News editorial: State should regulate medical marijuana providers." *Mercurynews.com*. 14 February 2011 http://www.mercurynews.com/opinion/ci_17387269?nclick_check=1.

"Obama: drug abuse requires broader policy response." *Reuters*. 28 January 2011 http://www.reuters.com/article/2011/01/28/us-obama-drugs-idUSTRE70Q8XR20110128.

Patton, George C, et al. "Cannabis use and mental health in young people: cohort study." *BMJ: British Medical Journal* 325.7374 (23 Nov. 2002): 1195. *Academic Search Complete*. EBSCO. 28 July 2008 http://search.ebscohost.com/login.aspx?direct=true&db=a9h&AN=8593613&site=ehost-live.

The Editors. "Marijuana Research." *Scientific American* 291.1 : 8. *Points of View Reference Center*. EBSCO. 28 July 2008 http://search.ebscohost.com/login.aspx?direct=true&db=pwh&AN=15024907&site=pov-live.

Thies, Clifford F., and Charles A. Register. "Decriminalization of marijuana and the demand for alcohol, marijuana and cocaine." *Social Science Journal* 30.4 (Oct. 1993): 385. *Academic Search Complete*. EBSCO. 28 July 2008 http://search.ebscohost.com/login.aspx?direct=true&db=a9h&AN=9404150766&site=ehost-live.

Thompson, Brian. "Law in Limbo, But Operators Sign Up to Sell Medical Marijuana in NJ." *nbcnewyork.com*. 15 February 2011 http://www.nbcnewyork.com/news/local-beat/Law-in-Limbo-but-Operators-Sign-Up-to-Sell-Medical-Marijuana-in-NJ-116191704.html.

Websites

InfoFacts—Marijuana. National Institutes of Health, National Institute On Drug Abuse. 28 July 2008. http://www.nida.nih.gov/infofacts/marijuana.html

War on Drugs a Global Failure, London School of Economics Says

By Janelle Jordan
CBC News, May 9, 2014

The war on drugs must end and the battle to change international drug policies must begin, says a new report from the London School of Economics.

Five Nobel Prize-winning economists signed off on the 84-page report entitled *Ending the Drug Wars: Report of the LSE Expert Group on the Economics of Drug Policy* authored by leading drug policy experts and supported by political figures from around the world calling for drug law reform.

The authors offer compelling evidence that achieving a "drug-free world" based solely on a prohibitionist model is an expensive and wasted effort. According to John Collins, co-ordinator of LSE IDEAS International Drug Policy Project and editor of the report, the drug policy experts' recommendations show how the war on drugs is a failure requiring a "major rethink of international drug policies."

Toronto health economist Dr. Claire de Oliveira, who works at the Centre for Addiction and Mental Health, agrees going in a new direction to achieve different results is needed to tackle drug policy reform.

"This is also the type of approach I take in my work and when proposing any policy recommendation— to implement policies that have been shown to work and that are based on rigorous, scientific evidence."

Collateral Damage

Based on rigorous economic and social analyses of primarily the U.S., Latin America, West Africa and Asia, the authors urge that global resources shift from prosecution and imprisonment to more "effective evidence-based polices" such as harm reduction, treatment and public health strategies. Similar recommendations are suggested for Canada, Australia and the United Kingdom.

The report also says the drug war epidemic has produced "negative outcomes and collateral damage." Prohibition helps push illicit drug prices up exorbitantly compared to what they would cost in a legally controlled market.

Current policies have helped push the black market drug trade to as much as $300 billion, and 40 of the world's nine million prison inmates are jailed for drug-related offences—a figure that jumps to 59 percent in the U.S. Moreover, between 70 and 85 percent of American inmates are in need of substance abuse treatment.

"Drug-Free" World Idealistic

The report emphasizes that while prohibition holds some value in decreasing drug dependence, the harm to society is gravely outweighed due to violence, government corruption and collateral damage associated with the drug war, especially in drug-producing countries like Mexico, Colombia and Guatemala.

Dr. Benedikt Fischer, the Applied Public Health Research Chair and professor in the Faculty of Health Sciences at Simon Fraser University in B.C. thinks prohibition is an outdated weapon to fight the modern war on drugs.

"The advocates of prohibition had about a century to prove that their approach is actually effective and we're still waiting for the positive evidence," he says. "I think it's fair game to now say, look let's give some alternative approaches a chance and on an evidence base, not based on ideology."

Fischer also says the argument that decriminalization leads to more drug use is a fallacy, and he points to the world's most popular drug—marijuana—as an example.

"Everyone that wants to use cannabis is using cannabis today," he says. "[There's no] evidence that there are people who are waiting just for this to be regulated, then all of a sudden will decide that they will now start using."

Benefits to Decriminalization

Even though Ottawa is considering making pot possession a ticketable offence (not a criminal one) Canada still lags the world on the issue of decriminalization.

Donald MacPherson, executive director of the Canadian Drug Policy Coalition, says governments, including Canada, need to rethink their drug policies.

"For too long, they overemphasized a sort of failed policy approach of prohibition and a failed policy of criminalization of people who use drugs," he says.

The report says decriminalization would cut incarceration and health-care costs for taxpayers everywhere. Countries with the harshest drug laws tend to have higher incarceration rates and higher HIV infection rates. Of the one million HIV-positive people in America, almost a quarter of them are in jail every year—which costs U.S. prisons $25 million a year for medical treatment, the report notes.

"This report clearly says we're spending way too much, we're over-prioritizing expenditures on enforcement and we need to look at scaling up a broader array of public health interventions . . . to improve the health of Canadians that have drug problems," MacPherson says.

Harm Reduction—a Possible Solution

MacPherson says society needs to stop merely jailing its drug users.

"Implementing a public health approach globally," he says, "you would see a shift in resources, a shift in outcomes and fewer people incarcerated, fewer criminalized and you would see a much more positive outcome."

Fischer agrees that harm reduction is only part of the larger picture in minimizing drug dependence. "No one can pretend that these problems will entirely disappear, but the assumption of a fundamentally different public health-oriented approach is that a lot of these problems will be significantly reduced to the benefit of both users and society at large."

Change Takes Time

The LSE report is a primer to the conversation on global drug reform policy for the United Nations General Assembly Special Session on Drugs 2016, the main policy making arm of the UN.

MacPherson hopes the report leads to a frank global debate on drug policies everywhere.

"It really is an opportunity to have a very open, honest, evidenced and informed discussion about the way forward post-2016," he says.

Until then, Fischer advocates a slow and steady approach to drug reform.

"The LSE report emphasizes advocating for regulatory experiments, [so] we need to experiment in a very cautious and sensible way to give these alternative approaches a chance."

Legally Green

By Suzanne Weiss
State Legislatures, February 2013

Got pot? Colorado and Washington do. In the wake of last November's election, the two states face an enormous and once-unthinkable challenge. They must transform the marijuana black market into an above-ground, regulated and taxed commercial enterprise.

Ballot measures approved by voters in Colorado and Washington create the most permissive pot laws in the nation. They not only explicitly allow citizens to use cannabis for recreational purposes, but demand state involvement in establishing systems for the drug to be sold much like alcohol.

Officials in both states have a number of months to craft and enact a regulatory framework for commercial marijuana cultivation and distribution—provided the U.S. Justice Department does not block them from doing so.

The federal Controlled Substances Act of 1970 classifies marijuana as a Schedule I drug, meaning that it has a high potential for abuse and no acceptable medical use, and thus it prohibits the possession, use, purchase, sale and/or cultivation of marijuana.

The federal government may choose to stymie implementation of the new laws, but it cannot make the two states recriminalize marijuana possession. And the states have no obligation to enforce federal marijuana laws. At press time, the U.S. Department of Justice was still reviewing the new state laws.

"We have no model for how to deal with this," says Colorado Representative Frank McNulty (R), who served as House Speaker in the past two sessions. "Even when Prohibition was repealed, it involved a product that had previously been legal. In this case, we're really starting from square one."

In Colorado, Governor John Hickenlooper (D) has pledged to respect the wishes of voters despite his opposition to legalization. Shortly after the election, he appointed a 24-member task force—comprising legislators, cabinet officials, civic leaders, employers, attorneys and marijuana advocates—to work out a variety of policy, legal and procedural issues associated with establishing a commercial marijuana market. The new law includes language requiring the legislature to address some of those issues during the 2013 session, including:

- Amending current laws regarding the possession, sale, distribution or transfer of marijuana.

- Clarifying the impact of legalization on workplace drug policies.

From *State Legislatures* 39.2 (February 2013): 14–18. Copyright © 2013 by National Conference of State Legislatures. Reprinted with permission. All rights reserved.

- Establishing new regulations in areas ranging from product labeling to security requirements for wholesale and retail marijuana establishments.

- Deciding whether to set a standard for marijuana impairment while driving, similar to the blood-alcohol standard for drunken driving.

- Integrating the existing medical marijuana system into the new commercial market.

- Submitting a proposal to voters to impose a 15 percent excise tax on wholesale marijuana sales.

McNulty says he and a number of other legislators remain opposed to legalization, but that there likely will be "broad agreement" on implementing the major provisions of Amendment 64. The most contentious issue will be the provision requiring legislators to refer an excise tax proposal to the voters. Many lawmakers on both sides of the aisle question "whether we can be compelled to cast our vote a certain way," he says.

By contrast, Washington's voter-approved marijuana law leaves the legislative branch largely out of the loop, and gives the State Liquor Control Board responsibility for coming up with a system for licensing, regulating and taxing marijuana growers, processors and retail stores.

Washington Senate Republican Leader Mark Schoesler says he doesn't expect the issue of marijuana legalization to get much attention during the 2013 session.

Legislative leaders of both parties "have committed ourselves to a narrowly focused agenda—jobs, education and the budget," Schoesler says. "So we've got a lot of work ahead of us, and can't afford to go off on other issues."

Besides, he notes, "amending the provisions of an initiative approved by voters requires a two-thirds vote of both chambers. That's a huge threshold, and I just don't see it happening."

Schoesler says the biggest question related to implementation of the new marijuana law "is how much leeway the other Washington is going to give us."

Groundbreakers

Politically and culturally, Colorado and Washington offered fertile ground for legalization advocates. Both have a history with marijuana law reform; more than a decade ago, they were among the first to approve the use of marijuana for medicinal purposes. Denver was the first major city in the country to legalize adult possession of pot, in 2005, and voters in Seattle several years ago passed a measure urging marijuana cases to be the "lowest law enforcement priority."

But when it came to full legalization, pro-pot activists had a harder fight. Colorado voters in 2006 rejected a measure to legalize up to an ounce of marijuana. And just two years ago, reform advocates in Washington weren't able to make the ballot with a measure that would have removed criminal penalties for marijuana.

What seemed to make the difference this time around were well-orchestrated campaigns with focused messaging that took advantage of wealthy backers and improbable big-name supporters, ranging from travel-show host Rick Steves to veteran law enforcement officials to conservative politicians like former Colorado Congressman Tom Tancredo.

Television ads featured a middle-aged mom saying she didn't like marijuana, but that taxing it would bring in much-needed money for schools and health care and free up police resources.

"What we figured out is that your average person doesn't necessarily favor using marijuana, but there's this untapped desire by voters to end the drug war," says Brian Vicente, a Denver lawyer who helped write Colorado's amendment.

Of the $8.5 million raised by legalization advocates, more than half came from billionaire George Soros, a longtime benefactor of liberal causes, and Peter Lewis, the founder of Progressive Insurance, whose support stems from his use of cannabis for pain relief after the partial amputation of his leg in 1998.

By contrast, opponents of legalization in Washington raised just $16,000. In Colorado, anti-Amendment 64 forces put up a stronger fight, mounting a $690,000 campaign with backing from an evangelical Christian group and businessman Mel Sembler, who runs the Drug Free America Foundation. The major arguments put forth by opponents ranged from the adverse health effects of smoking marijuana to the possibility of the two states becoming "drug meccas."

Growing Support

"Something is happening, and it's not just happening in Washington and Colorado," Andy Ko, who leads the Open Society Foundation's Campaign for a New Drug Policy, told the Associated Press. "Marijuana reform is going to happen in this country as older voters fade away and younger voters show up."

Another national advocacy group, the Marijuana Policy Project, recently predicted that legalization proposals will be taken up by state lawmakers or placed on the ballot through petition drives in a half-dozen states over the next two years.

First out of the block will be Maine, where Representative Diane Russell (D) is leading the charge to place a proposal on the November ballot that would legalize and tax the sale of marijuana.

"I think the people are way ahead of the politicians on this issue," Russell says. "Legislators can choose to bury their heads in the sand, or they can do the smart thing and recognize that [legalization] is inevitable."

Russell believes that one way or the other—through legislative action or citizens' initiative—Maine voters will have the opportunity to decide the issue in the fall. The chief advantage of having the legislature take the lead, she says, "is that would give us the opportunity to hold public hearings, to work out the details in a responsible and rational way, and put a well-thought-out proposal on the ballot."

In addition to their victories in Colorado and Washington last November 6, pro-marijuana advocates prevailed in Massachusetts, where 63 percent of voters approved eliminating criminal and civil penalties related to the possession and use of up to a 60-day supply of cannabis for medical purposes. It also requires the state to create and regulate up to 35 facilities to produce and dispense marijuana to approved patients. Massachusetts became the 18th state since 1996 to authorize the physician-recommended use of cannibis. (The District of Columbia also has a medical marijuana law.)

In Arkansas, a statewide ballot measure to legalize the therapeutic use of cannabis failed, but only by a narrow margin, 49 percent to 51 percent. And in Oregon, where pro-pot activists didn't wage much of a campaign, a proposal that would have allowed the state-licensed production and retail sale of cannabis to adults garnered 47 percent of the vote.

The Medical Marijuana Model

As more and more states take up the issue of marijuana reform, the prevailing view among legalization advocates is that Colorado will be the leader in developing model policies and practices.

"The thing that Colorado really has going for it is that there is already a high level of comfort and familiarity with the state licensing, taxing and regulating the above-ground distribution of marijuana," says Ethan Nadelmann, executive director of the Drug Policy Alliance. "People have become accustomed to the notion that this can be a source of tax revenue, and that police can play a role in ensuring effective regulation rather than just arresting anyone they can."

Vicente, who helped write Amendment 64, says he is hopeful that the federal government will hold off and allow Colorado to build on its existing medical marijuana regulations. "The state has a very strict level of oversight that we call seed-to-sale tracking, and this system has worked quite well," he says.

Currently, nearly 110,000 Coloradans are enrolled in the state's medical-marijuana registry, which issues "red cards" to qualified patients. The vast majority of enrollees list severe pain, nausea or muscle spasms as their primary ailment. Men account for about 68 percent of the registry, with the average age hovering around 41.

Over the past several years, more than 500 medical-marijuana dispensaries—which are required to obtain both state and local licenses—have sprung up across Colorado, along with dozens of authorized growers.

Under current regulations, every step in the growing process is rigorously overseen and continuously filmed by video cameras monitored by the state's Medical Marijuana Enforcement Division. No video blind spots are allowed, and truck shipments must detail the total weight of all marijuana products, as well as the times of their arrivals and departures. In addition, every marijuana worker must be licensed.

Vicente doesn't think legalization will lead to an explosion of new businesses selling pot.

"Probably the only retail marijuana shops will be pre-existing dispensaries that decide to opt in to this new system," he says. "What we've found is that communities across Colorado have strictly limited the number of dispensaries through zoning and other regulations, and they're not likely to expand much beyond that."

To date, 86 Colorado communities have banned pot dispensaries, either by popular vote or city council ordinances. But in a dozen other communities, ranging from

Denver to Grand Junction to the tiny mountain town of Nederland, commercial strips are dotted with neon green crosses signifying medical marijuana businesses.

On a recent segment of *60 Minutes,* correspondent Steve Kroft visited several of Denver's 204 medical marijuana dispensaries, noting that they "outnumber Starbucks and McDonald's combined by nearly threefold."

With two states blazing the trail by legalizing marijuana, and public acceptance of the drug on an upward trajectory, it's clear state lawmakers will be grappling with the social, economic and political ramifications of cannabis for some time.

A Growing Tolerance for Pot

A survey by Public Policy Polling several weeks after the November 6 election suggests that other states may be ready to follow Washington and Colorado's example. It found that 58 percent of registered voters favor legalizing pot, the highest level of support ever recorded in a national poll. And a strong plurality (47 percent) of respondents said they think the Obama administration should allow Colorado and Washington to establish the ballot measures approved by voters to regulate and tax marijuana like alcohol.

The change in opinion about legalizing marijuana has followed a slow but steady course, rising from 12 percent in a 1969 Gallup poll to a record 50 percent in 2011. While support for legalization dipped a bit during the anti-pot backlash of the "Just Say No" era in the 1980s, it began rising again in the 1990s.

Generational differences in opinions about marijuana legalization reflect generational differences in its use. According to the 2011 National Survey on Drug Use and Health, most Americans between the ages of 12 and 60 have tried marijuana, while most Americans in their 60s or older have not.

Shifts in public opinion are increasingly at odds with the longstanding prohibition on marijuana at the federal and state levels. Of the 1.5 million drug-related arrests in the United States in 2011, 43 percent were for marijuana possession, according to the FBI's annual Uniform Crime Report. The vast majority of those arrested for simple possession end up paying misdemeanor fines or, in some cases, serving a sentence in county jail, the Marijuana Policy Project has reported.

The Million-Dollar Revenue Question

A key selling point for marijuana legalization in Colorado and Washington was the potential for a major new stream of revenue in the form of licensing fees and taxes on the cultivation, processing and sale of cannabis. But estimates of the revenues likely to flow into state and local government coffers vary widely.

In Colorado, estimates range from between $5 million and $20 million a year (according to the nonpartisan voter guide prepared by the Colorado Legislative Council) to a high of between $40 million and $60 million (according to a study done by the Colorado Center on Law and Policy, a Denver think tank).

Those revenues would come from two sources: state and local sales taxes that patrons of marijuana stores would pay on their purchases, and a 15 percent excise tax that store owners would pay when buying marijuana from licensed wholesale growers.

Under the provisions of Amendment 64, the first $40 million collected each year from the excise tax would be put toward public-school construction. Any revenues above that would go into the state's general fund.

Revenue projections are considerably higher in Washington, where marijuana will be subject to a hefty 25 percent tax at every stage—cultivation, processing and sale. A study by legalization advocates during the campaign estimated those taxes would generate up to $500 million a year. The new Washington law calls for 40 percent of the revenues to go to the state general fund and local budgets, and the remainder to education, health care and substance-abuse programs.

But how much revenue will be generated in the two states depends on a variety of factors, says Beau Kilmer, co-director of the Rand Drug Policy Research Center: the demand for legal marijuana; the price of marijuana, which could plummet with legalization; the number of people who choose to stay in the two states' medical-marijuana system, where cannabis isn't taxed at such high rates; and the number of marijuana dealers who decide to stay underground and avoid taxes.

"If the taxes are set too high, you still have to worry about a black market," Kilmer says.

On the other hand, some factors could boost revenue numbers, according to Carnegie Mellon professor and drug-policy expert Jonathan Caulkins. For instance, if Colorado and Washington become hubs for marijuana tourism, demand at marijuana stores would not only increase, but those tourists would also spend money on hotels, restaurants and rental cars.

"It's possible that could have a bigger impact than excise and sales taxes," Caulkins says.

Washington's Initiative 502

Initiative 502 removes criminal sanctions for anyone 21 or older possessing one ounce or less of marijuana for personal use. It also legalizes possession of up to 16 ounces of solid cannabis-infused goods—such as brownies or cookies—and up to 72 ounces of marijuana-infused sodas, teas or juices.

The new law does not allow home growing, and selling marijuana remains illegal. The state has until the end of 2013 to come up with a system of state-licensed growers, processors and retail stores, with the marijuana taxed at 25 percent at each stage (cultivation, processing and sale).

Initiative 502 also sets a new standard for marijuana impairment while driving at 5 nanograms of THC per milliliter of whole blood.

Colorado's Amendment 64

Amendment 64 allows anyone over age 21 to purchase up to one ounce of marijuana from specialty marijuana dispensaries. Selling marijuana without a license, purchasing marijuana from a party who is not licensed and public use of marijuana remains illegal.

Unlike the new Washington law, Amendment 64 also allows residents to grow up to six marijuana plants and keep all of the harvest. The grower may give away as much as an ounce at a time to others "without remuneration." The measure also allows people to join together to grow marijuana, meaning people could form large-scale cooperatives that produce marijuana by the pound without needing a license as long as none of the marijuana is sold.

The Colorado Department of Revenue, which currently regulates the state's medical marijuana dispensaries, is tasked with writing regulations for marijuana retailers by July 2013, to begin processing license applications by October 2013 and to start issuing licenses by January 2014.

Amendment 64 requires the state to ask voters to approve a 15 percent excise tax on wholesale marijuana sales, with the first $40 million in revenue every year earmarked for building public schools.

The 3 Worst Arguments for Legalizing Marijuana

By Mike Riggs
Reason, March 23, 2012

When Gallup first asked Americans how they felt about marijuana in 1969, only 12 percent of respondents favored the legalization of weed. That number has increased steadily with each passing decade, and in October 2011, Gallup reported that 50 percent of Americans favor the legalization of marijuana, the country's most popular illicit drug.

The shift in popular opinion reflects not just decades of scientific research showing that marijuana is relatively safer than both alcohol and harder drugs (including many prescription pills), but also the savvy PR efforts of drug reform wonks and activists. When even conservative Christians such as The 700 Club's Pat Robertson are calling for legalizing pot, you know that the war on the War on Drugs is not just winnable, but practically over.

But that doesn't mean all arguments in favor of legalization are equally good, effective, or factual. Here are the three weakest arguments for legalizing marijuana. As you work to convince the shrinking ranks of drug prohibitionists—we're looking at you, Mr. President!—don't make these rookie mistakes when arguing for changing the legal status of cannabis.

3. Legalizing Marijuana Will End Cartel Violence in Northern Mexico

The election of Mexican President Felipe Calderon in 2006 ushered in a new era of prohibition-fueled drug violence. Six years and 50,000 drug-war deaths later, the argument that repealing marijuana prohibition could stem the violence in Mexico and along the U.S. border is ubiquitous. The claim was a major selling point for Proposition 19 in California, which would have legalized marijuana and subjected its sale to taxation and regulation, and has been made repeatedly by drug reform advocates in the two years since.

"We have created an illegal marketplace with such mind-boggling profits that no enforcement measures will ever overcome the motivation, resources and determination of the cartels," Libertarian Party presidential candidate Gary Johnson wrote in a 2011 op-ed for *The Washington Times*. Legalizing pot, he added, would deny the cartels "their largest profit center and dramatically reduce not only the role of the United States in their business plans, but also the motivation for waging war along our southern border."

But there are objections to that claim. In October 2010, the RAND Corporation released a study saying that Mexican cartels derived only 16 percent of their revenue from marijuana. (As pointed out by NORML, that number conflicted with the ONDCP's estimate that 61 percent of cartel revenue comes from marijuana.)

In June 2011, Mexico analyst Sylvia Longmire argued that cartels have diversified to the point that legalizing marijuana might dent their war chests, but it won't stop them; they'd still make money stealing oil from pipelines, pirating and selling contraband intellectual property, extorting small businesses, bribing politicians, ransoming kidnap victims, manufacturing and moving harder drugs such as cocaine, heroin, and meth, and trafficking undocumented immigrants and sex workers.

In 2011, David Borden, executive director of StoptheDrugWar.org, emailed me with objections to Longmire's argument: "Some of the other criminal enterprises that cartels are involved in (enterprises they've been able to enter because of having drug cash and organizations built by drug cash) are less straightforwardly tied to demand, such as kidnapping for ransom, but they have their limits—for all we know they are already doing as much of those things as they think could be sustained, and the more profit they continue to make from drugs, the more money they are going to invest in all kinds of enterprises, both illicit and licit."

"Will the cartels vanish from the face of the earth because of marijuana legalization?" Borden continued. "Probably not. Would even full legalization of all drugs accomplish that? Unclear."

That lack of clarity is exactly why marijuana reformers should be careful when promising what legalizing pot can and can't do for Mexico. The war on drugs has weakened the country's political institutions, corrupted its military and police forces, and devastated its economy. While pot legalization in the U.S. would allow users to divest from the cartels' brutality, pitching marijuana legalization as anything other than a baby step toward peace and stability in Mexico puts drug reformers on tenuous grounds.

2. Marijuana Should Be Taxed and Regulated Because It Is America's Largest Cash Crop

In 2006, ABC News reported that with "a value of $35.8 billion, marijuana exceeds the combined value of corn ($23.3 billion) and wheat ($7.5 billion)." That number came from a report published by Jon Gettman, director of the Coalition for Rescheduling Cannabis. Gettman arrived at this figure by multiplying the estimated number of metric tons of marijuana cultivated in the U.S. in 2005 (10,000 tons, or 20 million pounds) by a production value of $1,600 per pound.

Drug law reformers claimed Gettman's report was evidence that eradication and enforcement efforts had failed. In the intervening years, however, the statistic has been used to make the case that taxing and regulating marijuana would solve many of America's fiscal woes. The former argument is a sound one, the latter is not.

Here's why: Gettman's estimate of $1,600 per pound was conservative when compared to law enforcement agencies, which in 2005 cited the street value of marijuana at between $2,000 and $4,000 a pound. Marijuana cultivated in a post-prohibition market, however, would cost a fraction of that.

"To get a sense of the disparity in price between legal and illegal drugs," *Reason's* Jacob Sullum wrote in 2007, "compare the production value of marijuana—about $1,600 per pound, by Gettman's estimate—to the production value of tobacco, a legal psychoactive weed that U.S. farmers sell for less than $2 per pound."

Let's go back to 2005, make marijuana legal, and give it an astronomically high production value of $800 per pound, or half of Gettman's black market estimate: It would have tied with soy beans in 2006 as America's third largest cash crop, with an average production value of roughly $17 billion. If it had the same production value per pound as tobacco, or $2, its APV in 2005 would have been $44 million; or less than 10 percent of beans, 2005's 20th most valuable cash crop.

So while pointing to marijuana as America's largest cash crop is a good indicator of its popularity (and arguably, the safety of its use), it doesn't follow that taxation and regulation of the drug in a post-prohibition market would be an unlimited boon to government coffers, especially when factoring in the costs of an aggressive regulatory framework.

1. Marijuana Should Be Legal Because It's Medicine

There's no question that marijuana eases pain, stimulates the appetite, reduces nausea, and helps with a slew of other physical and psychological ailments. There is some question, however, as to whether promoting it as medicine is the best political strategy for making it fully available as a recreational drug.

Earlier this year, NORML Executive Director Allen St. Pierre wrote a searing critique of the medical marijuana strategy.

"If this were the 1920s, advocacy of today's 'medical' cannabis industry would sound like a lawyer back then fronting for the legal sellers of 'prescription' alcohol during Prohibition. Prescriptive alcohol was a sham then, and the 'medical' cannabis industry (not medical cannabis itself) is largely a sham now."

"Cannabis consumers," he continued, "who NORML represents, want good, affordable cannabis products without having to go through the insult and expense of 'qualifying' as a 'medical' patient by paying physicians and/or the state for some kind of get-out-of-jail-free card. How intellectually honest is all of this?"

One response is that successful medical marijuana ballot initiatives protect people who use marijuana for genuine medical reasons from harassment and imprisonment. But the problems with those laws—such as who counts as a caregiver, and the number of prescriptions given to people who are using it recreationally—don't reflect well on the political acumen of drug law reformers.

Legislators and regulators are wising up and changing tactics. Because most states that currently have medical marijuana laws make the bulk of their sales to people with chronic pain—the only ailment eligible for medical marijuana that doctors can't test for, and thus the ailment most likely to be cited by recreational users looking for safe access—Washington, D.C. decided to omit chronic pain from its list of ailments that qualify for medical marijuana. In the District, only people with cancer or a terminal illness will be able to get medical pot. In Colorado, where legislators claim only 20 percent of marijuana sales are to people with "legitimate" illnesses such as HIV/AIDS, cancer, Crohn's disease, and MS, legislators are looking for ways to limit the number of recommendations doctors can write to the other 80 percent of users.

In short, while medical marijuana laws initially gave more users safe access, anti-pot legislators now seem to know that the best way to limit marijuana sales is to treat it exactly like advocates claim to want: as medicine subject to a strict and invasive regulatory prescription scheme.

How Marijuana Legalization Leaves Mothers and Pregnant Women Behind

By Kristen Gwynne
RH Reality Check, May 12, 2014

It is no secret that marijuana legalization in Colorado and Washington ushered in internationally unprecedented progressive drug policy in the United States. What is lesser understood, however, is that these new "experimental" reforms do not necessarily peel back all of the many, punitive layers of drug war enforcement. Despite the prevailing notion that the consequences of marijuana prohibition are determined in criminal courts for crimes like possession and sale, some of the harshest punishments are steeped in ever-complicated family law and Child Protective Services (CPS).

Well-intentioned marijuana policy reform thus often leaves women, who are more likely to be their children's primary caretakers, behind. The effects of enforcing anti-drug family law go so far, in fact, as to punish women for child abuse and neglect crimes ostensibly committed on their fetuses—even in states where marijuana is explicitly legal for all adults 21 and older.

"Drug endangered children"—the term used to describe various programs, tactics, and other efforts to address child abuse via drug use—represents "the new way drug warriors are trying to continue their war on marijuana, and has become a multi-agency federal, state, and local tool, which the states and agencies may use to get even more funds," Sara Arnold, marijuana policy activist and founder of the Family Law Cannabis Alliance, told *RH Reality Check*. "Many cannabis [decriminalization] laws actually run the risk of making parents second-class citizens, because they end up being the only ones left who will face penalties for their cannabis use."

For Colorado mother Amber Buster, marijuana use was a seemingly legal, effective treatment for debilitating side effects of pregnancy. Buster was expecting her third child when she experienced "morning" sickness so severe that her nausea and vomiting lasted throughout the day.

"I couldn't even drink water or eat crackers," Buster said. She worried nutritional deficiencies might affect her pregnancy. Familiar with medical marijuana because her mother and spouse are state-licensed users, Buster found that smoking a little weed improved her appetite enough that she could keep some food and liquids down.

Unbeknownst to her, however, Colorado's marijuana law need not explicitly state exceptions to legalized adult marijuana use for such exceptions to exist. The complicated, incentive-based relationship between federal and state child abuse laws obscures parents' protections under legalization.

"As long as cannabis is a scheduled controlled substance under federal law, it will be included in laws regarding child abuse/neglect and come into conflict with state laws—and leave it up to CPS departments to decide which policy they follow, unless they are specifically stopped from doing so," Arnold explained in an email, adding that professionals, like doctors, who are tasked with reporting child abuse also have wide discretion. "Keep in mind that both mandated reporters [of child abuse] and CPS workers have qualified immunity; what this means is that they cannot be sued by parents who are wronged if they report or investigate a parent when they shouldn't, as long as it was in good faith (and it is always presumed to be so unless there is clear proof it was malicious)."

The Child Abuse Prevention and Treatment Act (CAPTA) requires states receiving federal grants to meet a series of standards. It mandates, for example, that states address the needs of infants "affected by illegal substance abuse or withdrawal symptoms resulting from prenatal drug exposure," and that "health care providers involved in the delivery or care of" drug-exposed infants notify CPS, regardless of whether the baby's health is threatened.

CAPTA's failure to further define terms like "affected by an illegal substance" leaves hospital staff incredible discretion in determining which mothers they perceive as potential addicts whose children should be tested, which babies are "affected," and even which drugs are "illegal."

This discretion, in turn, allows for an unpredictable system often guided by confusion and biases from individual reporters of abuse and neglect.

Buster informed her primary physician that she was using marijuana for nausea because she had been taught that doctors are "supposed to have the truth in case anything happens." The doctor thought of her marijuana use as the equivalent of smoking a cigarette, she said, and nonchalantly made a note of it. But nurses in the hospital where Buster gave birth were more concerned, and after discovering the note in her file, they notified the new mother that, despite an uncomplicated delivery and healthy infant, they were "required" to drug-test the baby. (There is no law explicitly requiring them to do so.)

The infant tested positive for THC, prompting three CPS visits to Buster's home followed by a notice indicating an official finding of child abuse and neglect, all thanks to a well-intended note neither she nor her physician expected to cause such a kerfuffle. To Buster, the entire ordeal was shocking proof that marijuana in Colorado is only legal for some.

Indra Lusero, a Colorado attorney focusing on civil rights related to childbirth, took on Buster's case. She argued that Buster's marijuana use was legal under Amendment 64, and that CPS agents failed to find additional evidence of an unfit environment. She won her appeal and had the child abuse finding expunged before

Buster went to trial. "The positive test for drug exposure basically became a de facto finding of abuse," said Lusero. Moreover, she said that she doubts Buster is alone.

"I am confident there are other women who are facing charges [similar to Buster's] and don't have access to legal help," said Lusero. "I am also confident that marijuana use is a factor in some complex cases where there are other variables related to abuse, and if parents had better access to legal help, marijuana use could be mitigated as an influential factor."

One such example is custody battles, during which marijuana use could be presented as evidence of an unfit parent.

In two marijuana-related child abuse and neglect cases Lusero successfully fought, drug tests at birth were the primary cause of investigation. The law here is fuzzy: Colorado considers a positive drug test for a Schedule I or II controlled substance (as defined by the state's Controlled Substance Act) an automatic finding of abuse or neglect, unless the Schedule II substance was taken legally as prescribed by a doctor. In Colorado, however, marijuana does not appear in the Schedule I or II category, creating a discrepancy between state and federal law (which does categorize marijuana as Schedule I) that individuals tasked with reporting child abuse have the leisure to define.

You see, CAPTA instructs states receiving funding to establish "mandatory reporters" of child abuse and neglect. In Colorado, these reporters range from marriage counselors to dental hygienists to clergy, all of whom are legally required to report maltreatment given "reasonable cause to know or suspect child abuse or neglect" or having observed "a child being subjected to circumstances or conditions that would reasonably result in abuse or neglect." At the same time, they are tasked with interpreting the laws and making decisions about home lives that, though often requiring a wealth of intimate knowledge, are based on the individual reporter's preconceived notions about drugs and who uses them, including a host of race- and class-based biases.

"It would be nice to have some kind of policy—even if I could have expected that on my delivery date I would be harassed and forced to get involved in CPS," said Buster. "It would be nice if maybe doctors would be required to tell you up-front that this could happen, that if you smoke marijuana and they end up testing your baby there's a lot of things that could happen. At the time, I thought patient confidentiality applied, that it would only be brought up in the case of an emergency."

Colorado legislators just introduced but failed to pass two bills tasked with "clarifying" the law in terms of drug-related child abuse and neglect, though not necessarily in a way that would have protected Buster.

The bills, SB 14-177 and SB 14-178, sought to define instances of a "drug-endangered child" while treating drug-endangerment as an automatic, punishable finding of child abuse and neglect. Concerning to Colorado legislators and marijuana policy activists alike, however, was that the bills were too sweeping to delicately address a complicated, yet exponentially important, issue. Critics' amendments significantly reduced the bills' oversight so that, by the time they reached the finish line, proponents argued the new legislation more narrowly defined drug-related child abuse than existing codes did.

Indeed, the new legislation added via amendments that de facto child abuse findings from drug endangerment can occur "only" when a child's welfare or health is threatened—a much-needed adjustment.

Still, the bills also expanded the existing code's de facto finding of child abuse in several ways. SB 14-177, for example, introduced to state law two new definitions by which parental drug use could legally endanger and abuse/neglect children: a child's "unrestricted access" to a controlled substance (including marijuana) and a parent's "impairment" due to use of a controlled substance or legal substance capable of causing impairment. Under these new de facto child abuse findings, mandatory reporters would be tasked with judging proper marijuana storage, not to mention acceptable levels of highs, both of which leave the door to discretion wide open.

SB 14-177 and SB 14-178 also tried to broaden the law's "manufacturing" focus on children near meth labs to consider parents who cultivated, produced, possessed, used, distributed, or obtained a controlled substance—such as voter-approved pot—where a child is present or resides, an automatic finding of child abuse. Amendments adding that abuse "only" exists amid threat of injury soothed but did not eradicate concerns that state-sanctioned home grows might be treated by some individual reporters as de facto child abuse.

Even in their amended state, however, these laws fail to acknowledge that, even when legislative language mandates evidence of a safety risk, linking drug use to abuse ignites a judgment of parenting that is difficult to reverse.

Buster, for example, says her marijuana use was treated as illegal "because they just presumed I was getting my baby high instead of [treating nausea]."

This notion—that a person who smokes marijuana while pregnant is causing abuse to her fetus—is one scientists have repeatedly rejected. In an affidavit related to a similar case, Dr. Peter Fried, a psychology professor at Carleton University in Canada who has dedicated much of his career to studying the effects of prenatal marijuana exposure on infants, wrote:

> Based on my 30 plus years of experience examining the newborn, infants, toddlers, children, adolescents and young adults born to women who used marihuana during pregnancy it is important to emphasize that to characterize an infant born to a woman who used marihuana during pregnancy as being "physically abused" and/or "neglected" is contrary to all scientific evidence (both mine and subsequent work by other researchers). The use of marijuana during pregnancy . . . has not been shown by any objective research to result in abuse or neglect.

Indeed, the legislative push to punish women for marijuana use during pregnancy is based not on science suggesting harm from which to protect children, but the notion of fetal rights.

Dorothy Roberts, University of Pennsylvania professor and author of *Killing the Black Body*, told *RH Reality Check*, "Punishing or monitoring a pregnant woman for drug use relies on a view of the fetus as not just a separate person apart from the mother, but as if their interests are in conflict," thus promoting the concept of fetal "personhood."

Roberts also explained that the "very discretionary, very discriminatory" practices of Child Protective Services are rooted in racial stereotypes about drug use and mothering that continue to affect the outcome of CPS cases today.

"Drug use during pregnancy became a crime because it was targeted at Black women," she said, acknowledging that "it has since moved to punish other women as well, but the conception of a public health problem as a crime relies on the vilification of Black women and their children."

It began during the crack era, says Roberts, along with which came anti-drug hysteria including "the myth of the pregnant crack addict, who was thought to have no maternal instinct, and the myth of the 'crack baby,' who was supposed to be destined to be a criminal, a welfare dependent, a drug addict, and every anti-social behavior imaginable."

The myth of the "crack baby," too, has been debunked in several well-regarded studies. One found, for example, that doctors could not tell the difference between babies born crack-exposed from those born poverty-stricken.

The science is clear: Drug-related accusations of child abuse and neglect for crimes committed against a fetus are unsubstantiated.

Fighting against this trend in Child Protective Services will require more than just marijuana legalization. But to move the drug policy reform conversation in a direction that benefits women, there will need to be more women in positions of authority in the marijuana legalization movement—which is often overwhelmingly represented by men.

To offer resources like model legislation, female drug policy reformers are stepping up and organizing their own women-led groups, like the NORML Women's Alliance and Sara Arnold's Family Law Cannabis Alliance. As we usher in a new tide of marijuana policy reform, their work is paramount to ensuring marijuana legalization remain dedicated to social and racial justice for men, women, and parents alike.

"This is the next major battle in the long fight of marijuana reform," said Arnold. "There is still some stigma about this issue even from marijuana reformers, and that has to change. The full might of marijuana reform needs to get behind this."

8 Lies We Have to Stop Telling Ourselves about Marijuana in America

By Tom McKay

PolicyMic, May 12, 2014

Legal marijuana will lead to criminals smashing through your door and stealing your money.

Marijuana has no medical use.

Do these claims sound familiar? Drug warriors have been extremely successful in alarming America about the dangers of marijuana for decades. But where they haven't been successful is spreading accurate information about ganja to the populace.

Here are 8 of the top myths people tell about marijuana, and how to rebut them.

1. Marijuana Is a Gateway Drug.

Marijuana's opponents claim marijuana is a "gateway drug"—that once someone smokes marijuana, they're much more likely to try other, harder drugs and eventually end up using something much more dangerous. There is, in fact, a correlation between marijuana use and other drugs: The National Institute on Drug Abuse claims that a person who smokes weed is 104× more likely to use cocaine than someone who never touched a joint.

But that's all it is—a correlation. As TIME's *Healthland* wrote all the way back in 2010, scientists have discarded the gateway hypothesis since the 90s. A report on the Institute of Medicine of the National Academy of Sciences in 1999 said that:

> In the sense that marijuana use typically precedes rather than follows initiation of other illicit drug use, it is indeed a "gateway" drug. But because underage smoking and alcohol use typically precede marijuana use, marijuana is not the most common, and is rarely the first, "gateway" to illicit drug use. There is no conclusive evidence that the drug effects of marijuana are causally linked to the subsequent abuse of other illicit drugs.

And the majority of marijuana users never touch cocaine or heroin. In 2009, 2.3 million people reported trying pot, compared to 617,000 for cocaine and 180,000 for heroin.

The Marijuana Policy Project says that 107 million Americans (nearly 40% of the country) have tried marijuana, while only 37 million have tried cocaine and less than 0.1% of Americans have used either coke or heroin in the past month.

Spokesman Morgan Fox says marijuana has never been demonstrated to have any chemical component that would make it particularly dangerous and that if there is a gateway, it's because dealers have an incentive to push other illegal drugs on buyers.

"When you go to a liquor store for a bottle of wine, there isn't a person there trying to sell you cocaine or other dangerous products," he says. "An illegal narcotics dealer has incentive to push dangerous drugs."

Another study of 12th graders published in the *Journal of School Health* indicated that if there is a "gateway drug," there's more evidence to point towards alcohol as the culprit. A 2012 review of the evidence in *Drug and Alcohol Dependence* for the gateway drug hypothesis noted that 83.2% of hard drug users in Japan had never touched cannabis, while noting that the theory of a variety of gateway behaviors stood up to more rigorous review.

Reason's Jacob Sullum wrote that the gateway drug hypothesis' "durability is largely due to its ambiguity: Because it's rarely clear what people mean when they say that pot smoking leads to the use of 'harder' drugs, the claim is difficult to disprove."

2. It's as Dangerous as LSD or Heroin.

This argument is based on the DEA's list of controlled substances, which places marijuana among "the most dangerous drugs," "with no currently accepted medical use and a high potential for abuse." Schedule I drugs are said to leave users with "potentially severe psychological or physical dependence," and in addition to weed, that list includes heroin, LSD, ecstasy, methaqualone, and peyote.

That's some pretty hefty, dangerous-sounding company. But in 2010, 38,329 people died from drug overdoses. Pharmaceutical drugs killed 22,134 people, of which opoid analgesics killed 16,651. An additional 25,692 people died from alcohol overdoses (for comparison, the CDC says that alcohol kills 88,000 a year including conditions like liver failure and drunken driving accidents).

But in not a single documented case has marijuana killed someone from overdose—technically, with a lethal dose that would require ingesting the THC of at least dozens and probably hundreds of pounds of marijuana or more, it's less lethal than water. Even the National Institute on Drug Abuse admits that it's "not very likely" you could overdose on marijuana, while still warning users they can experience anxiety attacks or get in marijuana-related accidents.

So by the most obvious metric of marijuana's danger—whether or not you can die or even be seriously injured through an overdose—the answer is plainly no.

Other Schedule I and even Schedule II drugs like meth and cocaine are plainly far more dangerous. That might explain why 38% of the country has tried it and walked away fine from the experience.

3. It's Causing an Epidemic of Car Crashes.

But if we were going to settle on another metric of how dangerous marijuana is— how many car crashes it causes—marijuana is still not anywhere near as dangerous as other illicit drugs. In general, the performance of drivers on THC is not impacted nearly as much as drivers on alcohol. A 2004 observational case study in *Accident Analysis and Prevention* found that "no increased risk for road trauma was found for drivers exposed to cannabis," while alcohol and benzodiazepines were linked to vehicular accidents.

There's some bad news here: a study published in the *American Journal of Epidemiology* that assessed 23,591 road fatalities found that the presence of cannabis in a dead driver rose from 4.2% in 1999 to 12.2% in 2010. But since THC can be present in blood for days after use, it's unclear how many drivers were actually high at the time of the accident. Furthermore, alcohol was found in over three times as many drivers—around 39.7%.

Additionally, car crash fatalities have been trending downwards for years. There were 51,091 fatalities in 1980, 41,945 in 2000, 37,171 in 2008, and 25,580 in 2012. So even if marijuana use has increased, American roads are still getting safer.

As Jenny Hollander writes for *Bustle*:

> Here's what we do know: Stoned drivers behave differently from drunk drivers. Stoned drivers are more aware that they're intoxicated—the opposite applies for drunk drivers—and so they tend to actually drive more slowly and carefully. Therefore, drivers who are a little stoned are generally safer drivers than those who are a little drunk. As a rule, drunk driving has been understood to be far more dangerous than driving when high.

So while no one would advise getting high and driving, there's no solid evidence that marijuana-related traffic fatalities are a major national epidemic.

4. Pot Smoking Leads to More Crime.

Sheriff Tom Allman of Mendocio County, Calif., had a warning for Colorado residents three months after they voted to legalize marijuana in Nov. 2012: "Thugs put on masks, they come to your house, they kick in your door. They point guns at you and say, 'Give me your marijuana, give me your money.'"

"Expect more crime, more kids using marijuana and pot for sale everywhere," said Douglas County Sheriff David Weaver in 2012. "I think our entire state will pay the price."

But Denver crime rates remained stable and in some places actually fell. (Arson was up 109% from the same period, but represented just 23 of 3,757 crimes—so if you want to blame every count on smouldering doobies, whatever.)

A study in *PLOS One* that examined states which legalized medical marijuana over the period 1990–2006 found that there were actually minor reductions in the homicide and aggravated assault rate.

It's debatable whether legalizing marijuana has a substantial downward effect on the crime rate. But what's clear is that looser marijuana laws have not been behind any noteworthy crime waves. And what's more, fewer people are going to jail in Colorado now that marijuana has been legalized.

5. It Makes You Lazy and Unsuccessful.

Opponents of marijuana reform point to studies like this one from researcher Christer Hyggen that linked marijuana use to lower motivation at work. During the study, 1,997 respondents born between 1965 and 1986 were tracked and found to have a statistically significant reduction in their work commitment. Sixty-three "repeat users" had an average score of 3.9 on questions of work commitment, compared to scores of 4.2 and 4.3 among limited users and those who hadn't tried it at all.

But that study wasn't able to finger pot as the culprit, saying it could have also been the social environment in which pot is used or whether the repeat pot-smokers were less committed to begin with. It also didn't tell us anything about the quality of lives of the smokers. And even if we assume that marijuana use was directly responsible for the decline in work commitment, habitual marijuana use might just be one of many contributing factors to below-average career commitment.

And many, many successful people have used pot at least once in their lives—from President Barack Obama and Supreme Court Justice Clarence Thomas to Microsoft CEO Bill Gates and former NYC Mayor Michael Bloomberg. Of all the anti-marijuana arguments, this one is the silliest, encompassing 38% of Americans.

6. It's Highly Addictive.

Studies have discovered cannabis to be less addictive than nicotine, alcohol and even caffeine. A large-scale survey in 1994 by epidemiologist James Anthony of the National Institute on Drug Abuse asked more than 8,000 people between the ages of 15 and 64 about their drug habits. They found that less than 9% of marijuana users ever fit a diagnosis of dependence, compared to 15% of drinkers, 17% of cocaine users, 23% of heroin users, and 32% of cigarette smokers. By and large, it seems marijuana is less addictive than a plethora of legal and illegal substances.

It's true that some 957,000 people aged 12 and over sought treatment for marijuana in 2012. But the large majority of treatment-seekers were referred by the criminal justice system, which has in many places decided referring marijuana users for drug programs instead of locking them up is a better use of public time and funds.

Psychology Today's Dr. J Wesley Boyd wrote that "the vast majority of marijuana users are neither addicted nor almost addicted to cannabis," comparing it to totally-legal alcohol. He also says that the current medical understanding is that physiological withdrawal symptoms from marijuana are "generally mild." CNN's Dr. Sanjay Gupta, a former opponent of medical marijuana, now admits that "It is hard to make a case that it has a high potential for abuse. The physical symptoms of marijuana addiction are nothing like those of the other drugs I've mentioned [morphine, heroin or cocaine]."

7. Legalization Will Lead to Mass Pot Usage.

Sorry, but that train has long since left the station. Some 19–25 million Americans claim to smoke marijuana at least once per year, all under a strict regime of prohibition across most of the country.

Decriminalization, however, has had little to no effect on consumption rates. One study found that while decriminalization pretty much had a negligible effect on prevalence of use, it generated substantial savings in the criminal justice system. A 2001 paper by Don Weatherburn and Craig Jones found that "Fear of arrest, fear of imprisonment, the cost of cannabis or its availability do not appear to exert much effect on the prevalence of cannabis use." And all this for the small minority of users who ingest marijuana regularly; they found that 54.2% of self-identified users use it "every few months" or less, while just 9.7% smoked every day.

A wide range of literature suggests that not only is marijuana prohibition not convincing people to abstain from drugs, its social costs may outweigh any perceived benefits. What's more, the anti-drug crowd has lost the faith of teenagers because they offer hyperbole and panic rather than factual explanations of marijuana and responsible use.

8. It Has No Medical Use.

This one ignores not just widespread medical evidence, but what the medical community itself says. WebMD found that 69% of doctors believe medical marijuana delivers benefits to patients, while 82% of oncologists and hematologists were in favor of medical marijuana. Another study published in the *New England Journal of Medicine* of 1,446 doctors from 72 countries and 56 states and provinces in North America found that 76% supported medical marijuana.

Doctors currently prescribe medical marijuana for pain, multiple sclerosis, chemotherapy-induced nausea, poor appetite and weight loss from chronic disease, seizure disorders, and Crohn's disease. It may even potentially help treat traumatic brain injury and Alzheimer's disease. Weed's illegal status and Schedule I classification means that patients have no federally recognized access to medical marijuana and doctors can't adequately study it.

How Not to Make a Hash out of Cannabis Legalization

By Mark Kleiman
Washington Monthly, March/April/May 2014

A majority of Americans, and an overwhelming majority of those under thirty, now support the legalization of marijuana. This change in public opinion, which has been building for years but has accelerated of late, is now generating policy changes.

In 2012, voters in Colorado and Washington state endorsed initiatives legalizing not just the use of cannabis but also its commercial production and sale to anyone over the age of twenty-one. That goes further than the "medical marijuana" provisions that are now the law in twenty states. Nonmedical retail sales started on January 1[2014] in Colorado and will begin in early summer in Washington. Similar propositions are likely to be on the ballot in 2014 and 2016 in as many as a dozen other states, including Alaska, Arizona, California, Nevada, and Oregon, and a legalization bill just narrowly passed in the New Hampshire House of Representatives, the first time either chamber of any state legislature has voted for such a bill. Unless something happens to reverse the trend in public opinion, it seems more likely than not that the federal law will change to make cannabis legally available at some point in the next two decades.

The state-by-state approach has generated some happy talk from both advocates and some neutral observers; Justice Louis Brandeis's praise for states as the "laboratories of democracy" has been widely quoted. Given how much we don't know about the consequences of legalization, there's a reasonable case for starting somewhere, rather than everywhere. Even some who oppose legalization are moderately comforted by the fact that the federal government isn't driving the process. "It's best that this be done state by state," said Pat Buchanan recently on *The McLaughlin Group*, "so you can have a national backlash if it doesn't work out."

But letting legalization unfold state by state, with the federal government a mostly helpless bystander, risks creating a monstrosity; Dr. Frankenstein also had a laboratory. Right now, officials in Washington and Colorado are busy issuing state licenses to cannabis growers and retailers to do things that remain drug-dealing felonies under federal law. The Justice Department could have shut down the process by going after all the license applicants. But doing so would have run the risk of having the two states drop their own enforcement efforts and challenge the feds to do the job alone, something the DEA simply doesn't have the bodies to handle:

Washington and Colorado alone have about four times as many state and local police as there are DEA agents worldwide. Faced with that risk, and with its statutory obligation to cooperate with the states on drug enforcement, Justice chose accommodation.

In August, the deputy U.S. attorney general issued a formal—though nonbinding—assurance that the feds would take a mostly hands-off approach. The memo says that as long as state governments pursue "strong and effective" regulation to prevent activities such as distribution to minors, dealing by gangs and cartels, dealing other drugs, selling across state lines, possession of weapons and use of violence, and drugged driving, and as long as marijuana growing and selling doesn't take place on public lands or federal property, enforcement against state-licensed cannabis activity will rank low on the federal priority list. Justice has even announced that it is working with the Treasury Department to reinterpret the banking laws to allow state-licensed cannabis businesses to have checking accounts and take credit cards, avoiding the robbery risks incident to all-cash businesses.

That leaves the brand-new cannabis businesses in Colorado and Washington in statutory limbo. They're quasi-pseudo-hemi-demi-legal: permitted under state law, but forbidden under a federal law that might not be enforced   until, say, the inauguration of President Huckabee, at which point growers and vendors, as well as their lawyers, accountants, and bankers, could go to prison for the things they're doing openly today.

But even if the federal-state legal issues get resolved, the state-level tax and regulation systems likely to emerge will be far from ideal. While they will probably do a good job of eliminating the illicit cannabis markets in those states, they'll be mediocre to lousy at preventing an upsurge of drug abuse as cheap, quality-tested, easily available legal pot replaces the more expensive, unreliable, and harder-to-find material the black market offers.

The systems being put into place in Washington and Colorado roughly resemble those imposed on alcohol after Prohibition ended in 1933. A set of competitive commercial enterprises produces the pot, and a set of competitive commercial enterprises sells it, under modest regulations: a limited number of licenses, no direct sales to minors, no marketing obviously directed at minors, purity/potency testing and labeling, security rules. The post-Prohibition restrictions on alcohol worked reasonably well for a while, but have been substantially undermined over the years as the beer and liquor industries consolidated and used their economies of scale to lower production costs and their lobbying muscle to loosen regulations and keep taxes low.

The same will likely happen with cannabis. As more and more states begin to legalize marijuana over the next few years, the cannabis industry will begin to get richer—and that means it will start to wield considerably more political power, not only over the states but over national policy, too.

That's how we could get locked into a bad system in which the primary downside of legalizing pot—increased drug abuse, especially by minors—will be greater than it needs to be, and the benefits, including tax revenues, smaller than they could be.

It's easy to imagine the cannabis equivalent of an Anheuser-Busch InBev peddling low-cost, high-octane cannabis in Super Bowl commercials. We can do better than that, but only if Congress takes action—and soon.

The standard framing of the cannabis legalization debate is simple: either you're for it or you're against it. Setting up the debate that way tempts proponents of legalization to deny all risks, while supporters of the status quo deny how bad the current situation is. Both sides deny the unknown. In truth, there's no way to gauge all the consequences of adopting unprecedented policies, so it's foolish to pretend to be 100 percent certain of anything. But it's possible to guess in advance some of the categories of gain and loss from policy change, even if the magnitudes are unknown, and to identify the complete wild cards: things that might get either better or worse.

The undeniable gains from legalization consist mostly of getting rid of the damage done by prohibition. (Indeed, as E. J. Dionne and William Galston have pointed out, polling suggests that support for legalization is driven more by discontent with prohibition than by enthusiasm for pot.) Right now, Americans spend about $35 billion a year on illegal cannabis. That money goes untaxed; the people working in the industry aren't gaining legitimate job experience or getting Social Security credit, and some of them spend time behind bars and wind up with felony criminal records. About 650,000 users a year get arrested for possession, something much more likely to happen to a black user than a white one.

We also spend about $1 billion annually in public money keeping roughly 40,000 growers and dealers behind bars at any one time. That's a small chunk of the incarceration problem, but it represents a lot of money and a lot of suffering. The enforcement effort, including the use of "dynamic entry" raids, imposes additional costs in money, liberty, police-community conflict, and, occasionally, lives. Cannabis dealing and enforcement don't contribute much to drug-related violence in the United States, but they make up a noticeable part of Mexico's problems.

Another gain from legalization would be to move the millions of Americans whose crimes begin and end with using illegal cannabis from the wrong side of the law to the right one, bringing an array of benefits to them and their communities in the form of a healthier relationship with the legal and political systems. Current cannabis users, and the millions of others who might choose to start using cannabis if the drug became legal, would also enjoy an increase in personal liberty and be able to pursue, without the fear of legal consequences, what is for most of them a harmless source of pleasure, comfort, relaxation, sociability, healing, creativity, or inspiration. For those people, legalization would also bring with it all the ordinary gains consumers derive from open competition: lower prices, easier access, and a wider range of available products and means of administration, held to quality standards the illicit market can't enforce.

To those real gains must be added the political lure of public revenue that comes without raising taxes on currently legal products or incomes. The revenue take could be substantial: legal production and distribution of the amount of cannabis now sold in the U.S. wouldn't cost more than 20 percent of the $35 billion now being paid for it. If prices were kept high and virtually all of the surplus was captured by taxation, it's possible that cannabis taxation could yield as much as $20 billion per year—around 1 percent of the revenues of all the state governments. Those are, of course, two big ifs. The current pricing and tax systems in Colorado and Washington, which between them account for about 5 percent of national cannabis use, won't give taxpayers there anything resembling the $1 billion a year that would be their prorated share of that hypothetical $20 billion.

So much for the upside. What about the downside?

The losses from legalization would mainly accrue to the minority of consumers who lose control of their cannabis use. About a quarter of the sixteen million Americans who report having used cannabis in the past month say they used it every day or almost every day. Those frequent users also use more cannabis per day of use than do less frequent users. About half of the daily- and near-daily-use population meets diagnostic criteria for substance abuse or dependence—that is, they find that their cannabis habit is interfering with other activities and bringing negative consequences, and that their attempts to cut back on the frequency or quantity of their cannabis use have failed. (Those estimates are based on users' own responses to surveys, so they probably underestimate the actual risks.)

And then, of course, there are the extreme cases. A substantial number of these daily users spend virtually every waking hour under the influence. Legal availability is likely to add both to their numbers and to the intensity of their problems. Jonathan Caulkins has done a calculation suggesting that legalization at low prices might increase the amount of time spent stoned by about fifteen billion person-hours per year, concentrated among frequent heavy users rather than among the more numerous Saturday-night partiers. Every year, hundreds of thousands of cannabis users visit emergency departments having unintentionally overdosed, experiencing anxiety, dysphoria, and sometimes panic. Presumably many others suffer very unpleasant experiences without seeking professional attention.

While a bad cannabis habit usually isn't nearly as destructive as a bad alcohol habit, it's plenty bad enough if it happens to you, or to your child or your sibling or your spouse or your parent.

Maybe you think the gains of legalizing marijuana will outweigh the costs; maybe you don't. But that's quickly becoming a moot point. Like it or not, legalization is on its way, unless something occurs to reverse the current trend in public opinion. In any case, it shouldn't be controversial to say that, if we are to legalize cannabis, the policy aim going forward should be to maximize the gains and minimize the disadvantages. But the systems being put in place in Colorado and Washington aren't well designed for that purpose, because they create a cannabis industry whose commercial interest is precisely opposite to the public interest.

Cannabis consumption, like alcohol consumption, follows the so-called 80/20 rule (sometimes called "Pareto's Law"): 20 percent of the users account for 80 percent of the volume. So from the perspective of cannabis vendors, drug abuse isn't the problem; it's the target demographic. Since we can expect the legal cannabis industry to be financially dependent on dependent consumers, we can also expect that the industry's marketing practices and lobbying agenda will be dedicated to creating and sustaining problem drug use patterns.

The trick to legalizing marijuana, then, is to keep at bay the logic of the market—its tendency to create and exploit people with substance abuse disorders. So far, the state-by-state, initiative-driven process doesn't seem up to that challenge. Neither the taxes nor the regulations will prevent substantial decreases in retail prices, which matter much more to very heavy users and to cash-constrained teenagers than they do to casual users. The industry's marketing efforts will be constrained only by rules against appealing explicitly to minors (rules that haven't kept the beer companies from sponsoring Extreme Fighting on television). And there's no guarantee that other states won't create even looser systems. In Oregon, a proposition on the 2012 ballot that was narrowly defeated (53 percent to 47 percent) would have mandated that five of the seven members of the commission to regulate the cannabis industry be chosen by the growers—industry capture, in other words, was written into the proposed law. It remains to be seen whether even the modest taxes and restrictions passed by the voters survive the inevitable industry pressure to weaken them legislatively.

There are three main policy levers that could check cannabis abuse while making the drug legally available. The first and most obvious is price. Roughly speaking, high-potency pot on the illegal market today costs about $10 to $15 per gram. (It's cheaper in the medical outlets in Colorado and Washington.) A joint, enough to get an occasional user stoned more than once, contains about four-tenths of a gram; that much cannabis costs about $5 at current prices. The price in Amsterdam, where retailing is tolerated but growing is still seriously illegal, is about the same, which helps explain why Dutch use hasn't exploded under quasi-legalization. If we too want to avoid a vast increase in heavy cannabis use under legalization, we should create policies to keep the price of the drug about where it is now.

The difficulty is that marijuana is both relatively cheap compared to other drugs and also easy to grow (thus the nickname "weed"), and will just get cheaper and easier to grow under legalization. According to RAND, legal production costs would be a small fraction of the current level, making the pre-tax value of the cannabis in a legally produced joint pennies rather than dollars.

Taxes are one way to keep prices up. But those taxes would have to be ferociously high, and they'd have to be determined by the ounce of pot or (better) by the gram of THC, as alcohol taxes now are, not as a percentage of retail price like a sales tax. Both Colorado and Washington have percentage-of-price taxes, which will fall along with market prices. In states where it was legal, cannabis taxes would have to be more than $200 an ounce to keep prices at current levels; no ballot measure now under consideration has taxes nearly that high.

Collecting such taxes wouldn't be easy in the face of interstate smuggling, as the tobacco markets illustrate. The total taxes on a pack of cigarettes in New York City run about $8 more than the taxes on the same pack in Virginia. Lo and behold, there's a massive illicit industry smuggling cigarettes north, with more than a third of the cigarettes sold in New York escaping New York taxes. Without federal intervention, interstate smuggling of cannabis would be even worse. Whichever state had the lowest cannabis taxes would effectively set prices for the whole country, and the supposed state option to keep the drug illegal would fall victim to inflows from neighboring states.

The other way to keep legal pot prices up is to limit supply. Colorado and Washington both plan to impose production limits on growers. If those limits were kept tight enough, scarcity would lead to a run-up in price. (That's happening right now in Colorado; prices in the limited number of commercial outlets open on January 1 were about 50 percent higher than prices in the medical outlets.) But those states are handing out production rights for modest fixed licensing fees, so any gain from scarcity pricing will go to the industry and encourage even more vigorous marketing. If, instead, production quotas were put up for auction, the gain could go to the taxpayers. Just as a cap-and-trade system for carbon emissions can be made to mimic the effects of a carbon tax, production quotas with an auction would be the equivalent of taxes.

The second policy lever government has is information: it can require or provide product labeling, point-of-sale communication, and outreach to prevent both drug abuse and impaired driving. In principle, posting information about, say, the known chemical composition of one type of cannabis versus another could help consumers use the drug more safely. How that plays out in practice depends on the details of policy design. Colorado and Washington require testing and labeling for chemical content, but techniques for helping consumers translate those numbers into safer consumption practices remain to be developed. The fact that more than 60 percent of cannabis user-days involve people with no more than a high school education creates an additional challenge, one often ignored by the advanced-degree holders who dominate the debate.

The government could also make sure consumers are able to get high-quality information and advice from cannabis vendors. In Uruguay, for example, which is now legalizing on the national level, the current proposal requires cannabis vendors to be registered pharmacists. Cannabis is, after all, a somewhat dangerous drug, and both much more complex chemically and less familiar culturally than beer or wine. In Washington and Colorado, by contrast, the person behind the counter will simply be a sales agent, with no required training about the pharmacology of cannabis and no professional obligation to promote safe use.

A more radical approach would be to enhance consumers' capacity to manage their own drug use with a program of user-determined periodic purchase limits.

All of these attempts by government to use information to limit abuse, however, could be overwhelmed by the determined marketing efforts of a deep-pocketed marijuana industry. And the courts' creation of a legal category called "commercial free speech" radically limits attempts to rein in those marketing efforts. The "commercial free speech" doctrine creates an absurd situation: both state governments and the federal government can constitutionally put people in prison for growing and selling cannabis, but they're constitutionally barred from legalizing cannabis with any sort of marketing restriction designed to prevent problem use.

Availability represents a third policy lever. Where can marijuana be sold? During what hours? In what form? There's a reason why stores put candy in the front by the checkout counters; impulse buying is a powerful phenomenon. The more restrictive the rules on marijuana, the fewer new people will start smoking and the fewer new cases of abuse we'll have. Colorado and Washington limit marijuana sales to government-licensed pot stores that have to abide by certain restrictions, such as not selling alcohol and not being located near schools. But they're free to advertise. And there's nothing to keep other states, or Colorado and Washington a few years from now, from allowing pot in any form to be sold in grocery stores or at the 7-Eleven. (Two years before legalizing cannabis, Washington's voters approved a Costco-sponsored initiative to break the state monopoly on sales of distilled spirits.)

To avoid getting locked into bad policies, lawmakers in Washington need to act, and quickly. I know it's hard to imagine anything good coming out of the current Congress, but there's no real alternative.

What's needed is federal legislation requiring states that legalize cannabis to structure their pot markets such that they won't get captured by commercial interests. There are any number of ways to do that, so the legislation wouldn't have to be overly prescriptive. States could, for instance, allow marijuana to be sold only through nonprofit outlets, or distributed via small consumer-owned co-ops. The most effective way, however, would be through a system of state-run retail stores.

There's plenty of precedent for this: states from Utah to Pennsylvania to Alabama restrict hard liquor sales to state-operated or state-controlled outlets. Such "ABC" ("alcoholic beverage control") stores date back to the end of Prohibition, and operationally they work fine. Similar "pot control" stores could work fine for marijuana, too. A "state store" system would also allow the states to control the pot supply chain. By contracting with many small growers, rather than a few giant ones, states could check the industry's political power (concentrated industries are almost always more effective at lobbying than those comprised of many small companies) and maintain consumer choice by avoiding a beer-like oligopoly offering virtually interchangeable products.

States could also insist that the private growers sign contracts forbidding them from marketing to the public. Imposing that rule as part of a vendor agreement rather than as a regulation might avoid the "commercial free speech" issue, thus eliminating the specter of manipulative marijuana advertising filling the airwaves and covering highway billboards. To prevent interstate smuggling, the federal government should do what it has failed to do with cigarettes: mandate a minimum retail price.

Of course, there's a danger that states themselves, hungry for tax dollars, could abuse their monopoly power over pot, just as they have with state lotteries. To avert that outcome, states should avoid the mistake they made with lotteries: housing them in state revenue departments, which focus on maximizing state income. Instead, the new marijuana control programs should reside in state health departments and be overseen by boards with a majority of health care and substance-abuse professionals. Politicians eager for revenue might still press for higher pot sales than would be good for public health, but they'd at least have to fight a resistant bureaucracy.

How could the federal government get the states to structure their pot markets in ways like these? By giving a new twist to a tried-and-true tool that the Obama administration has wielded particularly effectively: the policy waiver. The federal government would recognize the legal status of cannabis under a state system—making the activities permitted under that system actually legal, not merely tolerated, under federal law—only if the state system contained adequate controls to protect public health and safety, as determined by the attorney general and the secretary of the department of health and human services. That would change the politics of legalization at the state level, with legalization advocates and the cannabis industry supporting tight controls in order to get, and keep, the all-important waiver. Then we would see the laboratories of democracy doing some serious experimentation.

Could such a plan garner enough support in Washington to become law? Certainly not now, given a dysfunctional Congress, an administration with no taste for engaging one more culture war issue, and in the absence of a powerful national organization with a nuanced view of cannabis policy and the muscle to make that view politically salient. But there is a mutually beneficial deal waiting to be made. Though legalization has made headway in states with strong initiative provisions in their constitutions, it's been slow going in other states in which legalization has to go through the legislature, where anti-pot law enforcement groups can easily block it. So it could be many years before legalization reaches the rest of the country or gets formal federal approval that removes the stigma of (even unpunished) lawbreaking from cannabis users. Rather than wait, legalization advocates might be willing to accept something short of full commercialization; some of them actually prefer a noncommercial system. Meanwhile, those who have been opponents of legalization heretofore might—with the writing now on the wall—decide that a tightly regulated and potentially reversible system of legal availability is the least-bad outcome available.

The current political situation seems anomalous. Public opinion continues to move against cannabis prohibition, but no national-level figure of any standing is willing to speak out for change. That's unlikely to last. Soon enough, candidates for president are going to be asked their positions on marijuana legalization. They're going to need a good answer. I suggest something like this: "I'm not against all legalization; I'm against *dumb* legalization."

Obama: Marijuana Is Not "More Dangerous Than Alcohol"

By Eyder Peralta
NPR, January 19, 2014

The New Yorker has just dropped an extensive profile of President Obama by David Remnick, who wrote a major book on the president published in 2011.

It's nuanced and touches on issues like gay marriage and Israel and Palestine. But Obama also drops this bombshell about marijuana: "I don't think it is more dangerous than alcohol."

Obama goes on to add more nuance to the statement. Here's the context for the statement:

> "When I asked Obama about another area of shifting public opinion—the legalization of marijuana—he seemed even less eager to evolve with any dispatch and get in front of the issue. 'As has been well documented, I smoked pot as a kid, and I view it as a bad habit and a vice, not very different from the cigarettes that I smoked as a young person up through a big chunk of my adult life. I don't think it is more dangerous than alcohol.'

> "Is it *less* dangerous? I asked.

> "Obama leaned back and let a moment go by. That's one of his moves. When he is interviewed, particularly for print, he has the habit of slowing himself down, and the result is a spool of cautious lucidity. He speaks in paragraphs and with moments of revision. Sometimes he will stop in the middle of a sentence and say, 'Scratch that,' or, 'I think the grammar was all screwed up in that sentence, so let me start again.'

> "Less dangerous,' he said, 'in terms of its impact on the individual consumer. It's not something I encourage, and I've told my daughters I think it's a bad idea, a waste of time, not very healthy.' What clearly *does* trouble him is the radically disproportionate arrests and incarcerations for marijuana among minorities. 'Middle-class kids don't get locked up for smoking pot, and poor kids do,' he said. 'And African-American kids and Latino kids are more likely to be poor and less likely to have the resources and the support to avoid unduly harsh penalties.' But, he said, 'we should not be locking up kids or individual users for long stretches of jail time when some of the folks who are writing those laws have probably done the same thing.' Accordingly, he said of the legalization of

marijuana in Colorado and Washington that 'it's important for it to go forward because it's important for society not to have a situation in which a large portion of people have at one time or another broken the law and only a select few get punished.'"

We'll also note that Obama's statement about how pot use is policed differently depending on class and race, is in line with his policy.

It was Obama, remember, who signed into the law the Fair Sentencing Act, which dealt with the disparity with which the justice system dealt with powder cocaine and crack cocaine. Obama also issued commutations to eight people who were convicted of drug crimes, saying their terms were unusually harsh in the pre-Fair Sentencing Act days.

In August, Obama's Justice Department also issued guidance to federal prosecutors, telling them to "focus on cartels, criminal enterprises and those who sell the drug to children, not on casual marijuana users."

Is Marijuana as Safe as— or Safer Than—Alcohol?

By Jen Christensen and Jacque Wilson
CNN, January 22, 2014

Looks like the ongoing debate about marijuana legalization in the United States has reached a new high: President Barack Obama's White House.

"As has been well-documented, I smoked pot as a kid, and I view it as a bad habit and a vice, not very different from the cigarettes that I smoked as a young person up through a big chunk of my adult life," Obama told *New Yorker* Editor David Remnick. "I don't think it is more dangerous than alcohol."

Alcohol is the most commonly used addictive substance in the United States, according to the National Institute on Alcohol Abuse and Alcoholism. It's legal for those 21 and older. Only about 22% of adult women and 11% of adult men are lifetime alcohol abstainers.

Marijuana, on the other hand, is classified by the Drug Enforcement Agency as a Schedule 1 substance —the same category as heroin, LSD and Ecstasy—and is illegal in almost all states for recreational use. As such, comprehensive data on the drug's use and misuse in the United States is limited.

Obama speaks candidly on race and pot. Obama: Weed no worse than alcohol. Pot stocks are hot on Wall Street. Obama to his girls: Pot is "bad"

Here's what we do know:

Addiction

Alcohol's addictive qualities are well-documented. Approximately 17.6 million people, or one in every 12 adults, suffer from alcohol abuse or dependence, according to the NIAA [National Institute on Alcohol Abuse and Alcoholism]. Alcoholics in withdrawal can suffer from anxiety and depression, headaches, insomnia, nausea, fever and even seizures.

The addictive qualities of marijuana are not yet fully understood. The National Institute on Drug Abuse estimates 9% of people who use marijuana will become addicted to it. For comparison's sake, cocaine hooks about 20% of those who use it.

"There is clear evidence that in some people, marijuana use can lead to withdrawal symptoms, including insomnia, anxiety and nausea," CNN Chief Medical Correspondent Dr. Sanjay Gupta wrote in his story, "Why I Changed My Mind on Weed," referring to medical marijuana.

"Even considering this, it is hard to make a case that it has a high potential for abuse. The physical symptoms of marijuana addiction are nothing like those of the other drugs I've mentioned."

Driving under the Influence

Every hour, one person is killed and 20 are injured in crashes involving a drunken driver, according to the National Transportation Safety Board.

A new study found that even slightly "buzzed" drivers—drivers with a blood alcohol level of 0.01%, meaning someone who has had even one drink—are 46% more likely to be blamed for a crash when they collide with a sober driver.

The jury is still out on the impact of people who use marijuana and drive. Early studies showed marijuana had a slight impact on the psychomotor skills needed to drive, but these studies were seen as limited since they were done in lab situations.

A recent study review published in the *British Medical Journal* found people who used marijuana within three hours of driving were nearly twice as likely to cause a crash as sober drivers. People who use marijuana in combination with other drugs or alcohol also pose an increased crash risk, research suggests.

Munchies and Beer Bellies

It seems logical to think that alcohol would make you gain weight. One shot of liquor has about 100 calories; a beer usually contains around 150. Plus, alcohol lowers your inhibitions, encouraging you to binge on pizza and nachos.

As for marijuana, even cops know it gives you the munchies.

Yet some studies on whether alcohol or marijuana really cause weight gain have been contradictory.

One study of more than 19,000 women showed those who drank alcohol in moderation actually weighed less than those who didn't over 12 years. Others have linked obesity and alcoholism; frequent drinkers seem to be more at risk.

Marijuana smokers seem to be skinnier than those who don't smoke. A study published in the *American Journal of Epidemiology* found that rates of obesity are lower by roughly a third in people who smoke pot at least three times a week, compared with those who don't use marijuana at all.

The Desire's There . . .

Drinking reduces your inhibitions and can certainly make you feel more relaxed in social situations. But those lower inhibitions can also lead you to engage in risky sexual behavior, studies show. Unprotected sex can increase your risk of catching a sexually transmitted disease or infection and increase your chances for an unplanned pregnancy.

And while serving as a social lubricant, drinking alcohol actually leaves you dehydrated. The body needs a certain level of hydration and blood flow for sexual arousal. Drinking too much makes it difficult for men to have an erection and for women to feel pleasure from natural lubrication, studies have shown.

Marijuana may have a similar impact as alcohol in lowering your inhibitions and reducing your anxiety, but some studies have shown men have a harder time finding pleasure during sex under the influence.

A couple of studies found that men who use marijuana regularly had more problems with erectile dysfunction and needed medication to counteract that side effect. There are no similar studies that look at women's sexual satisfaction under the influence of pot.

Long-Term Health Risks

Over time, drinking can lead to liver disease, neurological problems, certain psychiatric issues and may increase your risk of several types of cancer.

Smoking marijuana is more dangerous than smoking cigarettes, experts say. The tar in joints contains a much higher concentration of the chemicals linked to lung cancer compared with tobacco tar. And smoking marijuana deposits four times more tar in the lungs than smoking an equivalent amount of tobacco, according to the National Institute on Drug Abuse.

High doses of marijuana can also cause temporary psychotic reactions, such as hallucinations and paranoia in some people. Younger people with a family history of schizophrenia are at a higher risk of developing the disorder after using marijuana, seven studies showed.

Death

About 88,000 Americans die each year because of excessive alcohol use, according to the CDC. Nearly half of those deaths are from chronic alcohol use—liver failure, for example—while the other half are attributable to acute situations, such as alcohol poisoning or a drunken driving accident. There is an average of 1,600 alcohol poisoning deaths, or overdoses, each year.

Weed can kill you too, as this drug dealer showed.

In all seriousness, marijuana affects your reflexes, hindering your motor skills. So, marijuana-related car fatalities are not unheard of.

And one study found marijuana users have a 4.8-fold increase in risk of a heart attack during the first hour after smoking because of the drug's effect on your heart rate.

That said, scientists believe that a marijuana overdose is highly unlikely. One study found it was safe for animals to consume about 30% of their body weight in cannabis without overdosing; that's the equivalent of a 160-pound person eating 48 pounds of weed at one time.

Student Views Shifting on Risks of Marijuana

By Evie Blad

Education Week, January 8, 2014

Campaigns in individual states to legalize marijuana use may be contributing to a drop in the percentages of teenagers nationwide who see risk in regular use of the drug and to an increase in its use by students themselves, public-health leaders say.

Experts say that shifting attitudes about the drug complicate schools' drug-abuse-prevention classes, where teachers must navigate conflicts between state and federal drug laws, disputes about the effects of marijuana, and, increasingly, a contrast between how marijuana is discussed in the classroom and how it is discussed in students' homes.

The changes in students' attitudes toward marijuana were highlighted last month by findings from the National Institutes of Health's annual Monitoring the Future Survey, a nationally representative study of teenagers' drug use and attitudes toward drugs.

In 2013, 39.5 percent of 12th grade respondents said they viewed regular marijuana use as harmful, a drop from 44.1 percent the previous year and a steep decline from 72.5 percent 20 years earlier, the study said. Among 10th graders, the figure dropped from 78.5 percent in 1993 to 46.5 last year. For 8th graders, it went from 79.6 percent to 61 percent.

While federal researchers saw declines in teenagers' use of many of the drugs the survey tracks, including alcohol and cigarettes, they saw an increase in marijuana use, they said. That use could continue to grow if young people's attitudes keep shifting, researchers said.

"We've seen, in various historical periods, a strong correlation between changes in an attitude toward a drug and patterns of use," Lloyd D. Johnston, the report's lead investigator, said in a Dec. 18 conference call on the results. Of the seniors surveyed, 6.5 percent reported daily marijuana use in 2013, compared with 6 percent in 2003 and 2.4 percent in 1993. Nearly 23 percent of the seniors reported using the drug in the preceding month, compared with 15.5 percent in 1993. And 36.4 percent said they had used it in the past year, up from 26 percent in 1993.

Among 10th graders, 4 percent reported daily marijuana use, compared with 1 percent in 1993; 18 percent said they'd used it in the past month, compared with 10.9 percent in 1993; and 29.8 percent said they'd used it in the past year, compared with 19.2 percent 20 years ago. And 12.7 percent of 8th graders said they'd used marijuana in the year preceding the survey, versus 9.2 percent in 1993.

The 2013 survey was administered on paper to 41,765 students in grades 8, 10, and 12 in 389 public and private schools around the country.

Noting Progress

The research also showed some positive downward trends. Of 12th grade respondents, 39.2 percent reported using alcohol in the month before the survey, compared with 48.6 percent in 1993; and 16.3 percent reported smoking a cigarette in the previous month, compared with 29.9 percent in 1993.

Teenagers' use of illicit drugs excluding marijuana, such as cocaine, crack, and heroin, has remained relatively constant over the last 20 years, with a slight increase in usage rates at all grade levels in the late 1990s and early 2000s. In 2013, 8.4 percent of surveyed seniors reported use of an illicit drug other than marijuana in the previous month, compared with 7.9 percent in 1993.

But federal officials focused much of their discussion on marijuana in unveiling the findings.

The shifts in attitudes toward marijuana follow changes that have eased state marijuana laws. Since 1996, 20 states and the District of Columbia have enacted laws that allow marijuana use for medicinal purposes, according to the National Conference of State Legislatures. They include Colorado and Washington, which also approved measures allowing recreational use of marijuana in 2012.

State medical and recreational marijuana laws, which conflict with a federal prohibition on the drug's sale and use, place varying restrictions on marijuana possession.

Proponents of nationwide marijuana legalization said it is wrong for federal officials to attribute teenagers' increased use of the drug to legalization campaigns, and they emphasized their support for prohibiting marijuana use below age 21.

"It's very similar to the way that we deal with alcohol," said Morgan E. Fox, a spokesman for the Marijuana Policy Project, a Washington, D.C., group that supports legalization efforts. "Parents can drink around kids and are able to educate them that this can be an unsafe behavior. Parents should be able to do the same with marijuana."

Legalizing marijuana would allow states to regulate and better control its use, Mr. Fox said.

"Broken Promises"

But R. Gil Kerlikowske, the director of the federal Office of National Drug Control Policy, said many successful medical-marijuana efforts have "broken promises" to voters by implementing ineffective controls that haven't prevented minors from obtaining the drug improperly.

Of marijuana-using 12th graders living in states with laws allowing medical use of the drug, 34 percent said they had obtained the drug with someone else's prescription, and 6 percent said they have prescriptions of their own, the survey found.

The conflict between federal authorities and legalization advocates is increasingly making its way into family conversations and opening up rifts in attitudes between educators and students, according to drug experts.

Because most decisions about drug education efforts are made by districts, it is difficult to detect curricular trends in how marijuana is discussed in states with relaxed laws, representatives of those states' education departments said. But the leaders of some of the nation's most popular school drug-abuse-prevention programs said they have not changed their approaches, despite shifts in state laws surrounding marijuana legalization.

Even before recent legalization efforts, anti-drug curricula had trended away from exhorting students to avoid taboo substances and toward a social and emotional approach that teaches students to assess what substances are drugs and the consequences of using them, said Michael L. Hecht, a communications professor at Pennsylvania State University. He wrote the Keepin' It Real curriculum used by D.A.R.E., a widely used Los Angeles-based provider of drug-abuse-prevention education.

"It's a move toward developing healthy, effective people," Mr. Hecht said. "When you have those kinds of people, they make good decisions of all types."

Potential for Harm

While some advocates see little harm in marijuana use for adults, federal officials say that it is still necessary for schools to emphasize abstinence from the drug, and that, to be effective, those efforts should be age-sensitive, comprehensive, and carried out over multiple years.

Chemicals in marijuana bond to cannabinoid receptors in the brain, blocking its normal functions, medical experts said. The teenage brain, which is still developing, has more cannabinoid receptors than the adult brain, and those receptors are concentrated in parts of the brain that regulate memory, problem-solving, and learning, said Dr. Nora Volkow, the director of the National Institute on Drug Abuse, a federal research institute based in Bethesda, Md.

Weakening the brain's ability to retain and process information can rob students of crucial learning time and slow students' academic attainment, she said.

"Adolescents are more sensitive to the effects of the drug on the brain because the brain is still developing," Dr. Volkow said.

Mr. Hecht said that skilled drug-abuse-prevention educators will adapt classroom conversations to the concerns of students, and that the same principles that apply to other drugs apply to marijuana, regardless of its legal status.

"Remember that the two most frequently used drugs are alcohol and tobacco, and they're not legal for the kids in any of the states," he said.

Poll: Marijuana Legalization Inevitable

By Kristen Wyatt
Associated Press, April 2, 2014

Marijuana legalization in the U.S. seems inevitable to three-fourths of Americans, whether they support it or not, according to a new poll out Wednesday.

The Pew Research Center survey on the nation's shifting attitudes about drug policy also showed increased support for moving away from mandatory sentences for non-violent drug offenders.

The telephone survey found that 75 percent of respondents—including majorities of both supporters and opponents of legal marijuana—think that the sale and use of pot eventually will be legal nationwide. It was the first time that question had been asked.

Some 39 percent of respondents said pot should be legal for personal adult use. Forty-four percent of those surveyed said it should be legal only for medicinal use. Just 16 percent said it should not be legal at all.

The responses come as two states have legalized recreational marijuana, with more than 20 states and Washington, D.C., allowing some medical use of the drug.

"It's just a matter of time before it's in more states," said Steve Pratley of Denver, a 51-year-old pipefitter who voted for legalization in Colorado in 2012.

Pratley, who did not participate in the Pew survey, agreed with 76 percent of respondents who said people who use small amounts of marijuana shouldn't go to jail.

"If marijuana isn't legalized, it fills up the jails, and that's just stupid," Pratley said.

Legalization opponents, however, drew a distinction between making pot legal for all and thinking that pot users belong in jail.

"It's an illegal drug, period. I don't see it spreading," said Laura Sanchez, a 55-year-old retiree in Denver who voted against legalization. She agreed that pot smokers don't belong in jail, but she disagreed with legalization.

"I've seen no proof that it's good for anybody," said Sanchez, who also did not participate in the survey.

The poll suggested that despite shifting attitudes on legalization, the public remains concerned about drug abuse, with 32 percent of those surveyed calling it a crisis and 55 percent of respondents viewing it as a serious national problem.

And a narrow majority, 54 percent, said marijuana legalization would lead to more underage people trying it.

As for mandatory minimum sentences, public attitudes have been shifting for years.

In 2001, the survey was about evenly divided on whether it was a good thing or bad thing for states to move away from mandatory minimum sentences for non-violent drug offenders. In 2014, poll respondents favored the move by a nearly 2-to-1 margin, or 63 percent to 32 percent. The other 5 percent either didn't respond or said they didn't know.

Public officials are well aware of the public's shifting attitudes on drug penalties.

Just last month, U.S. Attorney General Eric Holder testified in support of proposed sentence reductions for some non-violent drug traffickers in an effort to reserve the "the harshest penalties for the most serious drug offenders."

"Certain types of cases result in too many Americans going to prison for too long, and at times for no truly good public safety reason," Holder said last month at the U.S. Sentencing Commission.

Drug legalization activists said the Pew results come as no surprise.

"We see a growing bipartisan recognition that mandatory minimums went too far and did more harm than good," said Ethan Nadelmann, head of the New York-based Drug Policy Alliance, which opposes criminal penalties for non-violent drug users.

Marijuana legalization opponents saw signs of hope in the survey, too.

Kevin Sabet, co-founder of Smart Approaches to Marijuana, which opposes pot legalization, pointed to the fact that 63 percent said it would bother them if people used marijuana openly in their neighborhood.

"Saying that we don't want people to serve prison time for marijuana is very different from saying I want a pot shop in my neighborhood selling cookies and candies and putting coupons in the paper," Sabet said.

The poll of 1,821 adults was conducted Feb. 14–23. The survey had a margin of error of plus or minus 2.6 percentage points.

Don't Fear the Reefer!

Momentum Builds for Lone Star Legalization
of Marijuana

By Jordan Smith
The Austin Chronicle, March 14, 2014

For more than a decade, Austin Democratic state Representative Elliott Naishtat has brought to his Capitol colleagues a modest proposal: Create an affirmative defense to prosecution on pot possession charges for seriously ill Texans.

For seven sessions now—that's every other year since 2001—he's either authored or sponsored a measure that would give bona fide patients—those suffering, for example, from AIDS, multiple sclerosis, glaucoma, cancer—the ability to have a judge decide if a criminal charge for pot possession should be dismissed. Naishtat's proposal would also protect doctors who suggest their patients try marijuana as medicine to alleviate the debilitating symptoms of disease.

And he's been clear, at every turn, that this is *all* the bill would do. He hasn't suggested that the state legalize medical marijuana—as 20 states and the District of Columbia have done—let alone that Texas follow the lead of Colorado and Washington and legalize marijuana outright for all uses. "I try to be moderate," he says, and proposed this bill, specifically, because "I thought it would have a snowball's chance."

That isn't exactly how it's played out. The measure has only three times been assigned a committee hearing—once by the House Criminal Jurisprudence Committee (back in 2001) and then by the House Public Health Committee, in 2005 and again in 2013. No version of the bill has ever received a vote in committee, let alone made it to the House floor for consideration.

It's frustrating, certainly, but Naishtat is unsurprised and remains undaunted by the repeated roadblocks. In part, that's because he knows what lawmakers say to him in hushed tones on the floor: Sure, what you're doing makes sense, and it's the right thing to do, but I can't vote for it. "I have members come up to me and say, 'I know what you're trying to do here, but I can't vote for it because my cousin in Harlingen is a deputy sheriff,' or because 'I can't look weak on crime. Maybe in another six years.'"

Yet if recent poll numbers are to be believed, it shouldn't take anywhere near six years to get this done. According to a September 2013 poll commissioned by the Marijuana Policy Project, a majority of all Texas voters—men and women,

Democrats, Republicans, and independents—support legalizing medi-pot. In a *Texas Tribune*/UT poll released in February, 49% of voters favor making at least small amounts of pot legal for any purpose, and another 28% favor legalizing medi-mari—thus, a clear 77% of all voters (a slight majority of those polled were Republican) favor legalizing medi-pot, and most certainly would favor Naishtat's bill. He says, "I'm saying with more confidence it's just a matter of time until it's legalized."

Indeed, since January, when Governor Rick Perry said (during a panel discussion of the World Economic Forum in Switzerland) that he supports marijuana decriminalization—and the right of individual states to legalize the drug outright—the Texas media has been trolling for more. *The Dallas Morning News* asked Democratic gubernatorial candidate Wendy Davis about her views in a recent interview; she would support medi-pot, she responded, and the right of voters to consider legalization (though she said she's not sure how she'd vote on that question). Land Commissioner and recent GOP lite guv candidate Jerry Patterson told public television station KERA, without hesitation, that he would support legalizing medical marijuana; and author/musician Kinky Friedman's all-pot-all-the-time race for agriculture commissioner netted him 38% of Democratic party voters, the most in the three-way race, sending him to a May run-off.

These are among the recent and public shifts that veteran lawmakers and advocates for drug-law reform consider harbingers of big things to come for the Lone Star State. It's just a matter of time, they say, before Texas goes all in for lasting marijuana-law reform. The question is how quickly things will move, and what shape the future will take.

Change Follows Experience

The way state Representative Harold Dutton, D-Houston, sees it, all this talk about changing pot laws was inevitable. As Naishtat has fought long and hard to protect medical marijuana patients, so too Dutton has pressed—and pressed and pressed—to decriminalize possession of small amounts of pot, making possession of up to an ounce a fine-only offense. "[I]t appears that everyone else is getting as smart as I am," he said. "It's like you take a match and strike it and somehow or another the forest catches on fire and you have no idea how that happened. But it's a good thing. It focuses on what criminal laws are designed to do: Protect people. How can you say that's what you're doing when you take a 20-year-old kid and arrest him [for possessing a joint]?" Dutton asks.

Like Naishtat's bill, Dutton's is a modest proposal (it keeps jail time on the table for possession of two ounces or more) that has gained only limited traction since 2005, when he first introduced it. Last year it made the most progress, voted out of the Criminal Jurisprudence Committee—with crucial Tea Partier support—before disappearing into the Calendars Committee, never to find a date with the House floor.

Nevertheless, Dutton remains confident that his bill, too, will soon pass. "You have to realize how the Legislature operates," he said. "Remember the 'blue laws'? Trying to repeal the blue laws, people would say, 'More people are going to go to hell if you can shop on Sunday!' I think we have as many people going to hell now, but it took seven sessions to get that done." In short, he said, "People get very conservative about holding on to past statutes"—even where they serve no good purpose. And like Naishtat, Dutton has heard his colleagues lament that they'd love to vote for his bill, but can't. Yet he insists that if he keeps pressing long enough, his colleagues will come around and the job will get done. "One [House] member called me and told me he was against [my bill, but] that when his son was arrested for marijuana, he changed his mind," Dutton recalled. "Once you get some real experience, it changes things."

No More Harm: "Legalize It"

For sure, decriminalizing—or even outright legalizing—marijuana in Texas would bring a lot of benefits, advocates say, such as a noticeable reduction in criminal justice expenses, including the cost to lock up non-violent low-level drug offenders popped for possession. According to the FBI, in 2012, 82.2% of all drug arrests in the U.S. were for possession only; of those, 42.4% were arrested for marijuana possession. In Texas the numbers are even starker: In 2012, according to the Texas Department of Public Safety, 57% of the 116,634 adult arrests for drug possession, and a whopping 81% of the 8,132 juvenile arrests for drug possession, were for possession of pot. Consider a low-level offender popped for pot and sentenced to a year in county jail—in Austin that costs taxpayers an average of $38,548 per inmate per year.

Those are the kinds of numbers that make retired narcotics officer Russell Jones shake his head. Jones, who worked for the San Jose, California, police department and did foreign intelligence work before retiring to Central Texas in 1994, now works with the drug-law reform advocacy group Law Enforcement Against Prohibition, as well as with the Drug Policy Forum of Texas, giving talks to anyone who wants to listen about why the War on Drugs is an utter and complete failure and should be put out of its misery.

Among the biggest reasons, Jones says, is that policing drugs does way more harm than the drugs themselves, particularly among youth and young adults who get caught up in the drug war dragnet. The consequences of a single possession arrest can be haunting—taking away the opportunity to go to college, to enter a profession of choice. And for what? "Throwing people in jail and saddling them with a drug conviction, you're doing a whole lot worse than the drug use" did, he said, particularly when the vast majority of people simply grow out of it. "The vast majority don't get addicted," he said. "So what's the least harmful way to deal with [drug use]?" To Jones the answer is to fully legalize it: Decriminalization, he says, still leaves production and distribution in the hands of the black market—including the cartels working up into Texas from the Mexico border. He believes that legalizing marijuana in Texas would impose order on an underground business and, quite literally, save lives. "When was the last time we had a drive-by shooting between Bud and Coors? It doesn't happen, because it's a legal product," he said. "We've got to stop ruining kids' lives over youthful indiscretions."

Jones, like Naishtat, believes strongly that it's only a matter of diminishing time before medical marijuana is legal in Texas; Dutton believes decriminalization is on tap for the 2015 legislative session. But all three are more skeptical of when, or if, Texas will actually go all in to legalize marijuana. "I can't imagine making it legal," said Dutton, "but I think decriminalization is something Texas is going to do next session."

The Tipping Point?

Despite Dutton's understandable skepticism, there's at least one deep-pocketed advocate who believes not only that Texas will legalize marijuana, but that change is right around the corner. That's Rob Kampia, co-founder and executive director of the Marijuana Policy Project, which has backed nearly every successful marijuana initiative since the group's founding in the mid-nineties and was the driving force behind the 2012 vote to legalize pot in Colorado.

Now, Kampia is bringing that winning spirit to Texas; beginning March 1, the group hired its first-ever Texas lobbyist and has committed to spending $200,000 a year here until the job is done. Like Dutton and Naishtat, Kampia's heard plenty of lawmakers list all the reasons why pot-law reform simply won't work in their state. He's been taken into closed-door meetings where lawmakers say in hushed tones, "I just don't know if I can support this." Sure you can, Kampia responds, because "marijuana polls better than you do." That has been the case in any number of states where MPP has, eventually, prevailed despite conventional wisdom to the contrary. Indeed, the recent *Texas Tribune*/UT poll results reflect that voters favor some form of legalization (49%) more strongly than they approve of the job Governor Rick Perry (42%) has done. "I've learned over the last 15 years, people in the state in question believe change is not possible in their state, but [is] possible in other states," he said. "We feel like legalizing marijuana in Texas—though people in Texas feel like it's impossible—I think it's possible in five years."

The tide is visibly turning against pot prohibition—at press time, legalization measures had been introduced or were pending in 17 states, while medi-pot legalization measures had made it into 14 state houses. Moreover, the rhetoric against marijuana-law reform has become increasingly tired, if not desperate. Case in point: In testifying against a legalization measure pending in Maryland, Annapolis Police Chief Michael Pristoop told lawmakers that more than 30 people overdosed on marijuana on the first day it was legalized in Colorado. In contrast, he said, "No one's overdosing on beer." Unfortunately for Pristoop, the Colorado "pot-OD" story was a hoax, created by the satirical website Daily Currant, and no one at all had "overdosed" on marijuana (virtually an impossibility). By contrast, according to the Centers for Disease Control, there are approximately 88,000 deaths each year attributable to excessive alcohol use—something a police chief should know well.

Pristoop subsequently apologized for mistaking the OD story as a factual account, but to reform advocates, the incident highlights the lengths to which some opponents would go to in order to avoid change. "This just underscores why we should not be treating drug issues with a law enforcement approach," says Tom Angell, founder of Marijuana Majority.

Kampia, who expects voters in as many as six states could legalize marijuana in the 2016 election cycle, says it's time to "take reality for what it is, and move forward." In Texas, he believes that time has come. "We're in and we're in for the long haul," he said. "We're ready to go."

Naishtat says he's talked with MPP about its plans, and he supports those efforts, although, for now at least, he'll continue to push his moderate measure in the hope that, finally, his colleagues will agree that seriously ill Texans deserve their support. "I think we're getting close to the tipping point, in light of what is happening across the country," he said. "Maybe . . . the eighth time [is the charm], or the ninth. But I know we're making progress."

How Far Can Ethan Nadelmann Push America's Drug Laws?

By Will Godfrey
The Fix, June 30, 2013

Maybe a little bit of rock star has rubbed off on Ethan Nadelmann, the executive director of the Drug Policy Alliance, after his recent profile in *Rolling Stone*. Due to address a conference at NYU, where, the program promises, he will "take us around the world in 20 minutes," Nadelmann shows up with seconds to spare, clutching a Coke Zero and a stick of gum. He hits the rostrum without breaking stride and delivers, notes-free, an adrenaline-pumped rundown of the harms of drug prohibition and the emergence of alternatives in Latin America, Europe and the US that has the respectful crowd of social work educators whooping in appreciation.

Nadelmann, 56, has been a drug policy reform activist for decades, from his teaching and research at Princeton in the '80s and early '90s to his founding in 1994 of the Lindesmith Center—a think tank funded by George Soros, which Nadelman merged with another group to form the Drug Policy Alliance in 2000. He's widely considered the most influential advocate in this field, and his efforts bore their most spectacular fruit to-date last November, when Colorado and Washington voted to legalize marijuana.

Pot hogs headlines, but Nadelmann stresses that most DPA efforts focus elsewhere. Pushing harm reduction in the broadest sense—everything from Good Samaritan laws to combat overdose, needle exchange and naloxone distribution to ending mandatory minimum drug sentences and ultimately drug decriminalization—is their overarching theme. In a later session at the NYU conference, Nadelmann details how harm reduction boosts public health and breaks stigma; he wraps up with a glowing endorsement of heroin maintenance programs.

In person Nadelmann, who has a PhD in political science from Harvard, a master's in international relations from the London School of Economics and a New *Yawk* accent, combines an engaging passion for his subject with a professorial grasp of it, frequently citing studies to support his points. Later on, as we finish our interview on a bench in Washington Square Park, whiffs of second-hand marijuana smoke drift by, forestalling any temptation to stray off-topic.

A ballot initiative, you say, is what you do when you think people are already on your side. But as you waited for the Colorado and Washington results to come in last November, how confident were you really, given that you were trying to do something unprecedented?

I did not think, just a few months in advance, that we would win both. Certainly not by those margins, where we got roughly 55% of the vote. It was only in the final week that we began to see polling and early voting in these states—in Colorado, we were deeply involved in the drafting and then in the ground game; in Washington, we were slightly involved in the drafting but deeply involved in the fundraising—and to sense that we were ahead. Even then, I didn't quite believe it.

You know, we had a little wave of momentum in the late '90s, and then with Bush/Cheney and 9/11, especially, we got pushed back. Now this acceleration of support for legalizing marijuana has caught me, and almost everybody else, by surprise.

Where in the US do you think we'll next see marijuana legalized?

I'm wondering whether Oregon has a shot to move forward in 2014; there the legislature can put an initiative on the ballot, so I think there's a chance. There's some possibility around Alaska in 2014. I'm curious about Washington, DC, and whether the city council, where views have really evolved, might be willing to do something. California, we're looking at 2016. And states like Arizona or Missouri might pop through.

***Rolling Stone* calls you "The Real Drug Czar." What's your assessment of Gil Kerlikowske and the Obama administration?**

I was hopeful with Gil Kerlikowske. He had been the police chief of Seattle, and they have Hempfest. He had gone to Vancouver, looked inside a safe-injection site and written a fair-minded memo. I met him as soon as he was appointed, and he was very friendly. But now on the marijuana issue he appears to be mimicking the verbiage of his predecessors. It's almost like he was captured by the people who pursue this absurd line of thinking. In that respect, it's a good sign that responsibility for marijuana policy appears to have been shifted to the justice department, which has to pursue a much more pragmatic policy.

I was pleasantly surprised during the first 18 months of Obama's administration. He made three commitments when he was running for president. One was that he would pull back on federal enforcement on medical marijuana in the states that had made it legal. The second was that he would approve federal funding for needle exchange programs. And the third was that he would push to roll back the mandatory minimum crack penalties. You know that 100-to-one issue? [*the former sentencing disparity between crack and powder cocaine*]

Now it's "only" 18-to-one, right?

Yeah. He made good on all three commitments. On medical marijuana, they put out the Ogden Memo in '09, which was cautious, but emboldened some of the state governments. On needle exchange, they did not lead, but he did approve it. [*Congress reinstated the federal funding ban in 2011.*] And on the crack/powder issue, they actually did lead, and pushed on one-to-one.

Unfortunately, they kind of peaked. Once the Republicans took over the House, it made it much more difficult, having some of the most reactionary Republicans in charge of these committees, so I can only blame the Obama administration so far.

Kerlikowske, after being very leery of the overdose issue, is now providing some leadership on that. But they're using our rhetoric about a public health approach, about reducing incarceration, and the budgets, the policies, don't match the rhetoric. The stigmas associated with addiction; the criminalization of pregnant women who test positive for drugs; legislation to roll back further mandatory minimums—he's just not present on that stuff. I see him trying to claim the mantle of public health. But you can't do that if you're not willing to talk about the kinds of innovations we see in Europe, if you continually insist on the criminalization of drug possession.

You don't just preach to the choir like at NYU today; you go and speak to people who oppose your goals. Where have you experienced the most hostility?

The people most hostile to my goals typically don't invite me to speak—especially in the law enforcement world. Questioning that approach raises existential issues for them. When you're spending your life enforcing these laws and you want to go home at night and look your kid in the eye and say, "Daddy's doing good," to have to step back and say, "Maybe Daddy's job is no different than the prohibition agents during the alcohol Prohibition"—it's a hard thing. I'm sensitive to that.

The tragedy is the so-called "blue wall of silence." I mean, this is a powerful issue right now. I'm one of the leaders of this movement. You'd think these guys would want to hear it from the horse's mouth. I think a lot of them are afraid that if they invited me to speak, their members might be persuaded. The only silver lining on perceiving their fear of debate is that it lets me know how incredibly vulnerable they feel about what they're trying to defend. They know deep down—the smarter ones—that they can't win, that there's something flawed in their way of thinking.

Who do you see as your most formidable opponents?

The most pernicious and powerful opponents we have are the prosecutors and the DAs. Where we're trying to get a Good Samaritan law passed, trying to get needle exchange laws through, expand access to methadone, they're the ones standing in the way. Their bloated power in American society and the extent to which they are unaccountable, and only care about their own self-empowerment—that is the single most dynamic element driving the drug war today. It's not about money. This is about power. The power to run for higher office. The power in squeezing some poor guy arrested for drug possession or low-level selling into making a deal and avoiding a massive sentence.

I am continually stunned by the lack of humanity and the disrespect for science and public health that I see in that world. It is pathetic and they need to be held accountable. When DAs engage in behavior that results in the deaths of large numbers of people, they are never sanctioned. They deserve to be. The only saving grace is the growing number of people in that world who are beginning to break off: David Soares, the DA of Albany County, and some others.

Where around the world have you been most inspired by drug policy reforms?

My first trip to Switzerland was 1992, and they just had approved proceeding with the heroin maintenance thing. I used to go the Netherlands in the late '80s, early '90s, to see what they were doing. I went to Portugal more recently, and to Vancouver—as an advisor, as well as to learn and ally with them. The European approach has always been a major inspiration. When I created the Lindesmith Center in '94, one of the ways I defined our mission was to educate Americans about the lessons and benefits of foreign approaches.

You've criticized America's "pig-headedness" against harm reduction approaches that work elsewhere. Has the relative dominance of the abstinence-based 12-step movement in the US been part of the reason that harm reduction has been less welcome here?

I don't have a simple answer. We were one of the only countries in the western world to prohibit alcohol. That attitude, the abstinence-only approach, preceded AA. Our instinctive reliance on criminalization is not inherent to AA. That really grew up in an American frame: Nixon's war on drugs, the way race issues played out in this country, the private prison industry.

The 12-step model has been problematic, I think, in two areas. The first is the way the criminal justice system and the for-profit drug treatment industry tried to capitalize. When you marry the 12-step abstinence-only approach with a criminal justice approach, when falling off the wagon has a criminal sanction attached, you can't just take one step at a time, and it's awfully hard to build peer groups based on trust. All these for-profit 28-day programs—many ended up doing relatively little good, at a tremendous cost.

Where the 12-step thing has the most to own up to is its role in impeding harm reduction interventions to stem the spread of HIV/AIDS. Why was it that Australia and England and the Netherlands were able to stop the spread, and keep the number for injecting drug users under 5–10%, and the US was not? It's that notion—that abstinence is the only permissible approach, that we are not going to "enable" a junkie by giving him a clean needle. There has to be a kind of owning up to that role in hundreds of thousands of people dying unnecessarily, even as people in recovery play a greater and greater role in drug policy reform.

But there can be a natural fit between 12-step recovery and your goals?

Yes. The 12 Steps and harm reduction share some things: The notion of one step at a time, one day at a time; the importance of peer groups; the important role that dignity plays. This is why I admire Howard Josepher—he has both harm reduction and recovery programs. Some of the most significant leaders of the harm reduction movement are in 12-step programs. They say, "I have hit a point where I realize I cannot drink or use drugs; the 12-step approach worked for me," but they've also seen many people where it did not work. They realized they needed a fallback strategy, and therefore see 12-step and harm reduction as complementary. On my board, on my staff, in the drug policy reform movement, one of the most dynamic and fast-growing elements is people in recovery.

Some feel they can't support decriminalization or legalization because of awful personal experiences with drugs. What would you say to that?

First, marijuana prohibition in the US has almost entirely failed to make marijuana less available to young people. There are three national surveys in which young people say it's easier to buy marijuana than alcohol. For anybody who is in recovery and used marijuana at some point, the prohibition laws failed to make it unavailable to them. What makes them think it's going to be any better in the future, to persist with this policy?

The experience of the Netherlands is that the percentage of young people who use cannabis and then go on to try other drugs is less than in the US. The Dutch, I think reasonably, explain that as being a result of having separated the cannabis market from other drug markets. Drug dealers in the Netherlands are less likely to carry marijuana than other drugs, whereas in the US, they're more likely to carry marijuana and other substances. Much of what accounts for the gateway theory is having a supply that sells multiple substances.

What about the decriminalization of other drugs?

Drug addiction can be a terrible thing—but so can arrest and incarceration. We have to focus on reducing both the risks and harms of addiction and the risks and harms of incarceration.

With respect to the decriminalization of all drug possession, which we sometimes call the "Portugal model"—they did not eliminate criminal sanctions but they basically stopped putting anybody who was in possession in jail, or penalizing them through the criminal justice system. If you look at the evidence from Portugal, drug use went a little up in some groups and down in some others, but basically remained constant. But HIV, Hep C, drug arrests, criminality, all the negative consequences of drug use and addiction went down. The decriminalization of drug possession appears to have no impact on the number of people who use drugs. What it does do is remove obstacles to treating addiction as a health issue, reduce arrests, reduce the money spent on criminal justice.

You're open about your own drug use: You're a longstanding but occasional marijuana user; you've used cocaine but aren't a fan. You seem much more enthusiastic about psychedelics. What did you mean when you told *Rolling Stone* that psychedelics are wasted on the young?

Oftentimes when you talk to younger people who've done psychedelics, it's all about the bright lights and colors and the funny sensations—and that's fine. Most of them do it and it's fun; maybe they learn something from it, some of them get hurt by doing it stupidly. I've not been a frequent psychedelics user. I've tried a variety of them. I think it's a good thing to do once a year, so long as one doesn't have issues with mental health.

Why do you think it's a good thing to do once a year?

Psychedelics are a powerful and effective way of asking deeper questions about one's life. I grew up the son of a rabbi but I'm not an advocate for organized religion—but there's a spiritual element to this. There are traditions of prayer and fasting and chanting. Other people do it through psychological counseling. I think that continuing to challenge oneself becomes more difficult as one gets older. Trying to stir up the emotional sediment that one acquires is a good thing.

My occasional use of psilocybin mushrooms—I've derived not just wonderful experiences, and occasionally gone to some dark places. But I also had some intellectual and emotional insights that I value decades afterwards. Having once done it in the context of the Santo Daime ceremony—you know, the Brazilian aya-huasca-based church—people who had been through serious trauma, violence, loss, it was about coming to grips with that. The recent research, done in government-funded studies with very rigorous research models, shows profound benefits when psychedelics are done in a responsible way.

You have a 24-year-old daughter; what have you told her about drugs?

The thing I've always stressed with my daughter was to keep the bottom line focused on safety. I don't have an ideological viewpoint vis-à-vis adolescents and drugs. I'm not a proponent of drug use; I'm perfectly happy with people who want to be what they regard as entirely sober or straight. My view to marijuana and other drugs was similar to my view about alcohol, which is, if you're going to do it, do it responsibly. I'd rather you wait till you got older; take care.

Like many people my age, I was less concerned about marijuana being used occasionally in late adolescence, but radically opposed to cigarettes . . . I *hate* ciga-rettes. My dad died at the age of 58 and his cigarette addiction may well have played a role. I think that adolescents that choose to use cigarettes in the face of all the evidence, that's an indication that they're willing to take risks that I think are not acceptable. Whereas young people who choose to drink occasionally, or to smoke marijuana—or even, depending on the age, do something like use MDMA—are actually being much more intelligent about the relative risks.

How could better policies have reduced the huge US toll from Rx opi-oid overdoses?

One of my frustrations is that DPA is now devoting as much staff time and al-most as many resources to overdose prevention as to marijuana reform, but all the media attention focuses on marijuana. We are playing a role of national leadership in passing Good Samaritan laws. We've led efforts in New York, California, New Mexico, Colorado and been deeply involved in Vermont and a host of other states. In New Jersey, we got that through and Governor Christie vetoed it—then we came back, mobilized parents and city councils and finally got Christie to realize he made a mistake. It's a personal passion—probably more of my staff at DPA are passionate on the naloxone issue than on marijuana.

The shame is, the knee-jerk response, at least until recently, is: Crack down—crack down on pill mills, crack down on doctors. So much focus is on the supply side, in the absence of any significant evidence that that's the most important place to focus. Meanwhile, you have this in-your-face evidence that naloxone—making it liberally available, making people aware of it—saves lives.

The DPA is a broad church, ranging from all-out libertarians to doubt-ful drug warriors, and you say you don't need to fight over what the ulti-mate objectives are . . .

There's all sorts. People who want to roll back the drug war, get rid of mandatory minimums, harm reduction focus, decriminalization of possession—there's still so much work to be done to get to that point that the internal disputes over what the ultimate policy should be are really just intellectual ones.

Does that mean you can't tell me what you want the ultimate goal to be?

I'm somewhat bounded in terms of representing DPA. But on the marijuana issue, I'm not fighting for the Marlborization or Budweiseration of marijuana. My focus is very much to legislate a responsible public health approach.

The DPA website talks about giving people sovereignty over their own bodies. Is there any way to do that without legalizing all drugs?

There's a fundamental distinction between saying we're no longer going to criminalize people, and saying we are going to legalize the *availability*. We don't have a position for or against the broader legalization of drugs other than cannabis. And that split between people who favor broader legalization and those who favor a more public health, harm reduction approach is in the DNA of Drug Policy Alliance.

Might it be argued that the concept of decriminalized drugs—as opposed to legalized—is a fudge? You won't be prosecuted for drug use, but in order to obtain those drugs, you'll still have to employ the services of someone who is breaking the law?

You can call it fudge, or you can call it incremental steps! Thinking in politically realistic terms: People ask, Is there a slippery slope from marijuana legalization to the legalization of other drugs? The answer seems pretty clearly, No—whether you like it or not. There's two pieces of evidence: One is the Netherlands, where you've had majority or close to majority support for the legal regulation of cannabis for a long time, but you don't see support for legalizing other drugs. The second is the American opinion polls. You see the rapid increase in support for legalizing marijuana, but when you ask people about legalizing other drugs, it hovers in that 10–15% level.

But those who advocate outright for legalization serve very important roles. The government, the drug czars, have an interest in *conflating* the harms of drugs and the harms of prohibitionist policies. One service of legalization advocacy is to put right up front: Here are the harms that flow *from treating this as an illegal market*— the crime, the corruption, the black market, the incarceration and human rights violations, the environmental harms of spraying crops in Latin America, even the fact that drugs are much more dangerous, adulterated, unregulated.

Another value of legalization advocacy is that it requires people to think hard about what is it they're really afraid of. That's a hard question. To what extent are our fears real, and to what extent are they phantoms? Asking people what it is they fear is also about highlighting how we see some of these drugs—heroin, cocaine, meth—as so much more dangerous than alcohol and cigarettes . . .

Like the somewhat spurious distinction between "hard" and "soft" drugs.

Exactly. Those things don't conform much with the available scientific evidence or the consensus conclusions of nationally appointed commissions of experts. The legalization advocacy is about a provocation to think afresh, instead of some belief that we're all going to be selling crack cocaine in the stores the way we do Marlboro today. Some people advocate that; libertarians will. DPA does not—it's about getting people to think hard about that, and to challenge their assumptions.

You often sound as if you're primarily a pragmatist, looking to do what helps, rather than basing what you do primarily on ideology. Is that fair?

Yes and no. My mission, and that of my organization, is to reduce the harms of drugs—death, disease, crime, suffering—*and* to reduce the harms of our prohibitionist policies. The optimal drug control policy is the one which most effectively balances those two objectives. So in that sense, it's very pragmatic. Most DPA resources are devoted to incremental reforms, which accomplish some good: Pass a needle exchange program, you reduce HIV/AIDS; get naloxone or Good Samaritan, you save lives; pass medical marijuana and patients get the chance to not be treated as criminals.

But each one of these steps is also part of a broader vision. Needle exchange is not just about reducing HIV/AIDS; it's about redefining injection drug users, from criminals to be persecuted to potential partners in a public health campaign. Medical marijuana is about saying that the first people who deserve not to be criminalized are people who use it as medicine, but it also helps to transform the discussion around marijuana regulation.

I define myself first and foremost as a human rights activist, who happens to be focusing in this area of human rights violations. That drives me, gives me the passion—but I'm not typically putting human rights arguments out there, because that's not what the public is open to. The public wants to hear about reducing disease, reducing fiscal costs of the drug war, better utilization of scarce criminal justice resources. So I am essentially an idealist, but the work is realistic and pragmatic.

You've been on this road for a long time. How do you assess your progress?

Obviously marijuana reform in the US, where we now have 18 going on 20 states that have legalized medical marijuana, one and a half to two million legal medical marijuana patients—that's remarkable. And Washington and Colorado are almost certainly just the first two of many.

The other incredible breakthrough is the evolution in elite opinion in Latin America. Beginning with the Latin American commission on drugs and democracy in 2009, with former presidents and Nobel Prize winners. And then the presidents calling for open debate. And more recently this OAS report last month, coming up with four scenarios of how drug policy might evolve, one of which was marijuana legalization. This is the first time any multilateral organization has considered marijuana legalization, harm reduction and decriminalization on an equal footing with a drug-war strategy. What the OAS did would have been inconceivable three years ago. Having sitting presidents talking how Santos in Colombia and Molina in Guatemala and Mujica in Uruguay are, is extraordinary. I'm grateful to have been in a position of advising and publicizing with these various commissions. Last year I had one-on-one meetings with Presidents Calderon and Molina and Santos to talk about this.

How do you see your mission evolving in the years ahead?

For DPA, something which is going to become a much greater priority is the decriminalization of drug possession, making a serious commitment to treating drug addiction as a health issue, the way we treat cigarette or (mostly) alcohol addiction. Of the 1.5 million or more Americans arrested for drug charges last year, something like three quarters were for possession only. The negative consequences—for public and personal health, the criminal justice costs—are our major priority.

Down the road, I think ultimately we need to accept that there is always going to be a small percentage of people who are absolutely determined to get their drug of choice. Heroin, cocaine, whatever. And for those people: Offer them treatment; offer them counseling; offer them help. But ultimately, we need to find a way to allow them legal access to the substance they want. It's looking at what the Europeans and Canadians have been doing with heroin maintenance and finding a way to scale that that does not present greater threats to public health and safety. In the long run, a decade from now, that's going to be the major challenge.

An MBA for Stoners: Get Ready for the Next Growth Industry

By Michelle Goodman
Salon, November 16, 2013

Molly Poiset has a lot to learn about pot. "I never was a smoker," the 58-year-old pastry chef said. "I don't even know how to use a bong." But she's taking steps to start a patisserie business specializing in marijuana-infused confections—essentially, gourmet medibles. She wants to give critically ill patients a decadent sweet that offers a bit of palliative care, something beyond the usual gummy worms and Rice Krispies treats crowding dispensary shelves.

Poiset became interested in weed two years ago when her 32-year-old daughter was diagnosed with leukemia and required a stem cell transplant, a grueling process that included nine weeks of quarantine. "I saw her suffer," Poiset said. "It changes you." While helping her daughter and grandchildren through the ordeal, she attended a caregivers group in Los Angeles. There, she learned about the many ways cancer patients can benefit from cannabis.

Poiset, who also plans to peddle pot-free treats, learned to bake at Le Cordon Bleu in Paris. This summer, after graduating, she moved to Seattle to establish residency in Washington State. In September, one of her pot truffles nabbed second place in the "best edible" category at Seattle's High Times Cannabis Cup. This month, she'll apply for a marijuana producer and processor license under the state's new recreational pot law. To rein in costs and ensure she can get her hands on a strain that's low in psychotropic THC but high in CDB, or cannabidiol, which offers a number of therapeutic effects, she plans to grow her own.

I met Poiset at the second annual National CannaBusiness Conference and Expo, held earlier this month at Emerald Downs, a thoroughbred racetrack half an hour south of Seattle. The bespectacled chef was one of 700 people from 31 states and 10 countries who attended the crash course in potpreneurship, put on by trade publication *Medical Marijuana Business Daily* and sponsored by leading pot lobbyists and companies. At the top of the conference agenda: teaching attendees to run a successful cannabis company without winding up in an orange jumpsuit.

Before becoming a pâtissier, Poiset ran her own interior design firm in Telluride, Colo., for 30 years. But starting a pot pastry business is a horse of a different color. To catch up, she's spent the past six months doing reefer recon: talking to industry insiders, devouring cultivation websites and perfecting recipes. Hence her presence at the cannabusiness conference. In her words, "This is the most professional, focused, investment-oriented, visionary event that takes place in this industry." It may also be the most surreal. Serving as the conference backdrop was Emerald Downs' outdoor race course, visible through 100-foot-tall gallery windows. Inside, betting windows lined the meeting hall, and TV screens for broadcasting the races hung from the ceiling. Still, at $600 a head, this three-day cannabis confab attracts a more serious breed of entrepreneur than, say, Seattle Hempfest. Many are wage slaves looking for more meaningful work, midlifers plotting their second act, serial business owners in search of their next venture. A good number show up in ties or heels. Some are in it for the money. Others consider themselves artisans, much like a craft brewer or cheesemonger. Most gush about making history.

The timing of the conference couldn't have been better. Two weeks earlier, a new Gallup poll reported that 58 percent of Americans now support legalization. Medical marijuana is legal in 20 states and Washington, D.C. In Colorado, the legal sale of recreational weed begins on Jan. 1. Washington State is poised to follow suit later in 2014. (*The New Yorker* just published a feature on the policy work that is going into Washington's great recreational pot experiment.) A study released this month by ArcView Market Research, the financial analysis arm of ArcView Group, a cannabis investor network based in San Francisco, predicts that in the next five years, 14 additional states will pass "adult use" legislation. And then there are the financial forecasts. ArcView puts the legal U.S. cannabis market at $1.43 billion this year and $2.34 billion in 2014, an increase of 64 percent. "At this rate, U.S. cannabis sales will outpace the worldwide growth of smartphone sales," read ArcView's breathless press release. ArcView also predicts that by 2018, the country's annual dope trade will be worth $10.2 billion.

As far as career paths go, many see cannabusiness as a winning ticket. "This is like a dream job, really. The money is great," said a fortyish Las Vegas grower I'll call "Raj." (Raj, who's also employed by a casino on the Vegas strip, didn't want his real name used.) I approached him between conference sessions after watching him take reams of notes. He told me he's here to schmooze and learn more about navigating the legal minefield of growing ganja. Back in Nevada, which permits medical marijuana, Raj feels like he's always looking over his shoulder. He's had his door kicked in by a SWAT team, his "assets" confiscated. It's too late for him to meet Washington and Colorado's residency requirements to start his own recreational weed business. (Colorado's new pot law requires two years of residency; Washington requires three months. Neither state has said whether it will open another licensing window in the future.) But he's interested in relocating to either state on the off chance he can find someone to hire him as a grower. "I don't come cheap," said Raj, who's spent nearly two decades perfecting his cultivation techniques. "I do really, really high quality. I don't know if I can be a Budweiser. I'm more of a Chateau Montenegro."

Jobs and dollars aren't all that's at stake. Also on the line: reshaping the image of an industry that's been underground for decades. "What happens in Washington and what happens in Colorado over the next few years will determine whether we roll prohibition back," Alison Holcomb, criminal justice director of Washington State's ACLU chapter and chief author of the state's recreational pot law, said in a session called "Getting Recreation Right." "All of us need to be really aware of the eyes that are watching us right now." To elevate the profile of modern potpreneurs, the conference's 30 speakers did their best to dispense handy takeaways: *Be a good neighbor! Volunteer in your community! Don't lie about the type of business you're running!* As with any business conference, snoozy PowerPoints crammed with lists and acronyms abounded.

Session topics ran the gamut: How to woo investors. How to manage your finances when no one will give you a bank account. How to find honest, reliable employees who don't just want to get high on your dime. The real action, however, was on the expo floor, where dozens of marijuana companies shilled their products and services. Think vaporizers, sodas, tinctures, dispensaries, hemp shampoo, botanical extractors, hydroponics shops, potency testing labs, mobile payment apps, child-proof containers, custom printed stash bags, lawyers, accountants, insurance brokers, and business consultants. Some have catered to the cannabis world for years. Others are just lining up at the starting gate. Everyone wants to win big. MJ Freeway, for example, a Colorado corporation that's been selling "seed to sale" tracking software since 2010, already serves 450 dispensaries in 12 states as well as Canada and Europe. "We want to be the IBM of marijuana," Amy Poinsett, the company's CEO, said.

Not all these stories will have a happy ending. "Howard," an unemployed Seattleite I met at the conference, had to declare bankruptcy after the DEA shut down his dispensary in May. (At the time, state law required 1,000 feet between pot shops and schools, playgrounds or daycare centers, measured by public roads and walkways. Federal law, however, defined this 1,000-foot buffer as the crow flies. Howard's shop met the first requirement but not the second. The state has since amended its 1,000-foot rule to match that of the federal government.) Before becoming a potpreneur, Howard spent a decade as a successful IT consultant. Now his home is in foreclosure and he's barely scraping by. Getting work in his former field has been difficult. Companies don't want to hire someone with a two-year gap on their résumé. Or someone who freely admits to having run a pot shop. "It's a crazy industry," the 51-year-old said. "I'm just about done with it all." So what was he doing at a cannabis conference? Research, for a consulting client he's helping apply for a recreational store license. If all goes well—and it may not, considering the state has a finite number of licenses available for reefer retailers—Howard's client will make him a full-time employee early in 2014. If not, he may move to Vegas to live with relatives. Howard remained upbeat as he spun his sad tale. Despite a couple of attempted robberies and dishonest employees, he enjoyed being a pot retailer. "I had a lot of true patients come in that we helped," he smiled. "I had a lot of stoners come in, too. But who cares? They're not hurting anyone."

Industry leaders are hopeful the growing legitimacy of the marijuana market will help put an end to DEA shutdown letters like the one Howard received. "Change happens exponentially," Aaron Smith, executive director of the National Cannabis

Industry Association, a non-profit trade association, said on the expo floor. "Just a few years ago, people wouldn't have thought that the Colorado and Washington experience would happen."

To usher in this new era of professionalism, smoking pot at the conference was verboten. But old habits die hard. One vendor arrived with his own party bus, conveniently parked near the building entrance. "Any time I want to medicate, he lets me on the bus," a young woman doing a lap around the expo floor said between bus breaks. Inside the bus, half a dozen people sat passing a vaporizer and eating M&Ms. A Canadian conference goer peered into the open doorway but declined to step inside. He worried he'd smell like dope while crossing the border on his way home.

Back in the conference, this juxtaposition of stoner and startup cultures was everywhere. One ancillary business owner on the podium stressed not writing off potential customers based on visual appearance. "A stoner can still be a qualified lead," he said. "Just be sure to get it in writing." Later, on a panel about finding capital, one investor implored the crowd to rise above the industry's stereotypes. "It drives me crazy when someone comes in to pitch me and I can smell the product on them," he said. During the next panel, which started at 4 p.m., the speaker made a feeble joke about how he'd understand if people needed to take a bathroom break at 4:20. At Hempfest, the crowd would have whooped and taken a collective hit. Here, they just gave a timid courtesy laugh and took notes.

U.S. Policy on Marijuana Fuels Push for Legalization Worldwide

By Gene Johnson
Associated Press, February 16, 2014

In a former colonial mansion in Jamaica, politicians huddle to discuss trying to ease marijuana laws in the land of the late reggae musician and cannabis evangelist Bob Marley. In Morocco, one of the world's top producers of the concentrated pot known as hashish, two leading political parties want to legalize its cultivation, at least for medical and industrial use. And in Mexico City, the vast metropolis of a country ravaged by horrific cartel bloodshed, lawmakers have proposed a plan to let stores sell the drug.

From the Americas to Europe to North Africa and beyond, the marijuana-legalization movement is gaining unprecedented traction—a nod to successful efforts in Colorado, Washington state and the small South American nation of Uruguay, which in December became the first country to approve nationwide pot legalization.

Leaders long weary of the drug war's violence and futility have been emboldened by changes in U.S. policy, even in the face of opposition from their own conservative populations. Some are eager to try an approach that focuses on public health instead of prohibition, and some see a potentially lucrative industry in cannabis regulation.

"A number of countries are saying, 'We've been curious about this, but we didn't think we could go this route,'" said Sam Kamin, a University of Denver law professor who helped write Colorado's marijuana regulations. "It's harder for the U.S. to look at other countries and say, 'You can't legalize, you can't decriminalize,' because it's going on here."

That's due largely to a White House that's more open to drug-war alternatives.

President Barack Obama recently told *The New Yorker* magazine that he doesn't think marijuana is any more dangerous than alcohol, and said it's important that the legalization experiments in Colorado and Washington go forward, especially because blacks are arrested for the drug at a greater rate than whites, despite similar levels of use.

His administration has criticized drug war-driven incarceration rates in the U.S. and announced that it will let banks do business with licensed marijuana operations, which have largely been cash-only because federal law forbids financial institutions from processing pot-related transactions.

Such actions underscore how the official U.S. position has changed in recent years. In 2009, the U.S. Department of Justice announced it wouldn't target medical marijuana patients. In August, the agency said it wouldn't interfere with the laws in Colorado and Washington, which regulate the growth and sale of taxed pot for recreational use.

Government officials and activists worldwide have taken note of the more open stance. Also not lost on them was the Obama administration's public silence before votes in both states and in Uruguay.

It creates a "sense that the U.S. is no longer quite the drug war-obsessed government it was" and that other nations have some political space to explore reform, said Ethan Nadelmann, head of the nonprofit Drug Policy Alliance, a pro-legalization group based in New York.

Anxiety over U.S. reprisals has previously doused reform efforts in Jamaica, including a 2001 attempt to approve private use of marijuana by adults.

Given America's evolution, "the discussion has changed," said Delano Seiveright, director of Ganja Law Reform Coalition-Jamaica.

Last summer, eight lawmakers, evenly split between the ruling People's National Party and the opposition Jamaica Labor Party, met with Nadelmann and local cannabis crusaders at a luxury hotel in Kingston's financial district and discussed the next steps, including an effort to decriminalize pot possession.

Officials are concerned about the roughly 300 young men each week who get criminal records for possessing small amounts of "ganja." Others in the debt-shackled nation worry about losing out on tourism dollars: For many, weed is synonymous with Marley's home country, where it has long been used as a medicinal herb by families, including as a cold remedy, and as a spiritual sacrament by Rastafarians.

Influential politicians are taking up the idea of loosening pot restrictions. Jamaica's health minister has said he is "fully on board" with medical marijuana.

"The cooperation on this issue far outweighs what I've seen before," Seiveright said. "Both sides are in agreement with the need to move forward."

In Morocco, lawmakers have been inspired by the experiments in Colorado, Washington and Uruguay to push forward their longstanding desire to allow cannabis to be grown for medical and industrial uses. They say such a law would help small farmers who survive on the crop but live at the mercy of drug lords and police attempts to eradicate it.

There's no general push to legalize marijuana in Mexico, where tens of thousands have died in cartel violence in recent years. But in liberal Mexico City, legislators on Thursday introduced a measure to let stores sell up to 5 grams of pot. It's supported by the mayor but could set up a fight with the conservative federal government.

"Rather than continue fighting a war that makes no sense, now we are joining a cutting-edge process," said Jorge Castaneda, a former Mexican foreign minister.

Global Green

Here's a look at how some countries are rethinking their approach to marijuana:

Brazil: In November, former Brazilian President Fernando Henrique Cardoso joined former U.N. Secretary General Kofi Annan in calling for the decriminalization of all drugs.

Uruguay: In December, Uruguay became the first nation to approve marijuana legalization and regulation.

Morocco: Two leading political parties want to legalize the cultivation of cannabis for medical and industrial uses.

Mexico: In liberal Mexico City, a metropolis of 8 million, lawmakers have introduced a measure to allow stores to sell up to 5 grams of pot.

Following Legalization in US, Uruguay, Marijuana Gets Second Look

By Associated Press
Associated Press, February 15, 2014

The marijuana legalization experiments underway in Washington state, Colorado and Uruguay have prompted or accelerated discussion about changing pot laws in many nations, and activists say momentum is building in advance of a special United Nations convention on drugs scheduled for 2016. Here's a look at how some countries are rethinking their approach to marijuana.

Argentina

Personal possession of controlled substances has been decriminalized, thanks to a Supreme Court ruling in 2009 that found imposing jail time for small amounts of drugs was a violation of Argentina's constitution, which protects private actions that don't harm others. Lawmakers have been working to amend the law since then, with proposals ranging from simple decriminalization in accordance with the ruling to a complete overhaul of the country's drug laws. In December, Father Juan Carlos Molina, a Catholic priest newly appointed as the nation's drug czar, said Argentina deserves a debate about whether to follow Uruguay in regulating marijuana.

Brazil

Brazil doesn't punish personal drug use, but trafficking or transporting small amounts of controlled substances is a criminal offense, punishable by drug abuse education or community service. Some advocates worry the law isn't clear about how much constitutes personal possession, and that can leave it up to a judge's discretion about whether someone should be punished. In November, former Brazilian President Fernando Henrique Cardoso joined former U.N. Secretary General Kofi Annan in calling for the decriminalization of all drugs and allowing countries to experiment with drug regulation.

Guatemala

President Otto Perez Molina of Guatemala, a hard-hit cocaine transit country, took the floor at the U.N. last fall to join a growing chorus of nations calling the drug war a failed strategy. He announced that his country would study different approaches and praised the "visionary" experiments in Washington and Colorado—as well as U.S. President Barack Obama's decision to let them go forward. Currently, prison terms of four months to two years can be imposed for the possession of drugs for personal use.

Jamaica

The island nation is a primary source of marijuana in the Caribbean. Possession remains illegal and can result in mandated treatment or rehabilitation, though usually the defendant pays a small fine and is not incarcerated. Nevertheless, many young men wind up with criminal records that affect their future employment options, and recent changes in the U.S. and Uruguay have given momentum to activists who hope to see marijuana decriminalization approved soon.

Mexico

In Mexico, where tens of thousands have been killed in drug war violence in the past seven years, there is no general push to legalize or regulate marijuana for recreational use. But in more liberal Mexico City, a metropolis of 8 million, lawmakers have introduced a measure to allow stores to sell up to 5 grams of pot. The plan has the mayor's support but could set up a fight with the federal government. Small amounts of marijuana and other drugs have been decriminalized in Mexico since 2009.

Morocco

Morocco is one of the world's leading hashish producers, and nearly all of it makes its way into Europe. Cannabis was legal to grow as late as the 1950s by order of the king. Two leading political parties want to re-legalize its cultivation for medical and industrial uses, with the goal of helping small farmers who survive on the crop but live at the mercy of drug lords and police attempts to eradicate it. There is little chance the conservative nation will legalize it for recreational use any time soon.

Netherlands

The Netherlands has long had some of the most liberal cannabis laws. Hoping to keep pot users away from dealers of harder drugs, the country in the late 1970s began allowing "coffee shops" to sell marijuana, which remains technically illegal. Since 2012 the federal government has clamped down, briefly requiring people to obtain a "weed pass" to buy cannabis and banning sales to tourists. Some cities, including Amsterdam, have declined to ban sales to tourists, however, and mayors of 35 cities have banded together to call for the legalization of marijuana growing.

United States

Long the drug war crusader, the U.S. was the driving force behind the 1961 treaty that formed the basis of international narcotics control. For decades the U.S. has required other nations to cooperate in the drug war or risk losing foreign aid, even as some Latin American countries ravaged by drug war violence criticized America for failing to curb its appetite for cocaine, marijuana and other substances. Since 1996, nearly half the states have allowed medical use of marijuana despite federal laws banning it, and some states are considering following the lead of Washington state and Colorado in legalizing recreational use.

Uruguay

In December, Uruguay became the first nation to approve marijuana legalization and regulation. President Jose Mujica said his goal is to drive drug traffickers out of the dope business and reduce consumption by creating a safe, legal and transparent environment in which the state closely monitors every aspect of marijuana use. By April, Uruguay is expected to have written the fine print on its regulations. Once registered and licensed, any Uruguayan adult will be allowed to choose one of three options: grow plants at home, or join a pot-growing club, or buy marijuana cigarettes from pharmacies.

2

Marijuana: Legalization versus Decriminalization

©Zurab Kurtsikidze/EPA/Landov

Protesters hold a poster during a protest rally for cannabis decriminalization in front of the former parliament building in Tbilisi, Georgia, June 2013.

The Evolving Legal History of Marijuana

Since its first uses as a recreational drug at the turn of the twentieth century, marijuana has been one of the most divisive issues in America's long-standing War on Drugs. Since attention was first paid to marijuana use, opponents have labeled the dried buds "evil" and a "menace." Marijuana has also become a common symbol of the counterculture movement, a trend that began in the 1960s and has since persisted.

While the debate over the morality of marijuana use has continued for more than a century, a more focused issue has developed. Since the drug's official classification as a narcotic, political leaders, law enforcement officials, and a wide range of interest groups have debated whether marijuana-related offenses should be criminal in nature—that is, punishable by criminal penalties such as jail time. This debate began in the 1970s, amid concerns that harsher enforcement measures would lead to overcrowded prisons, and disagreements about whether possession of small amounts of the drug was really all that serious. Although this particular debate relates more to the criminal justice system than to broader social issues, it is largely infused, from both sides, with the same attitudes and passions regarding marijuana use.

The Early Debate

The debate over decriminalization (removing criminal penalties but perhaps leaving in place lighter penalties such as fines) and legalization (removing all legal prohibitions) with regard to marijuana possession and use is rooted in a period in which the drug's use was particularly widespread: the 1960s. During this period, marijuana use was prevalent, especially among the growing number of middle-class youths. In decades prior, activists and political leaders alike railed against the recreational use of marijuana, suggesting that the drug led to violence, criminality, and even insanity. The outcry over marijuana (which included the 1936 propaganda film *Reefer Madness*) and its perceived impact on American society led political leaders to enact, in the 1940s and 1950s, a series of laws that set mandatory minimum sentences for possession of the drug. Such sentences included multiyear jail terms and severe fines.

In the 1960s, however, the counterculture continued to use marijuana in large quantities, even with the threat of criminal charges for possession. Its widespread use gave researchers the data they needed to prove the aforementioned theories about marijuana's influence on crime and mental health. Instead, however, the theories were largely debunked: criminal behavior and instances of mental illness could not be linked to marijuana use. This information was verified in multiple studies, including those conducted by the administrations of Presidents John F. Kennedy, Lyndon B. Johnson, and Richard Nixon. As the federal government aligned its various antidrug agencies to formulate a unified approach to combating drug use (in 1968, the Bureau of Narcotics and Dangerous Drugs was established but later merged with other agencies to create the Drug Enforcement Administration in 1973), marijuana was increasingly given separate attention from opiates and hallucinogens. Since law enforcement did not view marijuana as an immediate threat to society, state governments began pulling back on sentencing laws and instead issuing modest fines for possession of certain amounts.

The Push for Legalization

The successful decriminalization movement of the 1960s and 1970s was not enough for some Americans, however. The 1960s had seen a tremendous growth in the use of drugs, including marijuana. For some, the widespread use of marijuana was not an epidemic but a political and social backlash against an overbearing and increasingly intrusive federal government. Beat poets Allen Ginsberg and Ed Sanders were among a growing minority of individuals who dismissed the politically charged environment that gave rise to *Reefer Madness* and other forms of what they perceived as antimarijuana hysteria. In the mid-1960s, Ginsberg and Sanders formed an organization in New York dedicated to pushing not for decriminalization but for outright legalization of the leafy drug known as "pot."

Ginsberg and Sanders's New York Chapter of the Committee to Legalize Marijuana found some support, but its biggest impact was more symbolic than substantive. For Ginsberg and Sanders—as well as countless other advocates of both legalization and decriminalization—the issue of marijuana use was not hinged on scientific evidence or matters of law. Rather, it was a battlefield with two very distinct combatants: the government (or, in broader terms, the "establishment") and the nation's young people. These two groups had confronted each other on other fronts—most notably on the issue of the war in Vietnam—and marijuana use was yet another area in which the divide between "us" and "them" was evident.

Backlash: The War on Drugs

Perpetuating the conflict was the warlike rhetoric coming from the government itself. Nixon, an ardent antidrug president, frequently described efforts to curtail drug use as a "war." At the middle of the issue, groups like the National Organization for the Reform of Marijuana Laws (NORML) advocated for decriminalization and gained support from both sides of the political aisle (including that of conservative intellectual William F. Buckley). However, the efforts of NORML (which was also seeking to exempt marijuana from a list of federally banned substances, claiming that marijuana contained properties of value to modern medicine) were undone when the group's main ally in the administration of President Jimmy Carter, drug czar Peter Bourne, was revealed to have been present at a cocaine party in 1978. Without a mainstream advocate for decriminalization, the idea of marijuana law reform was undercut; pro-legalization advocates went back to their corner, and antidrug government leaders went back to theirs.

In the 1980s, the political gulf between the two sides continued to widen. Increased activism against drug use gave rise to President Ronald Reagan's relaunch of the War on Drugs initiated by Nixon. Reagan himself referred to marijuana as "the most dangerous drug in America," and set about using every resource available to combat the production, trafficking, and use of the drug. Brought back to the legal system were mandatory sentencing laws, as well as legal measures that enabled law enforcement to investigate and disrupt drug trafficking activity. The push for decriminalization was shelved, and the idea of full legalization relegated to the world of fantasy.

Medical Marijuana

Although the movements for decriminalization or full legalization of recreational marijuana use were stymied in the 1980s, the idea of using the drug for purely medicinal purposes slowly gained traction. A wide range of studies were conducted in the late 1980s and 1990s to explore whether the active ingredient of marijuana, tetrahydrocannabinol (THC), possesses properties of value to treating painful and degenerative diseases. There were claims that the THC in marijuana helped reduce the pressure on blood vessels in the eye and therefore mitigated the effects of glaucoma. Other claims suggested that THC could offset the wasting effects of diseases like AIDS (which had by this time taken center stage in American health circles). Of all of the studies conducted on the medicinal uses of marijuana, only the claim that use of the drug tends to stimulate appetite seems to have been verified. In light of the intense nausea and loss of appetite associated with treatments for cancer and AIDS, this latter property alone has popularized the drug's use for medicinal purposes.

Regardless of the actual value of marijuana for AIDS, cancer, and glaucoma patients (among others)—many researchers believe that these perceived THC effects may be duplicated and even improved upon by prescribing legal synthetic medications—attention to medical marijuana fostered a new interest in removing the drug from the same legal category as heroin, cocaine, and LSD. In 1996, the state of California took the bold step of embracing the idea of medical marijuana and passed Proposition 215, which allowed for the sale and use of marijuana purely for medicinal purposes. Of course, the new state law was in direct contradiction with federal laws banning the substance altogether.

Changing Public Views

The gulf between those advocating for legalized marijuana and those adamantly against the drug's use in any circle was firmly reestablished at the turn of the twenty-first century. Echoing the politics of the Nixon administration, President George W. Bush—two years into his first term in 2002—ratcheted up the War on Drugs, appointing his own drug czar and advocating the full prosecution of drug users and dealers alike. By this time, however, Bush and those who sought to continue the law that designated marijuana a Schedule I drug (a substance that has no medicinal value, is likely to be abused, and cannot be effectively regulated, as defined by Schedule I of the 1970 Controlled Substances Act) were in the minority. By 2002, according to a *Time*/CNN poll, 80 percent of Americans approved of the distribution of legalized medical marijuana, and 72 percent thought that an individual caught using marijuana for recreational purposes should get no more than a modest fine. Overall, according to that poll, 34 percent of Americans believed that marijuana should be legalized altogether (a poll asking the same question in 1986 saw only 17 percent of respondents in favor of legalization).

In light of the wave of support for legalized medical marijuana and decriminalization for recreational use, cities and states started passing ordinances and laws that supported both notions. During the 2002 midterm elections, in addition to selecting their respective congressional and state leaders, voters in San Francisco voted to allow their city to grow and distribute medical marijuana. In Ohio and Arizona, residents voted in favor of reducing marijuana sentences to rehabilitation and small fines. Between 1998 and 2011, fifteen states passed laws legalizing medical marijuana, including Arizona, which reapproved such programs three times during this period.

The main battlefield in the war on drugs was between the federal government, which clung to the Schedule I classification for marijuana, and the increasing number of states and localities that passed legalized medical marijuana statutes. Instead of focusing on the users in these areas, federal agents raided medical marijuana dispensaries. Nevertheless, tensions over marijuana policy between the states and the federal government continued to rise.

Recent Developments

In 2009, President Barack Obama's administration dialed back on such raids. Obama, who openly admitted to using the drug himself during his youth and demonstrated a more casual perspective on the issue than his predecessors, ordered federal agencies to reinvest their energies on more serious drug trafficking issues than medical marijuana dispensaries. At the same time, states continued to reexamine their own statutes concerning nonmedical marijuana use. Massachusetts (in 2008) and Connecticut (2011) were among the states voting to decriminalize marijuana possession for recreational purposes. In 2014, the legislatures of Texas and New Jersey passed into law measures decriminalizing possession of marijuana. As of 2014, twenty-seven states and the District of Columbia have passed laws allowing medical marijuana, decriminalizing possession, or both. Many more states are mulling similar legislative action. In January 2014, the boldest legislative measure to date took effect in Colorado, when marijuana production, distribution, and use was legalized altogether for people aged twenty-one and over, with regulations on quantity. A similar law in Washington state also took effect in 2014, with the first licensed retail locations opening in July.

The debate over marijuana legalization and decriminalization has not been quelled by the passage of the Colorado and Washington measures, and not every state is embracing legalization. In Texas, where Governor Rick Perry signed into law the 2014 decriminalization bill, questions abound over whether that state will be the next to legalize marijuana. Seventy-seven percent of Texas voters are in favor of decriminalization or some form of legalization, and 49 percent advocate for full legalization. In addition to the recreational benefits espoused by users, there are potential revenue sources to consider—marijuana sales in Colorado and Washington are skyrocketing, and the potential tax revenues from such sales are enticing to cash-strapped states.

The Colorado and Washington laws have also generated interest in one of the longest-standing issues surrounding marijuana use: crime. Questions abound among political leaders, law enforcement officers, and other observers; among them are whether legalized marijuana use will result in increased crime, or if there are public health or public safety risks associated with overuse. As of August 2014 both state-level legalization measures have been in effect for less than a year, and as a result, the answers to these questions are far from conclusive. Data is being gathered from Colorado, but such information is raw and can be manipulated for the benefit of both sides of the argument. Some studies show highway accidents in Colorado are down since the law was passed, for example, but over the same period, crime has increased 7 percent in Denver (with public intoxication up 237 percent). There are also questions as to whether the legal use of marijuana will cause an increase in birth defects and other health issues; such questions cannot be answered until more concrete data can be obtained.

The issues of marijuana legalization and decriminalization are, as they have been since the early twentieth century, continuously evolving. Politics and ignorance (on both sides of the marijuana debate) continue to fuel the issue. As research continues and more data is obtained from Colorado and Washington and possibly other states that opt for full legalization, the debate is expected to continue until more conclusive evidence is available.

—Michael P. Auerbach

Bibliography

Balko, Radley. "Since Marijuana Legalization, Highway Fatalities in Colorado Are at Near-Historic Lows." *Washington Post*. Washington Post, 5 Aug. 2014. Web. 15 Aug. 2014.

Garvey, Todd and Brian T. Yeh. "State Legalization of Recreational Marijuana: Selected Legal Issues." *Congressional Research Service*. Congressional Research Service, 13 Jan. 2014. Web. 15 Aug. 2014.

Gittens, Hasani. "High Times: The Next Five States to Tackle Pot Laws." *NBC News*. NBC News, 2 June 2014. Web. 15 Aug. 2014.

Gwynne, Kristen. "Turning the Tide on Drug Reform." *Nation* 18 Feb. 2013: 22–24. Print.

Hartnett, Edmund. "Drug Legalization: Why It Wouldn't Work in the United States." *Police Chief*. Intl. Assn. of Chiefs of Police, Mar. 2005. Web. 15 Aug. 2014.

Lee, Martin A. "Let a Thousand Flowers Bloom: The Populist Politics of Cannabis Reform." *Nation*. Nation, 30 Oct. 2013. Web. 15 Aug. 2014.

"Marijuana Law Reform Timeline". *NORML*. NORML, 2014. Web. 15 Aug. 2014.

"Medical Marijuana Policy in the United States." *HOPES: Huntington's Outreach Project for Education*. Stanford U, 15 May 2012. Web. 15 Aug. 2014.

Sabet, Kevin A. "Crime Is Up in Colorado: What That Tells Us about Pot Legalization and, Perhaps More Importantly, Lazy Reporting." *Huffington Post*. TheHuffingtonPost.com, 11 Aug. 2014. Web. 15 Aug. 2014.

Decriminalizing versus Legalizing Marijuana— Who's Right, and What's the Difference?

By Randy LoBasso
Philadelphia Weekly, February 20, 2014

When U.S. Representative and gubernatorial candidate Allyson Schwartz broke the news to *Philadelphia Weekly* that she'd support decriminalizing simple marijuana possession at the state level, most were a bit taken aback.

After all, Schwartz had never expressed any interest in decriminalizing the plant. Her most recent score by the National Organization to Reform Marijuana Laws was a -10, implying a "hard on drugs" stance from the advocacy organization.

The frontrunner in the PA governor's race told me "simple possession and personal use should not be criminalized." Her reasoning for that, in part: laws against marijuana use are "not applied very evenly," she said. In other words, though whites and blacks use marijuana at roughly the same rate, blacks are much more likely to be arrested for possession and use, in Pennsylvania and nationwide.

She was applauded by advocates throughout the state, and the story made the rounds nationwide, including on Fox News.

But not everyone's buying it.

"Decriminalization is simply false advertising," wrote fellow gubernatorial candidate John Hanger in a blog post on his campaign website after the story broke, "because it wouldn't decriminalize at all—it just reduces penalties."

He insists that decriminalization—which is supported by other Pennsylvania gubernatorial candidates, like Max Myers—would not actually end the mass incarceration that's gone along with marijuana prohibition since the 1930s. In fact, the candidate writes, only full legalization would put a stop to the sorts of problems often associated with marijuana sales and possession.

"Only legalization will stop the waste of $300 million in law enforcement resources Pennsylvania spends annually waging this senseless war. Only by the legal sale of marijuana will new revenues and new jobs be generated. And, importantly, legal sales in controlled, regulated settings will be a much more effective way to keep marijuana out of the hands of youngsters," said Hanger, who has been endorsed by NORML.

The idea of "decriminalization," it may seem, sounds a lot cooler than it actually is.

In Philadelphia, Councilman Jim Kenney has proposed a bill that would hit those caught with less than an ounce with a $200 fine and a 3-hour drug treatment class. This news is encouraging for pot advocates and those in favor of saving some time and judicial cash in the city, just as was Schwartz's and Myers' explanation that they'd like to see decriminalization happen at the state level.

But problems remain. Decriminalized possession in Philly or not, it will continue to be illegal to sell and buy marijuana. "Decriminalization sucks," cannabis and marijuana reform advocate Les Stark wrote on his Facebook page, regarding Kenney's bill. "You've got this ENORMOUS demand for weed in a city the size of Philly and yet all channels of distribution are illegal and therefore controlled by the black market."

Stark's vast research on cannabis cultivation in Pennsylvania was a large part of *Philadelphia Weekly*'s report this fall regarding marijuana legalization. He similarly notes that many of those advocating for decriminalization have gone so far to admit that pot is relatively harmless. Kenney has even described a situation in which pot is sold in state liquor stores.

"Within the mentality of that bill is the recognition that cannabis is relatively harmless, that the prohibition and criminal penalties do more harm than good and that there is a better way," he continued. "In other words, they know the truth."

Kenney's idea aside, many who advocate decriminalization are a bit vague on the details. But looking at what some other states have in place, it's easy to see where such a compromise could go wrong.

Possession and cultivation of less than 100 grams of marijuana has been decriminalized in Ohio since 1975. Rather, getting caught is a "minor misdemeanor" with a $150 punishment and a driver's license suspension.

Half-an-ounce in North Carolina is considered a misdemeanor, too, but the guilty can still spend up to 30 days in jail and pay a $200 fine

Marijuana has been decriminalized in New York City for decades.

And yet, in Ohio, 2007 alone saw 23,335 marijuana arrests.

North Carolina saw 20,983 marijuana-related arrests in 2010—with blacks arrested at a rate 3.4 times higher than whites.

More than 400,000 people were arrested for marijuana possession in New York City during Bloomberg's tenure alone.

And they all make up part of the 8 million people arrested for marijuana between 2000 and 2010—88 percent of whom were brought in for "simply having marijuana," according to the ACLU.

So is decriminalization something to celebrate? Sure. It implies politicians are catching up to the public and willing to toss out the rhetoric that smoking some weed is akin to hard drugs, which is how it's still classified by the federal government. But decriminalizing is mostly akin to President Obama saying marijuana is less bad for you than alcohol—it sounds great, but on its face, won't change the situation all that much.

FYI: Decriminalization of Cannabis Does Not Mean Weed Will Be Legal in Texas

By Angelica Leicht

Houston Press, January 31, 2014

Well, Rick Perry wants to decriminalize pot in the state of Texas. But don't start sparking up that celebratory joint just yet. It may not mean quite what you think it does.

If you haven't heard the news, Rick Perry threw out his support for marijuana decriminalization in Texas during the World Economic Forum in Switzerland recently, and it was a bit surprising, to say the least. In years past, Perry's stance on drugs has always been a bit, well, punitive, and that "decriminalization" talk sure did sound like a mighty big change of heart. But when it comes down to it, would the decriminalization that Perry is touting really mean huge policy changes on marijuana in the state of Texas?

Unfortunately, the short answer to that question is "no." Decriminalization is not equivalent to legalization of marijuana in any form or fashion, although the two terms are often used interchangeably. There are some big differences between the two terms, and they're differences you might want to know about, because the differences could mean rehab on one hand, and a thriving pot industry on the other.

When it comes to decriminalization, the term means what it sounds like. To decriminalize pot means that it would no longer be a crime for which you would face jail time for simply possessing pot, but pot as a substance is still completely illegal. If it's on you, you can still be punished for it, just not in criminal court. And if you're selling it—even in a less shady "pot shop"—you can still face criminal charges, because selling pot remains a criminal offense under decriminalization.

And legalization is a term that also means what it sounds like. To legalize pot is to allow the sale and use of cannabis to adults, with regulations on the sale of marijuana, much like the ones that exist for the sale of alcohol. Under legalization, pot is legal, you can use it if you're an adult, and if you're a licensed, taxed and regulated business, you can sell it. Legalization is worlds away from decriminalization.

Removing criminality by way of decriminalization, which is what Perry is talking about, when it comes to pot is great and all, at least in theory. No jail time for a dime bag of weed seems like a huge step. But it's not legalization, and it seems a bit dishonest to use the terms interchangeably.

So given that decriminalization, which is what Perry is proposing for Texas, has a vastly different protocol than legalization, it's important to know how it will affect our state. Let's take a look at what decriminalization would really look like for Texas, shall we?

Decriminalization in Texas means that pot possession "doesn't *necessarily* mean jail time," but you'll still face rehab or fines if you're caught with it.

Weed isn't legal under decriminalization laws. You can't have it on you. But if you aren't a violent criminal, a dealer or in possession of a large amount of pot, under decriminalization, there's a good chance you won't go to jail for simple possession. It doesn't mean you won't face incarceration by way of treatment in rehab, though. And according to Perry's camp, it can also mean more of a financial punishment, by way of fines associated with possession. So you probably won't go to jail—although you still could—but even if you don't, you probably won't like where you're headed.

Decriminalization still involves the court system if you're caught with weed.

Sure, you won't be labeled as a hardened criminal for having weed on you. But under the guidelines proposed by Perry, you'll still have to go to court. Only this time it will be "drug court," which will offer alternative penalties, which are "softer" and will be more likely to order treatment. So basically the drug court could send you to rehab for smoking pot, and that still seems like an utter waste of time and resources.

Federal guidelines may still come into play with decriminalization, even if the state says you're not a criminal.

Decriminalization doesn't legalize pot, but it still begs the question as to the role federal guidelines would play in conjunction with changes to state law. Would someone be allowed to receive federal aid for education in Texas with a pot charge once it is no longer a criminal offense? Or do the federal guidelines still prohibit folks with drug charges from receiving financial aid?

If pot possession is no longer a criminal offense in Texas, it would seem logical that a person should no longer be punitively kept from receiving money for higher education, considering that a stint in rehab hardly begs for such a harsh federal punishment.

But things are sticky when it comes to decriminalization and legalization, and the murky guidelines that come with decriminalization don't really help to clear up the confusion. If pot possession is not a crime in Texas, but it's still illegal, it seems like it would be straddling both sides of the fence federally.

Street dealers, not regulated businesses, will still be the suppliers of pot.

Without weed being "legal," decriminalization still forces pot sales to go underground, which leaves the same old issues of pot sales to minors, shady street-level sources and financial benefit for drug cartels, who just so happen to be the major suppliers. Oh, and weed dealers will still face jail time and a criminal record, even if they're just dealing pot.

Not to mention the fact that it would be a whole lot safer to license and regulate growers to ensure the safety of a product that people are going to consume, despite its legal or illegal standing. Folks are going to smoke pot. The least we could do is make sure it isn't the bathtub gin version of weed and that it's safe to consume. Safety first, folks.

Manpower is still needed to enforce the punitive nature of decriminalization, but we don't even see the added benefit of pot tax revenue.

Want to know what costs money? Courts. Drug courts won't run themselves, and rehabs won't pay themselves. No one works for free, you know. So while—in theory—drug courts may sound logical, it is questionable as to how they would be funded. Social welfare programs are still costly alternatives, despite not being incarceration.

That pretty little pot shop industry that has popped up in Colorado wouldn't be an option for Texas under decriminalization. Those businesses would still be illegal, and we would still be wasting manpower to shut them down. Regulation also has its costs, but it also has its payoffs by way of taxes and small-business growth. It's apples to weed oranges, really.

Marijuana research is still stifled.

So that weed may not earn you a few days in the pokey, but we still can't conduct scientific research on the medical benefits of marijuana if it's freakin' illegal. No scientist is going to risk his license to conduct research on a substance that is illegal to possess, even if there are lesser criminal consequences to be had, so we're still holding back some really important medical research. Ask any cancer patient about his or her thoughts on stifling cannabis research. You may learn quite a bit. Or you may regret asking them, if you're really against the idea of legalization.

Bottom line is, pot is theorized to help treat a plethora of medical conditions, but we really don't have a clue about its limitations or full benefits until we can legally study it in the United States rather than overseas. And under decriminalization guidelines, we still wouldn't be able to study it.

The reality is that the only way to remove the criminal aspect of pot is to legalize it, not decriminalize it. Decriminalization may be a good first step, but it is by no means interchangeable with a legal, regulated pot industry in Texas, nor should it be thought of as such.

Legalizing Marijuana: Why Citizens Should Just Say No

By Charles "Cully" Stimson
The Heritage Foundation, September 13, 2010

Abstract: *This November, California voters will consider a ballot initiative, the Regulate, Control and Tax Cannabis Act of 2010. Scientific research is clear that marijuana is addictive and that its use significantly impairs bodily and mental functions. Even where decriminalized, marijuana trafficking remains a source of violence, crime, and social disintegration. Furthermore, studies have shown that legalized marijuana will provide nowhere near the economic windfall proclaimed by some proponents. The RCTCA addresses neither the practical problems of implementation nor the fact that federal law prohibits marijuana production, distribution, and possession. There is strong evidence to suggest that legalizing marijuana would serve little purpose other than to worsen the state's drug problems—addiction, violence, disorder, and death. While long on rhetoric, the legalization movement, by contrast, is short on facts.*

The scientific literature is clear that marijuana is addictive and that its use significantly impairs bodily and mental functions. Marijuana use is associated with memory loss, cancer, immune system deficiencies, heart disease, and birth defects, among other conditions. Even where decriminalized, marijuana trafficking remains a source of violence, crime, and social disintegration.[1]

Nonetheless, this November, California voters will consider a ballot initiative, the Regulate, Control and Tax Cannabis Act of 2010 (RCTCA),[2] that would legalize most marijuana distribution and use under state law. (These activities would remain federal crimes.) This vote is the culmination of an organized campaign by pro-marijuana activists stretching back decades.

The current campaign, like previous efforts, downplays the well-documented harms of marijuana trafficking and use while promising benefits ranging from reduced crime to additional tax revenue. In particular, supporters of the initiative make five bold claims:

1. "Marijuana is safe and non-addictive."

2. "Marijuana prohibition makes no more sense than alcohol prohibition did in the early 1900s."

3. "The government's efforts to combat illegal drugs have been a total failure."

4. "The money spent on government efforts to combat the illegal drug trade

can be better spent on substance abuse and treatment for the allegedly few marijuana users who abuse the drug."

5. "Tax revenue collected from marijuana sales would substantially outweigh the social costs of legalization."[3]

As this [article] details, all five claims are demonstrably false or, based on the best evidence, highly dubious.

Further, supporters of the initiative simply ignore the mechanics of decriminalization—that is, how it would directly affect law enforcement, crime, and communities. Among the important questions left unanswered are:

- How would the state law fit into a federal regime that prohibits marijuana production, distribution, and possession?

- Would decriminalization, especially if combined with taxation, expand market opportunities for the gangs and cartels that currently dominate drug distribution?

- Would existing zoning laws prohibit marijuana cultivation in residential neighborhoods, and if not, what measures would growers have to undertake to keep children from the plants?

- Would transportation providers be prohibited from firing bus drivers because they smoke marijuana?

No one knows the specifics of how marijuana decriminalization would work in practice or what measures would be necessary to prevent children, teenagers, criminals, and addicts from obtaining the drug.

The federal government shares these concerns. Gil Kerlikowske, Director of the White House Office of National Drug Control Policy (ONDCP), recently stated, "Marijuana legalization, for any purpose, is a non-starter in the Obama Administration."[4] The Administration—widely viewed as more liberal than any other in recent memory and, for a time, as embodying the hopes of pro-legalization activists[5]—has weighed the costs and benefits and concluded that marijuana legalization would compromise public health and safety.

California's voters, if they take a fair-minded look at the evidence and the practical problems of legalization, should reach the same conclusion: Marijuana is a dangerous substance that should remain illegal under state law.

The Initiative

The RCTCA's purpose, as defined by advocates of legalization, is to regulate marijuana just as the government regulates alcohol. The law would allow anyone 21 years of age or older to possess, process, share, or transport up to one full ounce of marijuana "for personal consumption." Individuals could possess an unlimited number of living and harvested marijuana plants on the premises where they were grown. Individual landowners or lawful occupants of private property could cultivate marijuana plants "for personal consumption" in an area of not more than 25 square feet per private residence or parcel.

The RCTCA would legalize drug-related paraphernalia and tools and would license establishments for on-site smoking and other consumption of marijuana. Supporters have included some alcohol-like restrictions against, for example, smoking marijuana while operating a vehicle.[6] Finally, the act authorizes the imposition and collection of taxes and fees associated with legalization of marijuana.

Unsafe in Any Amount: How Marijuana Is Not Like Alcohol

Marijuana advocates have had some success peddling the notion that marijuana is a "soft" drug, similar to alcohol, and fundamentally different from "hard" drugs like cocaine or heroin. It is true that marijuana is not the most dangerous of the commonly abused drugs, but that is not to say that it is safe. Indeed, marijuana shares more in common with the "hard" drugs than it does with alcohol.

A common argument for legalization is that smoking marijuana is no more dangerous than drinking alcohol and that prohibiting the use of marijuana is therefore no more justified than the prohibition of alcohol. As Jacob Sullum, author of *Saying Yes: In Defense of Drug Use*, writes:

> Americans understood the problems associated with alcohol abuse, but they also understood the problems associated with Prohibition, which included violence, organized crime, official corruption, the erosion of civil liberties, disrespect for the law, and injuries and deaths caused by tainted black-market booze. They decided that these unintended side effects far outweighed whatever harms Prohibition prevented by discouraging drinking. The same sort of analysis today would show that the harm caused by drug prohibition far outweighs the harm it prevents, even without taking into account the value to each individual of being sovereign over his own body and mind.[7]

At first blush, this argument is appealing, especially to those wary of over-regulation by government. But it overlooks the enormous difference between alcohol and marijuana.

Legalization advocates claim that marijuana and alcohol are mild intoxicants and so should be regulated similarly; but as the experience of nearly every culture, over the thousands of years of human history, demonstrates, alcohol is different. Nearly every culture has its own alcoholic preparations, and nearly all have successfully regulated alcohol consumption through cultural norms. The same cannot be said of marijuana. There are several possible explanations for alcohol's unique status: For most people, it is not addictive; it is rarely consumed to the point of intoxication; low-level consumption is consistent with most manual and intellectual tasks; it has several positive health benefits; and it is formed by the fermentation of many common substances and easily metabolized by the body.

To be sure, there are costs associated with alcohol abuse, such as drunk driving and disease associated with excessive consumption. A few cultures—and this nation for a short while during Prohibition—have concluded that the benefits of alcohol consumption are not worth the costs. But they are the exception; most cultures have concluded that it is acceptable in moderation. No other intoxicant shares that status.

Alcohol differs from marijuana in several crucial respects. First, marijuana is far more likely to cause addiction. Second, it is usually consumed to the point of intoxication. Third, it has no known general healthful properties, though it may have some palliative effects. Fourth, it is toxic and deleterious to health. Thus, while it is true that both alcohol and marijuana are less intoxicating than other mood-altering drugs, that is not to say that marijuana is especially similar to alcohol or that its use is healthy or even safe.

In fact, compared to alcohol, marijuana is not safe. Long-term, moderate consumption of alcohol carries few health risks and even offers some significant benefits. For example, a glass of wine (or other alcoholic drink) with dinner actually improves health.[8] Dozens of peer-reviewed medical studies suggest that drinking moderate amounts of alcohol reduces the risk of heart disease, strokes, gallstones, diabetes, and death from a heart attack.[9] According to the Mayo Clinic, among many others, moderate use of alcohol (defined as two drinks a day) "seems to offer some health benefits, particularly for the heart."[10] Countless articles in medical journals and other scientific literature confirm the positive health effects of moderate alcohol consumption.

The effects of regular marijuana consumption are quite different. For example, the National Institute on Drug Abuse (a division of the National Institutes of Health) has released studies showing that use of marijuana has wide-ranging negative health effects. Long-term marijuana consumption "impairs the ability of T-cells in the lungs' immune system to fight off some infections."[11] These studies have also found that marijuana consumption impairs short-term memory, making it difficult to learn and retain information or perform complex tasks; slows reaction time and impairs motor coordination; increases heart rate by 20 percent to 100 percent, thus elevating the risk of heart attack; and alters moods, resulting in artificial euphoria, calmness, or (in high doses) anxiety or paranoia.[12] And it gets worse: Marijuana has toxic properties that can result in birth defects, pain, respiratory system damage, brain damage, and stroke.[13]

Further, prolonged use of marijuana may cause cognitive degradation and is "associated with lower test scores and lower educational attainment because during periods of intoxication the drug affects the ability to learn and process information, thus influencing attention, concentration, and short-term memory."[14] Unlike alcohol, marijuana has been shown to have a residual effect on cognitive ability that persists beyond the period of intoxication.[15] According to the National Institute on Drug Abuse, whereas alcohol is broken down relatively quickly in the human body, THC (tetrahydrocannabinol, the main active chemical in marijuana) is stored in organs and fatty tissues, allowing it to remain in a user's body for days or even weeks after consumption.[16] Research has shown that marijuana consumption may also cause "psychotic symptoms."[17]

Marijuana's effects on the body are profound. According to the British Lung Foundation, "smoking three or four marijuana joints is as bad for your lungs as smoking twenty tobacco cigarettes."[18] Researchers in Canada found that marijuana smoke contains significantly higher levels of numerous toxic compounds, like ammonia and hydrogen cyanide, than regular tobacco smoke.[19] In fact, the study determined that ammonia was found in marijuana smoke at levels of up to 20 times the levels found in tobacco.[20] Similarly, hydrogen cyanide was found in marijuana smoke at concentrations three to five times greater than those found in tobacco smoke.[21]

Marijuana, like tobacco, is addictive. One study found that more than 30 percent of adults who used marijuana in the course of a year were dependent on the drug.[22] These individuals often show signs of withdrawal and compulsive behavior.[23] Marijuana dependence is also responsible for a large proportion of calls to drug abuse help lines and treatment centers.

To equate marijuana use with alcohol consumption is, at best, uninformed and, at worst, actively misleading. Only in the most superficial ways are the two substances alike and they differ in every way that counts: addictiveness, toxicity, health effects, and risk of intoxication.

Unintended Consequences

Today, marijuana trafficking is linked to a variety of crimes, from assault and murder to money laundering and smuggling. Legalization of marijuana would increase demand for the drug and almost certainly exacerbate drug-related crime, as well as cause a myriad of unintended but predictable consequences.

To begin with, an astonishingly high percentage of criminals are marijuana users. According to a study by the RAND Corporation, approximately 60 percent of arrestees test positive for marijuana use in the United States, England, and Australia. Further, marijuana metabolites are found in arrestees' urine more frequently than those of any other drug.[24]

Although some studies have shown marijuana to inhibit aggressive behavior and violence, the National Research Council concluded that the "long-term use of marijuana may alter the nervous system in ways that do promote violence."[25] No place serves as a better example than Amsterdam.

Marijuana advocates often point to the Netherlands as a well-functioning society with a relaxed attitude toward drugs, but they rarely mention that Amsterdam is one of Europe's most violent cities. In Amsterdam, officials are in the process of closing marijuana dispensaries, or "coffee shops," because of the crime associated with their operation.[26] Furthermore, the Dutch Ministry of Health, Welfare and Sport has expressed "concern about drug and alcohol use among young people and the social consequences, which range from poor school performance and truancy to serious impairment, including brain damage."[27]

Amsterdam's experience is already being duplicated in California under the current medical marijuana statute. In Los Angeles, police report that areas surrounding cannabis clubs have experienced a 200 percent increase in robberies, a 52.2 percent increase in burglaries, a 57.1 percent increase in aggravated assault, and a 130.8 percent increase in burglaries from automobiles. Current law requires a doctor's prescription to procure marijuana; full legalization would likely spark an even more acute increase in crime.

Legalization of marijuana would also inflict a series of negative consequences on neighborhoods and communities. The nuisance caused by the powerful odor of mature marijuana plants is already striking California municipalities. The City Council of Chico, California, has released a report detailing the situation and describing how citizens living near marijuana cultivators are disturbed by the incredible stink emanating from the plants.[28]

Perhaps worse than the smell, crime near growers is increasing, associated with "the theft of marijuana from yards where it is being grown."[29] As a result, housing prices near growers are sinking.

Theoretical arguments in favor of marijuana legalization usually overlook the practical matter of how the drug would be regulated and sold. It is the details of implementation, of course, that will determine the effect of legalization on families, schools, and communities. Most basically, how and where would marijuana be sold?

- Would neighborhoods become neon red-light districts like Amsterdam's, accompanied by the same crime and social disorder?

- If so, who decides what neighborhoods will be so afflicted—residents and landowners or far-off government officials?

- Or would marijuana sales be so widespread that users could add it to their grocery lists?

- If so, how would stores sell it, how would they store it, and how would they prevent it from being diverted into the gray market?

- Would stores dealing in marijuana have to fortify their facilities to reduce the risk of theft and assault?[30]

The most likely result is that the drug will not be sold in legitimate stores at all, because while the federal government is currently tolerating medical marijuana dispensaries, it will not tolerate wide-scale sales under general legalizational statutes. So marijuana will continue to be sold on the gray or black market.

The act does not answer these or other practical questions regarding implementation. Rather, it leaves those issues to localities. No doubt, those entities will pass a variety of laws in an attempt to deal with the many problems caused by legalization, unless the local laws are struck down by California courts as inconsistent with the underlying initiative, which would be even worse. At best, that patchwork of laws, differing from one locality to another, will be yet another unintended and predictable problem arising from legalization as envisioned under this act.

Citizens also should not overlook what may be the greatest harms of marijuana legalization: increased addiction to and use of harder drugs. In addition to marijuana's harmful effects on the body and relationship to criminal conduct, it is a gateway drug that can lead users to more dangerous drugs. Prosecutors, judges, police officers, detectives, parole or probation officers, and even defense attorneys know that the vast majority of defendants arrested for violent crimes test positive for illegal drugs, including marijuana. They also know that marijuana is the starter drug of choice for most criminals. Whereas millions of Americans consume moderate amounts of alcohol without ever "moving on" to dangerous drugs, marijuana use and cocaine use are strongly correlated.

While correlation does not necessarily reflect causation, and while the science is admittedly mixed as to whether it is the drug itself or the people the new user associates with who cause the move on to cocaine, heroin, LSD, or other drugs, the RAND Corporation reports that marijuana prices and cocaine use are directly linked, suggesting a substitution effect between the two drugs.[31] Moreover, according to RAND, legalization will cause marijuana prices to fall as much as 80 percent.[32] That can lead to significant consequences because "a 10-percent decrease in the price of marijuana would increase the prevalence of cocaine use by 4.4 to 4.9 percent."[33] As cheap marijuana floods the market both in and outside California, use of many different types of drugs will increase, as will marijuana use.

It is impossible to predict the precise consequences of legalization, but the experiences of places that have eased restrictions on marijuana are not positive. Already, California is suffering crime, dislocation, and increased drug use under its current regulatory scheme. Further liberalizing the law will only make matters worse.

Flouting Federal Law

Another area of great uncertainty is how a state law legalizing marijuana would fit in with federal law to the contrary. Congress has enacted a comprehensive regulatory scheme for restricting access to illicit drugs and other controlled substances. The Controlled Substances Act of 1970 prohibits the manufacture, distribution, and possession of all substances deemed to be Schedule I drugs—drugs like heroin, PCP, and cocaine. Because marijuana has no "currently accepted medical use in treatment in the United States," it is a Schedule I drug that cannot be bought, sold, possessed, or used without violating federal law.

Under the Supremacy Clause of the Constitution of the United States, the Controlled Substances Act is the supreme law of the land and cannot be superseded by state laws that purport to contradict or abrogate its terms. The RCTCA proposes to "reform California's cannabis laws in a way that will benefit our state" and "[r]egulate cannabis like we do alcohol."[34] But the act does not even purport to address the fundamental constitutional infirmity that it would be in direct conflict with federal law. If enacted and unchallenged by the federal government, it would call into question the government's ability to regulate all controlled substances, including drugs such as Oxycontin, methamphetamine, heroin, and powder and crack cocaine. More likely, however, the feds would challenge the law in court, and the courts would have no choice but to strike it down.

Congress has the power to change the Controlled Substances Act and remove marijuana from Schedule I. Yet after decades of lobbying, it has not, largely because of the paucity of scientific evidence in support of a delisting.

California, in fact, is already in direct violation of federal law. Today, its laws allow the use of marijuana as a treatment for a range of vaguely defined conditions, including chronic pain, nausea, lack of appetite, depression, anxiety, and glaucoma. "Marijuana doctors" are listed in the classified advertising sections of newspapers, and many are conveniently located adjacent to "dispensaries." At least one "doctor" writes prescriptions from a tiny hut beside the Venice Beach Boardwalk.

This "medical marijuana" law and similar ones in other states are premised on circumvention of the Food and Drug Administration (FDA) approval process. "FDA's drug approval process requires well-controlled clinical trials that provide the necessary scientific data upon which FDA makes its approval and labeling decisions."[35] Marijuana, even that supposedly used for medicinal purposes, has been rejected by the FDA because, among other reasons, it "has no currently accepted or proven medical use."[36]

The lack of FDA approval means that marijuana may come from unknown sources, may be adulterated with foreign substances, or may not even be marijuana at all. Pot buyers have no way to know what they are getting, and there is no regulatory authority with the ability to go after bogus manufacturers and dealers. Even if one overlooks its inherently harmful properties, marijuana that is commonly sold is likely to be far less safe than that studied in the lab or elsewhere.

Marijuana advocates claim that federal enforcement of drug laws, particularly in jurisdictions that allow the use of medical marijuana, violates states' rights. The Supreme Court, however, has held otherwise. In 2002, California resident Angel Raich produced and consumed marijuana, purportedly for medical purposes. Her actions, while in accordance with California's "medical marijuana" law,[37] clearly violated the Controlled Substances Act, and the local sheriff's department destroyed Raich's plants. Raich claimed that she needed to use marijuana, prescribed by her doctor, for medical purposes. She sued the federal government, asking the court to stop the government from interfering with her right to produce and use marijuana.

In 2006, the Supreme Court held in *Gonzales vs. Raich*[38] that the Commerce Clause confers on Congress the authority to ban the use of marijuana, even when a state approves it for "medical purposes" and it is produced in small quantities for personal consumption. Many legal scholars criticize the Court's extremely broad reading of the Commerce Clause as inconsistent with its original meaning, but the Court's decision nonetheless stands.

If the RCTCA were enacted, it would conflict with the provisions of the Controlled Substances Act and invite extensive litigation that would almost certainly result in its being struck down. Until that happened, state law enforcement officers would be forced into a position of uncertainty regarding their conflicting obligations under federal and state law and cooperation with federal authorities.

Bogus Economics

An innovation of the campaign in support of RCTCA is its touting of the potential benefit of legalization to the government, in terms of additional revenues from taxing marijuana and savings from backing down on the "war on drugs." The National Organization for the Reform of Marijuana Laws (NORML), for example, claims that legalization "could yield California taxpayers over $1.2 billion per year" in tax benefits.[39] According to a California NORML Report updated in October 2009, an excise tax of $50 per ounce would raise about $770 million to $900 million per year and save over $200 million in law enforcement costs per year.[40] It is worth noting that $900 million equates to 18 million ounces—enough marijuana for Californians to smoke one billion marijuana cigarettes each year.

But these projections are highly speculative and riddled with unfounded assumptions. Dr. Rosalie Liccardo Pacula, an expert with the RAND Corporation who has studied the economics of drug policy for over 15 years, has explained that the California "Board of Equalization's estimate of $1.4 billion [in] potential revenue for the state is based on a series of assumptions that are in some instances subject to tremendous uncertainty and in other cases not validated."[41] She urged the California Committee on Public Safety to conduct an honest and thorough cost-benefit analysis of the potential revenues and costs associated with legalizing marijuana. To date, no such realistic cost-benefit analysis has been done.

In her testimony before the committee, Dr. Pacula stated that prohibition raises the cost of production by at least 400 percent and that legalizing marijuana would cause the price of marijuana to fall considerably—much more than the 50 percent price reduction incorporated into the state's revenue model. Furthermore, she noted that a $50-per-ounce marijuana tax was not realistic, because it would represent a 100 percent tax on the cost of the product.

Under the state scheme, she testified, there would be "tremendous profit motive for the existing black market providers to stay in the market."[42] The only way California could effectively eliminate the black market for marijuana, according to Dr. Pacula, "is to take away the substantial profits in the market and allow the price of marijuana to fall to an amount close to the cost of production. Doing so, however, will mean substantially smaller tax revenue than currently anticipated from this change in policy."

The RCTCA, in fact, allows for so much individual production of marijuana that even the Board of Equalization's $1.4 billion per year revenue estimate seems unlikely. Under the law, any resident could grow marijuana for "personal use" in a plot at home up to 25 square feet in size. One ounce of marijuana is enough for 60 to 120 marijuana cigarettes. One plant produces one to five pounds, or 16 to 80 ounces, of marijuana each year, and 25 square feet of land can sustain about 25 plants. Therefore, an individual will be able to produce 24,000 to 240,000 joints legally each year.

Not only is this more than any individual could possibly consume; it is also enough to encourage individuals to grow and sell pot under the individual allowance. Who would buy marijuana from a state-regulated store and pay the $50 tax per ounce in addition to the sale price when they can either grow it themselves or buy it at a much lower price from a friend or neighbor? In this way, the RCTCA undermines its supporters' lavish revenue claims.

Other Negative Social Costs

In addition to its direct effects on individual health, even moderate marijuana use imposes significant long-term costs through the ways that it affects individual users. Marijuana use is associated with cognitive difficulties and influences attention, concentration, and short-term memory. This damage affects drug users' ability to work and can put others at risk. Even if critical workers—for example, police officers, airline pilots, and machine operators—used marijuana recreationally but remained sober on the job, the long-term cognitive deficiency that remained from regular drug use would sap productivity and place countless people in danger. Increased use would also send health care costs skyrocketing—costs borne not just by individual users, but also by the entire society.

For that reason, among others, the Obama Administration also rejects supporters' economic arguments. In his speech, Kerlikowske explained that tax revenue from cigarettes is far outweighed by their social costs: "Tobacco also does not carry its economic weight when we tax it; each year we spend more than $200 billion and collect only about $25 billion in taxes." If the heavy taxation of cigarettes is unable even to come close to making up for the health and other costs associated with their use, it seems doubtful at best that marijuana taxes would be sufficient to cover the costs of legalized marijuana—especially considering that, in addition to the other dangers of smoking marijuana, the physical health effects of just three to four joints are equivalent to those of an entire pack of cigarettes.

Other claims also do not measure up. One of the express purposes of the California initiative is to "put dangerous, underground street dealers out of business, so their influence in our communities will fade."[43] But as explained above, many black-market dealers would rationally choose to remain in the black market to avoid taxation and regulation. Vibrant gray markets have developed throughout the world for many products that are legal, regulated, and heavily taxed. Cigarettes in Eastern Europe, alcohol in Scandinavia, luxury automobiles in Russia, and DVDs in the Middle East are all legal goods traded in gray markets that are wracked with violence. In Canada, an attempt at a $3 per pack tax on cigarettes was greeted with the creation of a black market that "accounted for perhaps 30 percent of sales."[44]

Further, even if the RCTCA were to pass, marijuana would remain illegal in the entire United States under federal law while taxed only in California, a situation that would strengthen both California's gray market and the nationwide black market in illegal drugs. Fueled by generous growing allowances and an enormous supply in California, criminal sales operations would flourish as excess California marijuana was sold outside the state and, at the same time, out-of-state growers attempted to access the more permissive market inside the state.

In sum, legalization would put additional strain on an already faltering economy. In 2008, marijuana alone was involved in 375,000 emergency room visits.[45] Drug overdoses already outnumber gunshot deaths in America and are approaching motor vehicle crashes as the nation's leading cause of accidental death.[46] It is true that taxing marijuana sales would generate some tax revenue, but the cost of handling the influx of problems resulting from increased use would far outweigh any gain made by marijuana's taxation. Legalizing marijuana would serve only to compound the problems already associated with drug use.

Social Dislocation and Organized Crime

The final two arguments of those favoring legalization are intertwined. According to advocates of legalization, the government's efforts to combat the illegal drug trade have been an expensive failure. Consequently, they argue, focusing on substance abuse and treatment would be a more effective means of combating drug abuse while reducing the violence and social ills stemming from anti-drug enforcement efforts.

There is no doubt that if marijuana were legalized, more people, including juveniles, would consume it. Consider cigarettes: While their purchase by people under 18 is illegal, 20 percent of high school students admit to having smoked cigarettes in the past 30 days.[47] Marijuana's illegal status "keeps potential drug users from using" marijuana in a way that no legalization scheme can replicate "by virtue of the fear of arrest and the embarrassment of being caught."[48] With increased use comes increased abuse, as the fear of arrest and embarrassment will decrease.

Legalization advocates attempt to create in the minds of the public an image of a typical "responsible" user of marijuana: a person who is reasonable and accountable even when under the influence of marijuana. And for those few that don't fit that image? Society will treat them and restore them to full health. The facts, however, are much uglier.

The RAND Corporation projects a 50 percent increase in marijuana-related traffic fatalities under the RCTCA.[49] That alone should weigh heavily on California voters this fall. In a 2008 national survey, approximately 3 million Americans 12 years old or older started using illicit drugs in the past year— almost 8,000 new users per day. The most commonly used illicit drug is marijuana, especially among the 20 million Americans over 12 who were users in 2008. In California, 62 percent of all marijuana treatment cases are already individuals under 21.[50] Legalization will increase the number of underage users.

Keeping marijuana illegal will undoubtedly keep many young people from using it.[51] Eliminate that criminal sanction (and moral disapprobation), and more youth will use the drug, harming their potential and ratcheting up treatment costs.

Educators know that students using marijuana underperform when compared to their non-using peers. Teachers, coaches, guidance counselors, and school principals have seen the negative effect of marijuana on their students. The Rev. Dr. D. Stuart Dunnan, Headmaster of Saint James School in St. James, Maryland, says of marijuana use by students:

> The chemical effect of marijuana is to take away ambition. The social effect is to provide an escape from challenges and responsibilities with a like-minded group of teenagers who are doing the same thing. Using marijuana creates losers. At a time when we're concerned about our lack of academic achievement relative to other countries, legalizing marijuana will be disastrous.[52]

Additionally, making marijuana legal in California will fuel drug cartels and violence, particularly because the drug will still be illegal at the national level. The local demand will increase in California, but reputable growers, manufacturers, and retailers will still be unwilling—as they should be—to produce and distribute marijuana. Even without the federal prohibition, most reputable producers would not survive the tort liability from such a dangerous product. Thus, the vacuum will be filled by illegal drug cartels.

According to the Department of Justice's National Drug Threat Assessment for 2010, Mexican drug trafficking organizations (DTOs) "have expanded their cultivation operations in the United States, an ongoing trend for the past decade. . . .Well-organized criminal groups and DTOs that produce domestic marijuana do so because of the high profitability of and demand for marijuana in the United States."[53]

Legalize marijuana, and the demand for marijuana goes up substantially as the deterrence effect of law enforcement disappears. Yet not many suppliers will operate legally, refusing to subject themselves to the established state regulatory scheme— not to mention taxation—while still risking federal prosecution, conviction, and prison time. So who will fill the void?

Violent, brutal, and ruthless, Mexican DTOs will work to maintain their black-market profits at the expense of American citizens' safety. Every week, there are news articles cataloguing the murders, kidnappings, robberies, and other thuggish brutality employed by Mexican drug gangs along the border. It is nonsensical to argue that these gangs will simply give up producing marijuana when it is legalized; indeed, their profits might soar, depending on the actual tax in California and the economics of the interstate trade. While such profits might not be possible if marijuana was legalized at the national level and these gangs were undercut by mass production, that is unlikely ever to happen. Nor does anyone really believe that the gangs will subject themselves to state and local regulation, including taxation. And since the California ballot does nothing to eliminate the black market for marijuana—quite the opposite, in fact—legalizing marijuana will only incentivize Mexican DTOs to grow more marijuana to feed the demand and exploit the black market.

Furthermore, should California legalize marijuana, other entrepreneurs will inevitably attempt to enter the marketplace and game the system. In doing so, they will compete with Mexican DTOs and other criminal organizations. Inevitably, violence will follow, and unlike now, that violence will not be confined to the border as large-scale growers seek to protect their turf—turf that will necessarily include anywhere they grow, harvest, process, or sell marijuana. While this may sound far-fetched, Californians in Alameda County are already experiencing the reality of cartel-run marijuana farms on sometimes stolen land,[54] protected by "guys [who] are pretty heavily armed and willing to protect their merchandise."[55]

It is not uncommon for drugs with large illegal markets to be controlled by cartels despite attempts to roll them into the normal medical control scheme. For instance, cocaine has a medical purpose and can be prescribed by doctors as *Erythroxylum coca*, yet its true production and distribution are controlled by drug cartels and organized crime.[56] As competition from growers and dispensaries authorized by the

RCTCA cuts further into the Mexican DTOs' business, Californians will face a real possibility of bloodshed on their own soil as the cartels' profit-protection measures turn from defensive to offensive.

Thus, marijuana legalization will increase crime, drug use, and social dislocation across the state of California—the exact opposite of what pro-legalization advocates promise.

Conclusion

Pro-marijuana advocates promoting the Regulate, Control and Tax Cannabis Act of 2010 invite Californians to imagine a hypothetical and idyllic "pot market," but America's national approach to drug use, addiction, and crime must be serious, based on sound policy and solid evidence.

In 1982, President Ronald Reagan adopted a national drug strategy that took a comprehensive approach consisting of five components: international cooperation, research, strengthened law enforcement, treatment and rehabilitation, and prevention and education. It was remarkably successful: Illegal drug use by young adults dropped more than 50 percent.

Reagan was right to make drug control a major issue of his presidency. Illegal drugs such as marijuana are responsible for a disproportionate share of violence and social decline in America. Accordingly, federal law, representing the considered judgment of medical science and the nation's two political branches of government, takes the unequivocal position that marijuana is dangerous and has no significant beneficial uses.

California cannot repeal that law or somehow allow its citizens to contravene it. Thus, it has two options. By far the best option is to commit itself seriously to the federal approach and pursue a strategy that attempts to prevent illegal drug use in the first place and reduce the number of drug users. This may require changes in drug policy, and perhaps in sentencing guidelines for marijuana users charged with simple possession, but simply legalizing a harmful drug—that is, giving up—is not a responsible option.

The other option is to follow the above path in the short term while conducting further research and possibly working with other states in Congress to consider changes in federal law. Although those who oppose the legalization of marijuana have every reason to believe that further, legitimate scientific research will confirm the dangers of its use, no side should try to thwart the sober judgment of the national legislature and sister states.

In short, no state will likely be allowed to legalize marijuana on its own, with such serious, negative cross-state spillover effects. Yet even if California could act as if it were an island, the legalization route would still end very badly for the Golden State. There is strong evidence to suggest that legalizing marijuana would serve little purpose other than to worsen the state's drug problems—addiction, violence, disorder, and death. While long on rhetoric, the legalization movement, by contrast, is short on facts.

Notes

1. Stuart M. Butler, The Marijuana Epidemic, Heritage Foundation Background-er No. 140 (May 4, 1981), *available at* http://www.heritage.org/Research/Reports/1981/05/The-Marijuana-Epidemic.

2. Letter from Attorney James Wheaton, to Neil Amos, Initiative Coordinator, Office of the Attorney General (July 27, 2009), *available at* http://ag.ca.gov/cmsattachments/initiatives/pdfs/i821initiative09-0024amdt1-s.pdf.

3. For a preview of all potential arguments that the pro-legalization movement will make, one need go no further than the Web site of the Drug Policy Alliance. The Drug Policy Alliance: Alternatives to Marijuana Prohibition and the Drug War, http://www.drugpolicy.org (last visited August 31, 2010). The Web site contains a section titled "Myths and Facts About Marijuana." The Drug Policy Alliance: Myths and Facts About Marijuana, http://www.drugpolicy.org/marijuana/factsmyths/ (last visited August 31, 2010). According to their Web site, the Drug Policy Alliance Network is the "nation's leading organization promoting policy alternatives to the drug war that are grounded in science, compassion, health and human rights." George Soros is on the Board of the Drug Policy Alliance. The Drug Policy Alliance: Board of Directors, Drug Policy Alliance, http://www.drugpolicy.org/about/keystaff/boardofdirec/ (last visited August 31, 2010).

4. R. Gil Kerlikowske, ONDCP Director, Remarks to the California Police Chiefs Conference: Why Marijuana Legalization Would Compromise Public Health and Public Safety (March 4, 2010), *available at* http://www.ondcp.gov/news/speech10/030410_Chief.pdf.

5. On October 19, 2009, the Justice Department issued a memorandum to selected United States Attorneys regarding investigations and prosecutions in states authorizing the medical use of marijuana. See Memorandum from David W. Ogden, Deputy Attorney General, to Selected United States Attorneys (October 19, 2009), *available at* http://blogs.usdoj.gov/blog/archives/192.

6. The act prohibits unlicensed possession for sale; consumption in public, including consumption by an operator of any vehicle, boat, or aircraft; and smoking in any space while minors are present. The act provides for state regulations, local ordinances, and other official acts to control, license, regulate, permit, or otherwise authorize cultivation, retail sale, consumption, and transportation of marijuana. To read the entire act, see California Secretary of State, California General Election, Tuesday, November 2, 2010: Voter Information Guide 92 (August 10, 2010), *available at* http://www.voterguide.sos.ca.gov/pdf/english/text-proposed-laws.pdf.

7. Jacob Sullum, *Prohibition Didn't Work Then; It Isn't Working Now,* L.A. *Times,* April 21, 2008, available at http://www.latimes.com/news/opinion/la-op-sullum-stimson21apr21,0,7060990.story.

8. K. J. Mukamal et al., *Roles of Drinking Pattern and Type of Alcohol Consumed in Coronary Heart Disease in Men,* 348 New Eng. J. Med. 109–18 (2003).

9. Alcohol Use: If You Drink, Keep It Moderate, http://www.mayoclinic.com/ health/alcohol/SC00024 (last visited August 27, 2010).

10. *Id.*

11. National Institute on Drug Abuse, Marijuana: Facts Every Parents Needs to Know, http://www.drugabuse.gov/MarijBroch/parentpg13-14N.html (last visited August 27, 2010).

12. National Institute on Drug Abuse, Marijuana, http://www.drugabuse.gov/tib/ marijuana.html (last visited August 27, 2010).

13. *Id.*

14. *See* M. T. Lynskey & W. D. Hall, *The Effects of Adolescent Cannabis Use on Educational Attainment: A Review*, Addiction, 95(11) 1621–1630 (2000).

15. Harrison G. Pope and Deborah Yurgelun-Todd, *The Residual Cognitive Effects of Heavy Marijuana Use in College Students*, 275 jama 521–27 (1996).

16. *Marijuana: Facts for Teens*, Mar. 2008, at 7, *available at* http://www.drugabuse. gov/PDF/TEENS_Marijuana_brochure.pdf.

17. Robin Room et al., Cannabis Policy: Moving Beyond Stalemate (2009).

18. Office of National Drug Control Policy, What Americans Need to Know About Marijuana 3, *available at* http://www.ncjrs.gov/ondcppubs/publications/pdf/ mj_rev.pdf.

19. David Moir et al., A Comparison of Mainstream and Sidestream Marijuana and Tobacco Cigarette Smoke Produced Under Two Machine Smoking Conditions, Chem. Res. Toxicol. 21 (2) 494–502 (2008) *available at* http://pubs. acs.org/doi/pdfplus/10.1021/tx700275p.

20. *Id.*

21. *Id.*

22. W. M. Compton et al., *Prevalence of Marijuana Use Disorders in the United States: 1991–1992 and 2001–2002*, 291 jama 2114–2121 (2004).

23. A. J. Budney & J. R. Hughes, *The Cannabis Withdrawal Syndrome*, 19 Current Opinion in Psychiatry, 233–238 (2004); A. J. Budney et al., *Review of the Validity and Significance of Cannabis Withdrawal Syndrome*, 161 American Journal of Psychiatry, 1967–1977 (2004). *See also* R. Gil Kerlikowskc, *supra* note 4.

24. Rosalie Liccardo Pacula and Beau Kilmer, *Marijuana and Crime: Is There a Connection Beyond Prohibition?* (RAND Corporation Health Working Paper WR-125, Prepared for the National Institute on Drug Abuse, January 2004) *available at* http://www.rand.org/pubs/working_papers/2004/RAND_WR125. pdf.

25. David Moir et al., *supra* note 19.

26. Ministry of Health, Welfare and Sport, Government to Scale Down Coffee Shops (Sept. 11, 2009), http://english.minvws.nl/en/nieuwsberichten/ vgp/2009/government-to-scale-down-coffee-shops.asp.

27. *Id.*

28. Memorandum from Lori J. Barker, City Attorney, to Chico City Council (Oct. 6, 2009), *available at* http://www.chico.ca.us/government/minutes_agendas/ documents/SKMBT60010011114120.pdf.

29. *Id.*
30. California police provide evidence that attempts to burglarize dispensaries are already a problem. See Summit on the Impact of California's Medical Marijuana Laws: Dispensary Related Crime (April 23, 2009), *available at* http://www.californiapolicechiefs.org/nav_files/marijuana_files/files/DispensarySummitPresentation.ppt.
31. Beau Kilmer et al., Altered State? Assessing How Marijuana Legalization in California Could Influence Marijuana Consumption and Public Budgets(2010), *available at* http://www.rand.org/pubs/occasional_papers/2010/RAND_OP315.pdf.
32. *Id.*
33. *Id.* at 43.
34. *See* California Secretary of State, *supra* note 6.
35. Press Release, U.S. Food and Drug Administration, Inter-Agency Advisory Regarding Claims That Smoked Marijuana Is a Medicine (Apr. 20, 2006), *available at* http://www.fda.gov/NewsEvents/Newsroom/PressAnnouncements/2006/ucm108643.htm.
36. Gardiner Harris, F.D.A. Dismisses Medical Benefit from Marijuana, *N.Y. Times,* April 21, 2006, *available at* http://www.nytimes.com/2006/04/21/health/21marijuana.html.
37. In 1996, California passed the Compassionate Use Act, which legalized marijuana for medical use. The law conflicted with the Controlled Substances Act, which classifies marijuana as a Schedule I controlled dangerous substance and makes no exception for medical necessity.
38. 545 U.S. 1 (2005).
39. Dale Gieringer, Ph.D., Benefits of Marijuana Legalization in California, http://www.canorml.org/background/CA_legalization2.html (last visited Aug. 30, 2010).
40. *Id.*
41. Rosalie Liccardo Pacula, Legalizing Marijuana: Issues to Consider Before Reforming California State Law, Testimony Before the California State Assembly Public Safety Committee (Oct. 28, 2009), *available at* http://www.rand.org/pubs/testimonies/2009/RAND_CT334.pdf.
42. W. M. Compton et al., *supra* note 22.
43. The Regulate, Control and Tax Cannabis Act of 2010 § 2B5.
44. *See* California Secretary of State, *supra* note 6 at 20.
45. Drug Abuse Warning Network, http://dawninfo.samhsa.gov/default.asp (last visited August 31, 2010).
46. *See* Letter from Attorney James Wheaton, to Neil Amos, *supra* note 2.
47. Centers for Disease Control and Prevention, Faststats—Smoking, http://www.cdc.gov/nchs/fastats/smoking.htm (last visited August 31, 2010).
48. David G. Evans, In Support of the United Nations Drug Conventions, 10 (2d ed., 2009).
49. California Secretary of State, *supra* note 6 at 41.

50. California Secretary of State, *supra* note 6 at 36.

51. David G. Evans, *supra* note 48 at 10.

52. Telephone interview with Father Dunnan, A.B. (Harvard University), A.M. (Harvard University), M.A. (Oxford University), D.Phil. (Oxford University) (June 9, 2010).

53. U.S. Department of Justice, Marijuana Availability—National Drug Threat Assessment 2010, *available at* http://www.justice.gov/ndic/pubs38/38661/marijuana.htm#Marijuana.

54. While this paper does not express any position on the issue, it is interesting to note that, as one unintended consequence of these illegal marijuana farms, the legal owners of the plots of land occupied by cartel members could lose the land to the drug lords at some future date under California's adverse possession laws.

55. Aaron Swarts, "Pot 'Cartels' a Reality in Rural Alameda County" (Feb. 19, 2009), *available at* www.californiapolicechiefs.org/nav_files/marijuana_files/files/AaronSwarts.pdf.

56. Department of Justice, National Drug Threat Assessment 2009, 1, *available at* http://www.justice.gov/dea/concern/18862/ndic_2009.pdf.

Drug Legalization: Why It Wouldn't Work in the United States

By Edmund Hartnett
The Police Chief, March 2005

The issue of drug legalization is a complex one. Most Americans do not favor it, yet there is a strong and very vocal lobby in the United States that feels that legalization would be the proper course to take. When this vocal minority raises the issue in any community, citizens look to the police chief to speak to the issue. Police chiefs are encouraged to borrow from this article as they prepare their speeches.

Proponents' Arguments

Proponents of drug legalization believe that the current policies regarding drugs have been harmful to individuals, families, and society as a whole. They strongly oppose current drug laws and policies for a variety of reasons. Some see the laws as an impingement of individual freedoms. Some see them as a colossal waste of government resources citing the opinion that the legalization of drugs could produce millions in tax revenues while at the same time putting drug dealers out of business and ensuring quality controls in the production of drugs. Some feel that legalization would reduce overall crime. Some argue that the laws are a form of institutionalized racism designed to keep minorities as a permanent disenfranchised underclass by keeping them in prison, addicted, or completely dependent on government aid. Others take what they view as a humanitarian approach, arguing that certain substances should be made legal for medicinal purposes. Some have chosen to refer to the issue as harm reduction instead of drug legalization in an apparent effort to soften the issue and give it a more humanitarian tone. Still others view the prohibition against drugs as an inherently flawed and impossible strategy that has exacerbated crime and violence and has contributed to a sense of despair and hopelessness for millions of Americans.

It is also interesting to note that the proponents of legalization include supporters from across the political spectrum, from progressives on the far left to libertarians on the far right. Liberal Democratic Congressman Charles Rangel is adamantly opposed to drug legalization, while conservative icon and columnist William F. Buckley has long been a proponent of making drugs legal. Congressman Rangel has referred to legalization as "a very dangerous idea" that should "be put to rest once and for all."[1]

Opponents to Legalization

Although it is clear the majority of U.S. citizens are in favor of keeping the use, sale, and possession of drugs illegal, much of the writing from the antilegalization viewpoint comes from law enforcement and government officials. Former New York City Mayor Ed Koch once described drug legalization as "the equivalent of extinguishing a fire with napalm."[2] Although many acknowledge that the so-called war on drugs has had mixed success, they believe that the alternative would have catastrophic effects on the nation. They believe that the legalization of drugs would increase use, lead to more experimentation by youth, and exacerbate the existing deleterious effects that drugs have on society. They are of the opinion that government subsidization of addicts would have crippling effects on the economy. They also feel that legalization would help to create a large black market for drugs. Antilegalization proponents also point out that drug dealers and hardcore addicts would not suddenly become productive, law-abiding members of society. The antilegalization point of view is that dealers will still be involved in crime and violence and that users will still need to support themselves by engaging in criminal activity. Basically, they believe that the legalization of drugs would lead to increases, not reductions, in crime because there would be more addicts and because of the aforementioned black market. Also, opponents of legalization often cite statistics that show that drug prevention initiatives, drug awareness curricula in schools, and drug treatment programs are working. They point to the fact that there are fewer addicts today than there were 20 years ago.

Drugs and Crime

There are two schools of thought on the issue of drug legalization and crime. Do drugs cause crime? Does drug use inevitably lead to crime? If drugs were made legal, would there be less crime? If the government subsidized addicts, would they still engage in criminal conduct? What would happen to drug dealers and drug gangs if drugs were legalized? Although the issue is complex, both groups agree that drugs and crime are inexorably linked.

Many legalization supporters believe that property crime, particularly burglary, larceny from persons (purse snatchers, chain snatchers, and pickpockets), auto theft, theft from autos, and shoplifting would decrease by 40–50 percent if drugs were made legal. Similarly, many believe that the terms "drug-related murder" and "drive-by shooting" would become outdated once drugs were legalized. In their view, turf wars would be eliminated because there would no longer be a need to fight for one's turf.

Additionally, there are those who point out that drug enforcement is a waste of valuable law enforcement resources since statistically most drug users do not get caught. Thus, the deterrent effect of criminalization is lost. Todd Brenner uses the example of marijuana arrests. In 1987 approximately 25 million people in the United States used marijuana, the most easily detectable drug, yet only 378,000 arrests were made; roughly one arrest for every 63 users.[3] His point is that the public would be better served if the police targeted crimes in which they had a better success rate. Also, legalization supporters believe that once drugs were legalized, the government could pay less attention to drug-related crime and spend more time and money on treatment, rehabilitation, education, and job training programs. Other benefits cited would be reduced prison populations, more manageable caseloads for judges and attorneys, and better relations between the public and the police.

Many believe that traditional organized crime would be seriously affected by legalization. Benjamin and Miller write: "The Mafia would not disappear, because organized crime would be able to survive on other criminal activities, such as loan sharking, gambling, prostitution, and child pornography. But drug legalization would remove the backbone of organized crime's profits, causing it to diminish in importance."[4]

Opponents to legalization obviously do not see legalization as a panacea that will make crime go away. They see a clear connection between drug use and crime and, perhaps more importantly, between drug use and violence. Joseph Califano, the author and a member of President Johnson's cabinet, stated: "Drugs like marijuana and cocaine are not dangerous because they are illegal; they are illegal because they are dangerous."[5] The DEA reports that six times as many homicides are committed by persons under the influence of drugs than those looking for money to buy drugs and that most arrestees for violent crimes test positive for drugs at time of arrest.[6] Speaking to a Congressional subcommittee on drug policy in 1999, Donnie Marshall, then deputy administrator of DEA, spoke of drug use, crime, and violence. He said that there is "a misconception that most drug-related crimes involve people who are looking for money to buy drugs. The fact is that most drug-related crimes are committed by people whose brains have been messed up with mood-altering drugs."[7]

Legalization opponents are convinced that the violence caused by drug use "will not magically stop because the drugs are legal. Legal PCP isn't going to make a person less violent than illegally purchased PCP."[8] Susan Neiberg Terkel echoes these sentiments by saying that legalizing drugs "cannot change human nature. It cannot improve the social conditions that compel people to engage in crime, nor can it stop people from using drugs as an excuse to be violent."[9] The belief is that drugs, legal or not, often lead to violence. Erich Goode, a SUNY professor and a proponent of harm reduction, writes: "It is extremely unlikely that legalization will transform the violent nature of the world of heavy, chronic drug abuse very much. That violence is a part of the way that frequent, heavy drug users live their lives; it is systemic to their subculture."[10]

It is interesting to note that the federal approach to drugs and crime is not solely linked to arrest and incarceration. In Congressional testimony in 1999, Barry Mc-Caffrey, then-director of the U.S. Office of National Drug Control Policy, stated: "We cannot arrest our way out of our nation's drug problem. We need to break the cycle of addiction, crime, and prison through treatment and other diversion programs. Breaking the cycle is not soft on drugs; it is smart on defeating drugs and crime."[11]

Public Health Concerns

Opponents of legalization seem to be just as committed as the prolegalization lobby. They believe that the legalization of drugs would have devastating effects on public health, the economy, quality of life, American culture, and society as a whole.

The advocacy group Drug Watch International points out that drugs are illegal "because of their intoxicating effect on the brain, damaging impact on the body, adverse impact on behavior, and potential for abuse. Their use threatens the health, welfare, and safety of all people, of users and nonusers alike."[12] Legalization advocates contend that the same statement could be made about alcohol.

William J. Bennett, former director of the Office of National Drug Control Policy, responds to that claim, arguing "that legalized alcohol, which is responsible for some 100,000 deaths a year, is hardly the model for drug policy. As Charles Krauthammer has pointed out, the question is not which is worse, alcohol or drugs. The question is, can we accept both legalized alcohol and legalized drugs? The answer is no."[13] Morton M. Kondracke of the *New Republic* magazine discusses another comparison between drugs and alcohol: "Of the 115 million Americans who consume alcohol, 85 percent rarely become intoxicated; with drugs, intoxication is the whole idea."[14]

Legalization opponents believe that our already burdened health care industry would be overwhelmed if drugs were legal. This would come in the form of direct results of drug use (more overdoses, more AIDS patients, and more illness stemming from addiction) and indirect results of drugs (more injuries due to drug-related violence, accidents, and workplace incidents). They also believe that legalization would increase the number of emergency room visits, ambulance calls, and fire and police responses. The ONDCP reports that in 2002 direct health care costs attributable to illegal drug abuse were $52 billion.[15]

In addition, legalization opponents disagree with legalization advocates regarding whether legalization would increase drug use. Legalization opponents believe that drug use would increase dramatically if drugs were made legal and easy to obtain. William J. Bennett uses the example of crack cocaine. He writes: "When powder cocaine was expensive and hard to get, it was found almost exclusively in the circles of the rich, the famous, or the privileged. Only when cocaine was dumped into the country, and a $3 vial of crack could be bought on street corners, did we see cocaine use skyrocket—this time largely among the poor and disadvantaged."[16] The DEA also takes issue with the legalization lobby on the link between easier access to drugs and an increase in addiction from a humanitarian standpoint: "The question isn't whether legalization will increase addiction levels—it will—it's whether we care or not. The compassionate response is to do everything possible to prevent the destruction of addiction, not make it easier."[17]

Drugs Tied to Terrorism

In the aftermath of September 11, it was evident that enormous amounts of money were part of a global terrorist network. Much of this money was hidden in ostensibly legal outlets, primarily banks, investments, and charitable organizations. They were correctly targeted by law enforcement agencies and, in many cases, frozen; thereby denying terrorists access to the money. Many experts believe that terrorists are now using narcotics trafficking to fund their activities. Although much of this activity seems to be centered in the Afghanistan and Pakistan region (sometimes referred to as the Golden Crescent in law enforcement circles), all international narcotics investigations now have to add terrorism to their list of concerns. Legalization would only exacerbate this problem and put more money into the terrorists' bank accounts.

The DEA has identified links between drug suppliers and terrorism. Their investigations, again primarily in Afghanistan and Pakistan, have shown connections among traffickers in heroin and hashish, money launderers, and al Qaeda members. They also suspect a drug-related connection involving al Qaeda and the train bombings in Madrid. According to DEA, "The bombers swapped hashish and ecstasy for the 440 pounds of dynamite used in the blasts, which killed 191 people and injured more than 1,400 others. Money from the drugs also paid for an apartment hideout, a car, and the cell phones used to detonate the bombs."[18]

Economy Issues

Legalization advocates claim that if drugs are legal it will be a financial windfall for the American economy. They believe that all the public funds now wasted on the enforcement of drug laws and related matters could then be used for the good of society in areas such as education, health care, infrastructure, and social services. As mentioned earlier, some believe that drugs could eventually be taxed and thus create much-needed revenue. The DEA's response is: "Ask legalization proponents if the alleged profits from drug legalization would be enough to pay for the increased fetal defects, loss of workplace productivity, increased traffic fatalities and industrial accidents, increased domestic violence and the myriad other problems that would not only be high-cost items but extremely expensive in terms of social decay."[19]

Medical Marijuana

The antilegalization point of view rejecting the use of marijuana to ease the pain of those suffering from a variety of illnesses and conditions may appear harsh and insensitive. Their view is that there are safer, more effective drugs currently available and that there is therefore no need to rely on medicinal marijuana. The DEA states that the "clear weight of the evidence is that smoked marijuana is harmful. No matter what medical condition has been studied, other drugs have been shown to be more effective in promoting health than smoked marijuana."[20] They also believe that many proponents of the use of medicinal marijuana are disingenuous, exploiting the sick in order to win a victory in their overall fight to legalize drugs. They point to studies that show that marijuana smoke contains hundreds of toxins, similar to cigarettes, and that prolonged use can lead to serious lung damage. This, they feel, can only exacerbate existing health problems, especially for people with compromised immune systems. The DEA cites the fact that marijuana has been rejected as medicine by the American Medical Association, the American Glaucoma

Society, the American Academy of Ophthalmology, the International Federation of Multiple Sclerosis Societies, and the American Cancer Society.[21]

Harm Reduction

The term "harm reduction" is anathema to the antilegalization lobby. They believe that "harm reduction, a cover-all term coined by the legalizers, is a euphemism encompassing legalization and liberalized drug policy, and can best be defined as 'a variety of strategies for making illicit drug use safer and cheaper for drug users, at the expense of the rest of society, regardless of cost.'"[22] The passion surrounding the issue of harm reduction is illustrated by Drug Watch International: "Harm reduction abandons attempts to free current drug users and encourages future generations to try drugs. It asserts that drug use is natural and necessary. Rather than preventing harm and drug use, harm reduction feebly attempts to reduce the misery level for addicts. Harm reduction forsakes a portion of the population, often the poor and minorities, to lifetime abuse of drugs."[23]

Opponents of harm reduction see it as a very dangerous message. They complain that, instead of addressing and eventually eliminating the problems of addiction, harm reduction creates a situation that prolongs the agony of the addicted, their families and their community.

Public Reaction

A 1998 poll by the Family Research Council showed that eight out of 10 responders rejected the legalization of cocaine and heroin. The same poll asked whether they would support making these drugs legal in a manner similar to alcohol; 82 percent responded "no." A 1999 Gallup poll revealed that 69 percent of Americans are against the legalization of marijuana. In addition, another Gallup poll showed that 72 percent were in favor of drug testing in the workplace. However, one of the better indicators of the public's disdain for drugs is the fact that an estimated 50 million Americans who have used drugs in their youth have now rejected them.[24]

The U.S. Department of Justice National Drug Intelligence Center (NDIC) reveals some additional alarming statistics. In 2002 an estimated 35.1 million people aged 12 or older reported using an illegal drug within the past year; approximately 3.2 million people were drug-dependent or drug abusers.[25] Based on this set of figures, there is still a significant demand for drugs in America and multitudes willing to supply the drugs. It is this demand for drugs that is at the heart of the issue. Speaking from a law enforcement perspective, it is clear that we can make millions of drug arrests, but if we don't address the demand side of the problem, the best we can hope for is maintenance of the status quo.

Progress in this regard has been achieved and considerable inroads have been made through years of proactive prevention and education efforts. By 1999 the Office of National Drug Control Policy reported that drug use in America had been cut in half and cocaine use was reduced by 75 percent.[26] Nevertheless, in spite of these promising statistics, the across-the-board nature of the drug problem in America indicates that we are far from declaring victory.

Speaking Out

The process of completing this project has led to a reexamination of my personal opinions and values on the issue of drug legalization. I assume that it is normal to be introspective when exploring both sides of a broad and complex problem. As a parent, a citizen, and a law enforcement official, I am clearly a stakeholder in this issue. I was concerned that my views in light of my police background would make me sound like an ideologue. As a public administrator, I hope that I reinforced my opinions against the legalization of drugs with sound logic and analysis.

My research allowed me to see the issue from a broader outlook. I now understand the pro-legalization viewpoint much better. Although I am still strongly opposed to the notion of drug legalization, I realize that, for the most part, they are Americans, from a broad field, who are truly committed to a cause in which they believe. Although they are pursuing a course that is dangerous for America, I respect their passion and education. But they are woefully wrong on this issue.

I encourage police executives to speak out against drug legalization, and I hope the information in this article has provided some of the resources they need as they prepare to make these speeches.

Notes

1. Charles B. Rangel, "Legalizing Drugs: A 'Dangerous Idea,'" in *Drugs: Should We Legalize, Decriminalize, or Deregulate?*, ed. Jeffrey A. Schaler (New York: Prometheus, 1999), 74.
2. Susan Neiburg Terkel, *Should Drugs Be Legalized?* (New York: Franklin Watts, 1990), 16.
3. Todd Austin Brenner, "The Legalization of Drugs: Why Prolong the Inevitable?," in *Drug Legalization: For and Against*, ed. Rod L. Evans and Irwin M. Berent (LaSalle, Ill.: Open Court, 1992), 173.
4. Daniel K. Benjamin and Roger Leroy Miller, *Undoing Drugs* (New York: Basic Books, 1991), 175.
5. U.S. Department of Justice, Drug Enforcement Administration, "Fact 7," Speaking Out against Drug Legalization (Washington, D.C.: U.S. Government Printing Office, November 2002), 2; available at (www.usdoj.gov/dea/demand/speakout/index/html).
6. U.S. Department of Justice, Drug Enforcement Administration, "Fact 7," Speaking Out against Drug Legalization, 2.
7. Donnie Marshall, testimony before the U.S. House of Representatives, Committee on Government Reform, Subcommittee Criminal Justice, Drug Policy, and Human Resources, June 16, 1999; transcript available at (www.usdoj.gov/dea/pubs/cngrtest/ct061699.htm).

8. Carolyn C. Gargaro, "Drug Legalization? Drugs Should Not Be Legalized; Just Say No to Drug Legalization" (1999): 5; available at (www.gargaro.com).

9. Terkel, *Should Drugs Be Legalized?*, 91.

10. Erich Goode, *Between Politics and Reason: The Drug Legalization Debate* (New York: St. Martin's, 1997), 129; see text of chapter 7, available online at (www.druglibrary.org).

11. Barry R. McCaffrey, "The Drug Legalization Movement in America," testimony before the U.S. House of Representatives, Committee on Government Reform, Subcommittee on Criminal Justice, Drug Policy, and Human Resources, June 16,1999, 20; transcript available at (www.drugwatch.org).

12. Drug Watch International, "Drug Legalization," no. 3 in the "Truth and Lies" series (October 1995): 1; available online at (www.drugwatch.org).

13. William J. Bennett , "Mopping Up after the Legalizers: What the 'Intellectual' Chorus Fails to Tell You," in *Drug Legalization: For and Against*, ed. Rod L. Evans and Irwin M. Berent (LaSalle, Ill.: Open Court, 1992), 226.

14. Morton M. Kondracke, "Don't Legalize Drugs: The Costs Are Still Too High," in *Drug Legalization: For and Against*, ed. Rod L. Evans and Irwin M. Berent (LaSalle, Ill.: Open Court, 1992), 284.

15. U.S. Department of Justice, Drug Enforcement Administration, "The 'Secondhand Smoke' Effects of Drugs on Society": 5.

16. Bennett, "Mopping Up after the Legalizers": 225.

17. U.S. Department of Justice, Drug Enforcement Administration, "Fact 6," Speaking Out against Drug Legalization, 2.

18. U.S. Department of Justice, Drug Enforcement Administration, "Secondhand Smoke": 16.

19. U.S. Department of Justice, Drug Enforcement Administration, Speaking Out against Drug Legalization, 17.

20. U.S. Department of Justice, Drug Enforcement Administration, "The DEA Position on Medical Marihuana" (May 2004): 2.

21. U.S. Department of Justice, Drug Enforcement Administration, Speaking Out against Drug Legalization, 19.

22. Sandra S. Bennett, "The Drug Decriminalization Movement in America," testimony before the U.S. House of Representatives, Committee on Government Reform, Subcommittee on Criminal Justice, Drug Policy, and Human Resources, June 13, 1999; transcript available at (www.drugwatch.org).

23. Drug Watch International, "Harm Reduction," no. 2 in the "Truth and Lies" series (May 1995): 1; available at (www.drugwatch.org).

24. McCaffrey, "The Drug Legalization Movement in America": 5.

25. U.S. Department of Justice, National Drug Intelligence Center, National Drug Threat Assessment 2004.

26. McCaffrey, "The Drug Legalization Movement in America": 13.

Pot Reform's Race Problem

By Carl L. Hart
The Nation, November 18, 2013

Barack Obama, George W. Bush and Bill Clinton all acknowledge illicit marijuana use in their younger years. Of the three, who do you suppose was most at risk for arrest and all of the associated negative consequences, including truncating his political aspirations?

To most Americans, the answer is clear: the black guy, of course. For those for whom the answer is less obvious, consider a recent report by the American Civil Liberties Union showing that black people are two to over seven times more likely to be arrested for pot possession than their white counterparts, despite the fact that both groups use marijuana at similar rates. These disparities held up even when researchers controlled for household income. It's about race, not class.

As a neuropsychopharmacologist who has spent the past fifteen years studying the neurophysiological, psychological and behavioral effects of marijuana, I find this particular effect of pot prohibition most disturbing. Each year, there are more than 700,000 marijuana arrests, which account for more than half of all drug arrests. And now, largely because of the selective targeting of African-American males, one in three black boys born today will spend time in prison if we don't take action to end this type of discrimination. The gravity of this situation contributed to Attorney General Eric Holder's remarks about mass incarceration, which he described as "a kind of decimation of certain communities, in particular communities of color."

Throughout its study of marijuana, the scientific community has ignored this shameful marijuana-related effect. There are virtually no articles in the scientific literature addressing it. One possible reason is that the National Institutes of Health has not made it a priority to understand or prevent racial discrimination, even though the devastating impact of racism on health is well documented. The NIH, specifically the National Institute on Drug Abuse (NIDA), funds no less than 90 percent of the world's research on marijuana. If that doesn't include studies on race, then the research is not likely to be done.

Another reason for this blind spot is that the researchers themselves are overwhelmingly nonblack and thus shielded from this kind of segregation. The luxury afforded to scientists as a result of working in a racially homogeneous field is apathy and willful ignorance, while the price paid by black people is high rates of arrest and incarceration.

The NIDA could help remedy this situation by requesting research applications that focus explicitly on race—for example, trying to understand the long-term consequences of marijuana arrests on black people, especially as they relate to disrupting one's life trajectory.

Apathy about pot arrest racism is not unique to scientists. The major marijuana-law reform organizations, such as the Marijuana Policy Project and NORML, have also largely ignored this obvious injustice. About a month ago, I appeared on a Pacifica radio station in Washington, DC, with a director from one such group, who said: "We know there [are] stop-and-frisk policies and so forth that are terribly racially discriminatory, but we're looking at the big picture of public health." In his view, the racist enforcement of marijuana laws was not a "big picture" item. The more pressing issue, he explained, is correcting the erroneous belief that marijuana is a "gateway drug" to "harder" substances. I had to exercise a great deal of restraint as I listened incredulously to this person dismiss the grave injustice being perpetrated against black people.

But then I considered the racial composition of his and similar organizations. From their rank and file to their advisory boards, the membership consists almost exclusively of white, privileged and devoted marijuana smokers. Not that there's anything wrong with that, per se, but it helped me understand why racial equality is not a central priority for them. Most of these individuals would like to light up without fear of personal legal consequences—a self-interested goal that could make it difficult to empathize with those who are actually vulnerable to racially motivated marijuana law enforcement. Fifty years ago, Martin Luther King Jr. came to a similar conclusion in a Birmingham jail as he struggled to understand the apathy of his white fellow clergymen to the plight of their black brothers and sisters. "I guess I should have realized," he wrote, "that few members of a race that has oppressed another race can understand the deep groans and passionate yearnings of those who have been oppressed, and still fewer have the vision to see that injustice must be rooted out by strong, persistent and determined action."

There are exceptions, however. The Drug Policy Alliance (DPA), a relatively more racially diverse organization, has committed itself not only to reforming marijuana laws, but also to opposing all drug laws that selectively target people of color. Based in New York City, it played a vital role in dismantling the infamous Rockefeller drug laws and in bringing attention to the New York Police Department's racist stop-and-frisk policy.

I should note that I am a current DPA board member. This is less an acknowledgment of conflict or bias than it is evidence to support my point. In 2007, the DPA had two black board members—at least twice as many as other similar organizations. Concerned that this number was still too low, the leadership asked me to join the board. I accepted because the DPA understands that having a token black board member as window dressing is insufficient to affect the type of necessary change I have laid out here.

Combating racially discriminatory marijuana arrest practices will require a team effort across a variety of communities—scientific, advocacy and so on—and it is in this spirit of a shared purpose that I write. But perhaps I can be forgiven for my impatience with organizations that claim to be allies in this fight while also displaying blatant apathy concerning this issue. You see, I am the father of three black sons. I recognize that there is a high probability that they, like their white counterparts, may one day experiment with marijuana. Knowing the potential consequences if they are arrested, I cannot afford to remain silent.

I call on our allies to break their silence on this issue and make racial justice a central part of the fight against pot prohibition. The next generation is counting on you.

3

Seeking Relief:
Medicinal Marijuana

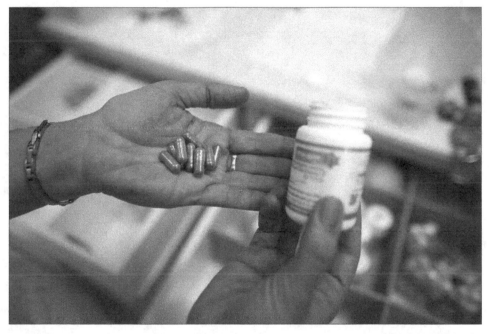

©Abir Sultan/EPA/Landov

Tikun Olam is a company that distributes cannabis for medicinal purposes to patients who received special permission from a doctor.

Marijuana as Medicine

For over five thousand years, marijuana has been used as a medicinal herb to treat ailments ranging from skin disorders to venereal disease. As a result of the drug prohibition movement of the early twentieth century, the medicinal use of marijuana was legally prohibited in the United States for nearly half a century. Beginning in 1996, several US states began adopting laws to legalize marijuana for medical development and use. By August 2014, twenty-three US states and the District of Columbia amended laws to allow for the growth, distribution, prescription, and use of marijuana as a therapeutic medicine.

Debate over the benefits and potential hazards of medical marijuana continues, with the Drug Enforcement Agency (DEA) maintaining its stance that marijuana is a dangerous drug and that even medicinal use could stimulate the illegal use and abuse of marijuana. Despite this, an increasing number of medical professionals support medical marijuana use while new research, enabled by legalization initiatives, has revealed a growing list of medicinal uses, including treatment of some of the world's most pressing health issues.

History of Medical Marijuana

The flowers, and to a lesser extent leaves, seeds, and stems of the marijuana plant (*Cannabis sativa* L.) have potent physiological effects, largely due to the presence of chemicals known as cannabinoids. Consumption of marijuana can result in intoxication and a number of physiological effects. Cannabinoids link with receptor molecules in the brain and stimulate the production of dopamine, thus stimulating feelings of euphoria and simultaneously easing pain responses. Cannabinoids also stimulate the appetite, have short-term effects on cognitive function, and interact with the cardiovascular and pulmonary systems.

The earliest known reference to the medicinal use of marijuana comes from documents from circa 2700 BCE attributed to the quasi-mystical Chinese Emperor Shen Nung a healer who played an important mythic role in the development of traditional Chinese medicine. In ancient China, developments more accurately ascribed to the collective discoveries of myriad individuals were often attributed to mytho-historic figures and the discovery of medicinal marijuana use followed this pattern; it was eaten or burned and inhaled for the treatment of ailments including malaria, gout, gynecological disorders, and rheumatism.

Medicinal use of marijuana spread to India, where the Vedas—compiled between 2000 and 1000 BCE—describe the physical benefits of marijuana use. Marijuana was also used as a sleeping aid, and may have been given to soldiers suffering from symptoms that today might be classified as stress disorders. Over time, marijuana cultivation spread to the Middle East and into Egypt, where documents from around the sixteenth century BCE, describe using marijuana as a component in various medical treatments.

Western Europe was familiar with marijuana as a source of fiber for textiles by the first century CE. Marijuana was imported to the United States as an industrial product, and became one of the most important crops of the 1700s, used to make rope, paper, clothing, and sails for ships. Irish doctor William O'Shaughnessy, a physician with the British East India Company, discovered the medicinal use of marijuana through research in India and began using it to treat rheumatism, nausea, rabies, and tetanus in the 1840s. O'Shaughnessy is credited with popularizing the medicinal use of marijuana in the United States and Europe. By the 1850s, doctors in the United States were using marijuana to treat disorders including pain, gout, depression, cholera, hysteria, and nervous conditions.

Prohibition and Return to Legality

By 1900, drug addiction and abuse had become a major problem in the United States, with about three hundred thousand Americans addicted to opioids, which were unregulated and used in a variety of medicines and curative solutions (of dubious benefit) sold across the country. The effort to eliminate substance abuse turned to marijuana, partially out of misinformation and fear, as recreational marijuana use was tied to increased Mexican immigration in the 1910s and 1920s.

Racism, xenophobia, and a lack of information contributed to a situation in which marijuana was mistakenly equated with the far more damaging abuse of narcotics. Driven by a powerful conservative lobby, states began making marijuana growth and use illegal in the 1930s. In 1937, the federal government followed suit, making growing, owning, and using marijuana illegal through the establishment of a new tax law. From the 1940s to the twenty-first century, a lobby to legalize marijuana emerged in the United States, and one aspect of this lobby was to legalize the use of marijuana as a medicinal aid.

The effectiveness of marijuana as a pain mediator and appetite stimulant for patients undergoing chemotherapy and HIV treatment was a major factor in turning the tide in favor of medical marijuana legalization. Throughout the 1990s, the development of non-smokable marijuana alternatives progressed, and the medical industry urged state governments to consider easing on marijuana-based treatments. In 1996, California voters passed Proposition 215, the first law in US history to make it legal to sell and use marijuana as a medicinal aid. The passage of Proposition 215 led to a gray market in marijuana sale and cultivation and a battle between the Drug Enforcement Agency (DEA) and the growing medical marijuana industry. By the end of the century, Oregon, Washington State, Maine, and Alaska joined suit, passing their own laws making medical marijuana legal. Between 2000 and 2014, twenty additional states and the District of Columbia legalized medical marijuana, while a number of other states were in the process of considering similar legislation.

Regulation and Medical Support

Each state has adopted different regulatory measures for the use and cultivation of medicinal marijuana. In Arizona, patients are restricted to possession of 2.5 ounces of usable marijuana and up to twelve plants, while New York restricts patients to possession of a thirty-day supply of non-smokable marijuana. Some states allow private citizens to grow marijuana, unlicensed, for sale to medical dispensaries and physicians, while other states are debating regulations that would standardize the methods of production, storage, and distribution, including more stringent licensing guidelines.

In many states where medical marijuana is legal, continued legislation has been required to clarify the law. For instance, in California, 2003 Senate Bill 420 amended Proposition 215, specifying that any patient with a legitimate doctor's note could own as many as six marijuana plants or possess a half-pound of processed marijuana for consumption. The law also legally permitted individuals identified by patients as primary caregivers to sell marijuana to be paid for helping the patient to obtain marijuana for medical use.

Over the eighteen years since California legalized medical marijuana, opposition from the DEA and other groups has continued, but an increasing number of medical professionals support medicinal legalization. A 2013 survey of doctors published by the *New England Journal of Medicine* indicated that 76 percent of doctors support medical marijuana treatment. Television correspondent and neuroscientist Sanjay Gupta became one of the best-known medical professionals to speak out in favor of marijuana in 2013, reversing (and apologizing for) his earlier opposition to legalization, which he said was based on misinformation rather than scholarship.

Research and Pharmacology

Since 1968, marijuana intended for scientific research has been grown at the University of Mississippi's Marijuana Research Project, the only facility approved by the National Institute on Drug Abuse (NIDA) to dispense marijuana. Those seeking to conduct research on the plant must first obtain permission from the DEA. As of August 2014, marijuana is classified as a Schedule 1 substance, which is a category of substances believed to have the highest risk of abuse and to have no verified medicinal uses. While the legalization debate continues, a more nuanced lobby is attempting to have marijuana reclassified, on the basis that it does not qualify as a Schedule 1 substance. Research stretching back to the 1940s supports reclassification, and there are no medical studies that currently support the Schedule 1 designation, however, the DEA and NIDA have so far opposed efforts to reclassify.

Medical and legal concerns about marijuana use can be legitimately tied to research indicating that marijuana has a number of potentially harmful side effects. Consumption results in temporary impairment of motor skills and cognitive abilities, which some believe has the potential to increase accidental death and automobile collisions. Consumption through combustion and inhalation results in the creation of carcinogenic compounds and can damage the pulmonary systems of users. Some studies indicate that marijuana use in young individuals may have developmental effects on the brain. A lack of reliable research on either detrimental or beneficial effects of marijuana consumption has become a cornerstone of the lobby to reclassify the drug to open doors to further study.

Despite restrictions, research has proliferated around the world and has resulted in the discovery that marijuana can be used effectively in the treatment of a wide variety of disorders. The reduction of nausea in cancer patients has been demonstrated by studies conducted from the 1970s to the 2000s, and remains one of the key justifications for the legalization of marijuana. Marijuana is also widely used to alleviate the side effects of HIV treatment.

In a more recent development, studies have indicated that cannabinoids may be useful in treating brain cancer. A 2009 study conducted at Complutense University in Spain and published in 2009 in the *Journal of Clinical Investigation* reported that THC may work to kill cancer cells within the brains of users. A number of studies support this assertion that THC can help to kill cancer cells in the brain while other studies, including a 2013 study from the *Journal of Pharmacy and Pharmacology* and conducted in Tokyo, Japan, indicate that THC may be effective in combating skin cancer.

Another branch of research indicates that marijuana is effective in combating depression and stress-related disorders. Studies conducted in Haifa, Israel, as well as similar studies in Europe, have investigated the utility of THC to treat Post Traumatic Stress Disorder (PTSD). In 2012, researchers at the Arizona College of Medicine proposed a study of marijuana's utility as a treatment for PTSD and were initially met with resistance from the NIDA, but they were eventually granted access to government marijuana stocks in March 2014. While government regulations have sometimes proved a hindrance to research, physicians in several states where medical marijuana has been legalized have begun prescribing marijuana for PTSD sufferers and those suffering from other stress disorders.

Another area of research suggests that cannabinoids are effective in preventing seizures. A 2013 study conducted by the British Pharmacological Society suggested that marijuana can act as a strong anticonvulsant and may therefore be useful in the treatment of seizures related to epilepsy and other disorders that commonly produce seizures in patients. In 2014, Illinois became the first state to legalize the prescription of non-smokable marijuana, with parental consent, for children suffering from seizures. This legislation is controversial because many feel that marijuana can have deleterious developmental effects on the brains of young users. Supporters of the law argue that marijuana's demonstrable effectiveness is combating seizures could revolutionize the treatment of childhood epilepsy.

Controversies and Futures

In addition to the controversial movement to extend marijuana treatment to underage patients, there are a number of other controversies surrounding the medical marijuana debate. Among the most pressing is the debate over whether marijuana should be permitted for palliative treatment, given to prevent the development of future disorders, rather than only to treat existing conditions. A unique feature of the marijuana debate is that the substance has been used for thousands of years as a treatment and the exploration of marijuana-based medicine is therefore also a historical investigation of medical history reaching back more than five thousand years. As humanity increasingly comes to reevaluate its past in hopes of improving the future, the marijuana debate has become a key issue in global politics, with the potential to affect the future of health and wellness for future generations.

—Micah Issitt

Bibliography

Adler, Jonathan N., and James A. Colbert. "Medical Use of Marijuana—Polling Results." *New England Journ. of Medicine*. Massachusetts Medical Society, 30 May 2013. Web. 15 Aug. 2014.

Brown, David T., ed. *Cannabis: The Genus Cannabis*. New York: Taylor, 1998. Print.

Buckley, Bruce, and Joan Buckley. "NIDA Study Cites Dangers of Marijuana Use in Teens." *Pharmacy Practice News*. McMahon, July 2014. Web. 15 Aug. 2014.

Clarke, Robert, and Mark Merlin. *Cannabis: Evolution and Ethnobotany*. Los Angeles: U of California P, 2013. Print.

Clarke, Robert Connell. *Marijuana Botany*. Berkeley: Ronin, 1981. Print.

Grant, Igor. "Medicinal Cannabis and Painful Sensory Neuropathy." *Virtual Mentor* 15.5 (2013): 466–69. Print.

Gupta, Sanjay. "Why I Changed my Mind on Weed." *CNN Health*. CNN, 8 Aug. 2013. Web. 18 Aug. 2014.

Halper, Evan, "Mississippi, Home to Federal Government's Official Stash of Marijuana." *Los Angeles Times*. Los Angeles Times, 28 May 2014. Web. 18 Aug. 2014.

Mulcahey, Martin, "The Case for Treating PTSD in Veterans with Medical Marijuana." *Atlantic*. Atlantic Monthly Group, 17 Jan. 2012. Web. 18 Aug. 2014.

Stack, Patrick, and Claire Suddath. "A Brief History of Medical Marijuana." *Time*. Time, 21 Oct. 2009. Web. 18 Aug. 2014.

Health Benefits of Medical Marijuana: 3 Major Ways Cannabis Helps Sick People Live Normal Lives

By Anthony Rivas
Medical Daily, May 19, 2014

To say that marijuana's making a comeback would be an understatement. Since California enacted a medical marijuana law in 1996, 20 other states and the District of Columbia have followed suit, with eight of them passing laws in the past four years alone. Two of them—Washington and Colorado—have even passed full-blown legalization of the drug. And none of that includes the many states that are currently in the process, such as New York and Minnesota. This huge shift in public opinion can be credited, in large part, to a wide range of studies and patient testimonies supporting the drug's health benefits. So, what are some of them?

Stress, Anxiety, and PTSD—It's a Mixed Bag

No matter how you ingest marijuana, there are possible side effects to the drug—pro-pot advocates will claim they're never as bad as pharmaceutical side effects—including anxiety and paranoia. These effects can subsequently lead to higher blood pressure, arrhythmia, and other effects common to anxiety. In this way, it's a gamble when taking marijuana. For those who know how much they're taking and what to expect, however, they may experience the opposite effect: calm, relaxation, and happiness.

For people with post-traumatic stress disorder (PTSD), one of the worst possible anxiety disorders, marijuana might be able to alleviate symptoms. Although there's a scarcity of human research into the association, anecdotal evidence is heavy, and states, such as Maine and New Hampshire, have begun allowing its use. The Department of Health and Human Services also signed off recently, on a study to test its benefits in PTSD patients.

The use of marijuana for anxiety disorders, and just plain stress, comes from the fact that the brain naturally produces cannabinoids, which are the active chemicals in marijuana—namely, delta-9 tetrahydrocannabinol, or THC—and what help regulate how fear is processed in the brain.

A May 2013 study found that people with PTSD showed lower levels of a certain endocannabinoid known as anandamide in the area of their brains associated with fear and anxiety. Thus, fewer cannabinoid receptors were being activated, spurring

PTSD along. In theory, using marijuana would boost concentrations of these beneficial cannabinoids, reducing symptoms of PTSD. "We know very well that people with PTSD who use marijuana often experience more relief from their symptoms than they do from antidepressants and other psychiatric medications," said lead author Dr. Alexander Neumeister, of the Departments of Psychiatry and Radiology at New York University, in a press release.

In part, these calming effects could be the reasons why marijuana use has been linked to a 10 percent reduction in suicide rates, while also being considered for use in some Swiss prisons.

Cerebral Palsy and Other Neurodegenerative Diseases

Neurodegenerative diseases affect millions of people in the U.S. Parkinson's disease, for example, affects an estimated one million people, while cerebral palsy affects as many as 764,000 children and adults. These diseases and more are all debilitating in their own way, as they affect the nervous system's ability to connect with the brain, therefore affecting a person's ability to move. Marijuana has shown *huge* promise in saving these people.

Multiple sclerosis (MS), which occurs when the immune system attacks the nerve's myelin sheaths, causes the nerves to become unable to communicate with each other. In turn, this causes weakness in limbs, partial to complete loss of vision, and tremors. Studies on marijuana use among animals with MS showed that THC and other cannabinoids were able to target the inflammation-causing cells produced by the immune system, subsequently leading to less destruction of myelin. Another UK study found that 12 weeks of marijuana treatment helped relieve muscle stiffness in 30 percent of almost 300 patients suffering from MS.

Marijuana has also been shown to reduce symptoms of Parkinson's disease (PD), which include rigid muscles, slow movement, and tremors. In a study of 22 patients who were all about 66 years old, tremor scores dropped after using marijuana. "The study suggests that cannabis might have a place in the therapeutic armamentarium of PD," the researchers wrote. "Larger, controlled studies are needed to verify the results."

In such patients, the results really do need to be seen to be believed. In December, *Medical Daily* reported the story of Jacqueline Patterson, a Missouri mother of four whose cerebral palsy had left her with a severe stutter caused by muscle stiffness, which has also caused her severe pain and the inability to use her right arm correctly. With marijuana, she becomes a totally different person, able to speak, move, and overall become less tense.

Cancer

The big one right here. Pretty much any state that legalizes marijuana for medical use lists cancer as one of the first conditions it can be used for. People undergoing chemotherapy for whatever their cancer may be often experience nausea, vomiting, loss of appetite, and pain, according to the National Institutes of Health (NIH).

Marijuana has been shown to alleviate all of these side effects. In fact, two FDA-approved medications, dronabinol and nabilone, are derived from THC and used in cancer patients and HIV/AIDS patients to treat nausea and vomiting. Dronabinol was also shown last year to ease pain in cancer patients. As for increasing appetite, well, they don't call it the munchies for nothing.

Beyond chemo, there's also evidence that marijuana can help prevent the growth of tumors. According to the NIH, another cannabinoid, cannabidiol, has been shown to relieve pain as well as lower inflammation. Cannabinoids such as these have been shown to block cell growth, prevent the growth of blood vessels that aid metastasis (the spread of tumors), and kill tumor cells. Some researchers have even found a way to harness this power without the psychoactive effects.

"Cannabinoids have a complex action; it hits a number of important processes that cancers need to survive," oncologist Dr. Wai Liu told *The Huffington Post.* "For that reason, it has really good potential over other drugs that only have one function. I am impressed by its activity profile, and feel it has a great future, especially if used with standard chemotherapies."

For Recreational Users

As marijuana becomes further engrained in American culture, some might ask, "Is it better to smoke weed or consume it through mediums like edibles and oils?" It is indeed better to eat it, as it doesn't involve inhaling the harmful tars produced through the combustion of rolling paper. But even eating it may have its caveats, as getting the proper dose can be difficult. By far, the best way to toke healthily is to use a vaporizer, which heats the cannabis just enough to release active cannabinoids without releasing smoke and toxins. "Vaporizer users are only 40 percent as likely to report respiratory symptoms as users who do not vaporize," researchers of a 2007 study wrote. "Regular users of joints, blunts, pipes, and water pipes might decrease respiratory symptoms by switching to a vaporizer."

Medical Marijuana: 4 Experts on Benefits versus Risks

By David Levine
Elsevier Connect, May 2, 2014

When I landed in Denver to attend the Association of Healthcare Journalists (AHCJ) annual meeting, the pilot announced, "Welcome to the mile-high city— although lately the emphasis has been on *high*."

The humorous references to the state's recent legalization of recreational marijuana sales continued into the conference March 27 to 30, which was attended by about 700.

Governor John Hickenlooper opened his keynote speech by denying he was seeking" higher" office.

He gave a report on how Colorado has fared since January 1, when the state legalized recreational marijuana use for adults 21 and older and implemented ways to regulate, tax and distribute cannabis products. He noted that the state issued 136 licenses for recreational marijuana sales in December. (Although recreational marijuana only started January 1, medical marijuana has been legal in Colorado since 2000.) "The world has not fallen apart. Crime is not rampant. We are not having tons of automobile accidents from stoned drivers," Governor Hickenlooper said. In the first month, he added, Colorado collected nearly $14 million in taxes from sales, mostly from Denver stores.

The governor said he was first offered marijuana in middle school: "Drugs are here whether there are laws or not. We have spent billions of dollars on the war on drugs in this country and it is not working." He said that since marijuana is around, it makes more sense to make it legal and educate the public about it.

He said his biggest concern was how the new law would affect children and young people. "We are spending a lot of money and effort to reach out to them." He noted that the state's marijuana website has a special section for parents to start a dialogue with their children and that his government is committed to working with state agencies and community partners over the coming months to develop a statewide public awareness campaign addressing the dangers of under-age marijuana use.

There were many questions from the audience of health journalists—including whether the governor had inhaled since the law took effect. His answer was no, but no one asked him whether he had consumed any products that contained marijuana, which are very popular in Colorado and can be found in every store selling it.

He said he wants to use the money raised by sales for education and research. He supports the proposal of Dr. Larry Wolk, executive director of the Colorado Department of Public Health and Environment, who is calling for the State Legislature to use tax revenues from marijuana sales to fund $10 million in human research trials.

Panelists Speak from Experience

Dr. Wolk took part in a panel discussion on the "Medical Ramifications of Legal Marijuana," which drew a huge crowd. The panel was moderated by Michael Booth, Managing Editor of *Health Elevations*, a quarterly journal published by the Colorado Health Foundation. It included Dr. J. Michael Bostwick, a psychiatrist at the Mayo Clinic; Dr. Kari L. Franson, Associate Dean for Professional Education at the University of Colorado Skaggs School of Pharmacy and Pharmaceutical Sciences; and Michael Elliot, Executive Director of the Marijuana Industry Group, which was founded in 2010 to protect and promote the Colorado medical marijuana regulatory framework, serve as a resource for policy makers, and protect the rights of medical marijuana patients.

Dr. Kari Franson: Still Much to Learn—and Be Careful When Eating It

Dr. Franson said marijuana is difficult to study in the lab, and there is still a lot to learn about its effects on the body. "There is a reason people take one or two aspirins. We know that works for most people," she said. "We don't know that about marijuana."

She pointed out that unlike prescription drugs, people take marijuana in many different forms, and there is a wide variation in how tetrahydrocannabinol (THC)— the active ingredient of marijuana—affects individuals when taken in oral form. "One day a person might need one dose, and another day four or more in order to get the same effect."

Dr. Franson noted that patients can also get into trouble when they ingest marijuana products because it can take between one to five hours to feel its effects.

Many patients prefer the convenience of the oral products, such as gummy bears and brownies, rather than smoking it. But they are used to inhaling weed, which takes effect almost immediately. Edible products have to be digested. And consuming more edible products doesn't cause marijuana to get into the system faster. But it can lead to increased anxiety and altered perceptions once it becomes effective.

Pediatrician Larry Wolk: Reports of '"Miracles" Are Overblown

Dr. Wolk said that despite marijuana being around for years, we don't know that much about it: "It is almost impossible to get funding from the federal government for studies. I see this as an opportunity in public health to study the health effects, both short- and long-term, of marijuana."

When asked by a member of the audience whether he was prepared for the rush of parents of epileptic children moving to Colorado to get medical marijuana, Dr. Wolk, who is a pediatrician, said there hasn't been a rush. In fact, he said that less than 300 of the 120,000 medical marijuana registrants were children. "Children with epilepsy and other seizure disorders have become the poster children for medical marijuana advocates, but the evidence is not there."

Dr. Wolk said the reports of the miracles for children who use a form of marijuana known as Charlotte's Web—named after Charlotte Figi, whose severe seizures were controlled by marijuana—have been overblown. "We only hear the success stories. It doesn't help everyone; in fact, we're not even sure if it helps the majority of children."

Dr. Wolk said he is very frustrated by the lack of response from doctors who treat patients: "I keep asking doctors to get me some data, show me your clinical notes or the EEGs and brain scans that show kids have responded clinically. Despite multiple requests, I've received no response."

Psychiatrist Michael Bostwick: One in 10 Users Meets Medical Criteria for Addiction

Dr. Bostwick, who specializes in addiction psychiatry, said that unlike alcohol, whose responses are well known, there is a lot of variability in response to marijuana.

There have not been good randomized trials on the effects of marijuana. There is no funding for it, and politicians are against it. But we need to know more.

He said, although it is almost impossible to overdose from marijuana, one in 10 marijuana users meet the medical criteria for addiction. "Although this is troubling given the vast amounts of people who use marijuana, it is still a low percentage compared to alcohol and nicotine."

He told the audience that his 20-year-old son needed treatment for marijuana use when he was 17. "It was absolute hell to figure out what was experimentation and what was going to destroy his life and his brain," Dr. Bostwick said. But his son's treatment worked. He has been substance-free for close to four years.

As a psychiatrist, Dr. Bostwick said he was disappointed that medical marijuana for PTSD is not among the eligible conditions approved by Colorado. "There is good evidence that for some patients with PTSD it is helpful," he said. (The eligible conditions include AIDS, HIV, cancer, glaucoma and any of the following symptoms that are caused by a chronic or debilitating disease or the treatment of such disease: cachexia (severe weight loss caused by a medical condition or its treatment), severe pain, severe nausea, seizures, or persistent muscle spasms.)

Advocate Michael Elliott: "We Embrace Regulation . . . and Taxation"

Elliott, an attorney, said his trade association, the Marijuana Industry Group, takes an opposite approach to the tobacco companies:

> We acknowledge safety concerns. We embrace regulation. They don't. We support taxation. They don't. The same is true for accountability, transparency and control. We want it because it makes the use of marijuana safer for both medical and recreational users.

He said his group supports using marijuana tax revenue to keep the substance away from children, deter driving while under the influence of marijuana and combat drug traffickers.

Elliott noted that laws in 20 states and the District of Columbia allow marijuana for medical use and that about a dozen other states are considering the legalization of marijuana in some form in the coming years.

My fellow attendees said they learned a lot from the panel discussion, and many expressed interest in seeing first-hand the stores that sold marijuana.

Visiting a Marijuana Store

During the conference, several AHCJ members bought marijuana products and paraphernalia and showed it to a group of us sitting around the bar. It was an Alice in Wonderland atmosphere—not because anyone used it, but because no one had to look over their shoulder while showing it.

I went with a fellow attendee to visit one of the marijuana stores. It was right near the hotel, an easy 10-minute walk. To find it, all you had to do was Google "marijuana stores," and it was the first to come up.

The store is named the Native Roots Apothecary, and it bills itself as an alternative wellness center. It is on the eight floor of an office building, and there are no signs on the street telling you to "buy marijuana here."

It is very professionally run. All of the workers are licensed by the state and wear their IDs. When you take the elevator to the Apothecary, you can't just walk in. You are buzzed in, and the receptionist asks you if you are there as a recreational user or as a patient. And you have to show the receptionist your driver's license, which is scanned (so you can't go from shop to shop) and looked at more closely than a TSA agent. You have to be 21 to buy any of the products.

If you are a resident of Colorado, you can buy one ounce of retail marijuana per transaction. If not, .25 ounces. You are allowed four transactions a day and can buy THC products such as THC lotion, topicals, elixirs and edibles (THC—tetrahydro-cannabinol—is the active ingredient of marijuana), as well as the traditional "grass" you can smoke.

Recreational users don't need anything but a license. Medical patients need a state registration card, which they can only get from a doctor.

Once you go in, you wait. I was given a number, the kind you get in a bakery, and waited about half an hour. No cell phones or pictures are allowed because of patient confidentiality. This establishment has been operational for four and a half years, previously as a medical marijuana dispensary.

When we were called in, the people behind the desk looked at our driver's licenses again then showed us the products in the recreational section. (I asked to see the patient products but was not allowed).

There were all kinds of products for sale. Marijuana varieties included Purple Flo, Tangerine Haze, Dark Dream and Lemon Sweet Skunk, with prices ranging from $30 to $35 for 1/8 of an ounce. Edibles included Love's Oven Magic Bars (150 mg of graham cracker, cannabis infused butter, coconut, sweetened condensed milk, semi-sweet chocolate, butterscotch and walnuts) for $14 each. You can see the full menu on the website. The person I went with bought marijuana chapstick, which she said didn't do anything.

The two people behind the counter were very knowledgeable and made recommendations to consumers based on whether they wanted to feel mellow or alert. But there was no joking around. They took their jobs seriously. And everyone there is certified by the State and has an ID issued by the state.

There was a photo of the staff with the rapper Snoop Dogg. There is a strain of marijuana named after him which is very popular.

You can't use marijuana in any public place. You can't even use it in the stores. (No one is sitting around getting stoned, if that was what you were wondering.)

And there is a lot of security, including guards and cameras. It is an all cash business. The federal government won't allow credit card transactions for marijuana, I was told, although Native Roots did allow debit card transactions.

I asked if they ever refused a sale. The clerk said, "If a person is impaired, either drunk or stoned, I have the power to refuse a sale."

Family Moving in Search of Medical Marijuana

By Taylor Shuck
The Baker Orange, April 3, 2014

Baldwin City native Ryan Reed lived in New York City when he and his wife, Salina native Kathy Reed, got engaged. They moved back to Lawrence [Kansas] to be close to their families. But now, they have to leave again.

In May, they will be moving to Colorado to seek medical marijuana treatment for their 2-year-old son's regular seizures.

"We need to speak up before we leave to let legislators know what we are doing and that we think it's not right that our state isn't allowing it for the sickest people, children, among us," Ryan said. "We don't have time to wait for the laws to change."

"Nothing Has Panned Out"

At nine weeks old, Otis Reed was diagnosed with intractable epilepsy, a disease resistant to any form of treatment. He has been through a hefty list of treatments, including all three of what the doctors call "the big guns" that are normally used to treat infantile spasms. The list of outcomes listed in his treatments package from the hospital says, "No change in seizure activity" and "enlarged heart and high blood pressure."

"We've tried everything and nothing has panned out," Ryan said. "Some of the drugs have made his seizures worse. The side effects from these medications that he has been on, some of them have been horrible."

For a while, Otis's parents were told by their neurologist to record how many times Otis would have a seizure in a day. Ryan assumes a safe bet would be 100 seizures in a day for Otis, which in his case, consists of a quick jerk lasting only a second or two. What might look like only a "funny kid move" to some has actually stunted Otis's development due to his constant erratic brain activity.

Otis can't walk, can't talk and is slowly falling behind other kids his age.

"The worst day I stopped counting at 600," Ryan said. "When he's having a cluster of seizures, he fights through them. He tries to go back to what he was doing before the fits. As a parent, it's awesome to see him struggle through it and fight back."

For two years he has been working on the "big third gun" that includes a high-fat diet, for which his parents have to weigh everything in grams before feeding it to Otis. But the diet weakened his bones to the point of breaking. When Ryan repositioned his immobile son in bed, Otis's leg broke. This is what Ryan calls "a pretty low point" in his family's struggle.

"I felt pretty guilty for that," Ryan said. "But we're glad that that's over. It was a rough time for us."

A New Home for New Hope

The idea for medical marijuana use finally came up in conversation when the Reeds realized they had gone through every legal option for their son, short of brain surgery. Doctors tell the Reeds that the marijuana procedure has a 50 percent chance of working, with possible positive results, ranging from one less seizure a day to complete freedom.

"If someone had told me when we started the process that I could either give my son heavy doses of steroids that caused ventricle hypertrophy or medical marijuana, I would have (chosen) medical marijuana," Ryan said. "But six months ago, I would have thought medical marijuana was a joke."

The couple has done extensive research on the effects of medical marijuana on children and is currently looking into a strain of the drug called "Charlotte's Web." Named after Charlotte Figi, a child who had symptoms somewhat similar to Otis's that were cured by this drug, this strain of marijuana is low in the psychoactive compound in marijuana. But it is high in cannabidiol, or CBD, which has medicinal properties.

They have joined medical marijuana support groups to talk about the disease that won't get better on its own. When testimonies say the only side effects are "less seizures" or "smiling more," the drug seems like a viable option for the couple.

"We've separated the idea of hope and expectations," Ryan said. "We hope this will help him get a better quality of life, but do we expect it to be Otis's miracle that will heal him? No. But we are just doing whatever we can to give him the best life possible."

Although many community members have shown the Reed family support, some still have reservations. The lack of research on the medicinal uses of marijuana makes the couple a bit hesitant. While he doesn't have a desire to fight the legalization of the recreational use of marijuana, Ryan said that the stigma surrounding its medicinal qualities needs to change in order to save lives.

"We need to be able to do the research to prove that it's not just anecdotal stories," Ryan said. "It's not just Charlotte, it's not just the kids in Colorado, it's science."

Turning Plan into Action

But before the two decided to move, they brought their case to the Kansas legislature. They talked to a dozen different members of the House and Senate but eventually became exhausted from the ordeal and lack of response.

"I think that most of them, if put in the same shoes, would make the same decision for their kids or grandkids," Ryan said. "But I don't think that was enough to put it into action for those people."

One person who took interest in the case was Representative John Wilson. Wilson attends the same church as the Reeds and had talked to his pastor about the case before it was even brought to his desk. So when Ryan presented his situation, Wilson told him he would do whatever he could to help.

"If people want to move to Colorado, they should move to hike or ski, not for medical care," Wilson said. "That's why I want to help them so that families like theirs don't have to leave the state because we didn't give them any other option."

But Wilson shares Ryan's dismal look on legalization, which he says "isn't just an issue about hippies with black light posters anymore." Wilson believes that the change has to come from both testimonies and scientific research, both of which are hard to get without legalization.

With an election in the fall, Wilson believes that new options could come up for families like the Reeds.

"It's going to take credible science, thoughtful success stories from families and organization to work the system," Wilson said. "That's my part in this - teaching the Reeds how to work the system."

Wilson said that because the majority party determines what bills will be brought to the table, it will take a speaker of the house willing to have an open conversation regarding the legalization of the drug. But with support from the house speaker, he believes all that would need to happen after that is a little bit of organization.

"People are seeing real benefits from medical marijuana use, but I think people need to be brought up to speed on what we are really talking about here," Wilson said.

So while the Reeds are disappointed to leave their family and friends, they hope this adventure changes their lives drastically.

"I love Kansas, but we aren't the most progressive state," Ryan said. "If the federal government would take it off as a criminal drug, states could stop hiding behind that, and we could make some changes. I think that for Kansas it will be a while, but stories like this won't go away. I think it's happening, but not fast enough for us."

Out of Options

By Jacob Jones
Inlander, March 27, 2014

Perched in his wheelchair with a blanket over his lap, 10-year-old Koa Kalua rocks in his seat, his arms outstretched to his mother as she offers him a sippy cup of water. Clutching the cup, the brown-haired boy moans in thanks and smiles broadly, his jaw and neck straining around the expression. He then turns quiet, more relaxed as he begins to drink.

"This is Koa," his mother Kim Kalua says. "Today's a really good day for him. He's relatively calm and happy."

Koa has suffered from Doose Syndrome, a severe and medication-resistant form of epilepsy, since age 2. Plagued by violent seizures and developmental delays, he struggles to communicate and control his motor functions. On bad days, he screams for hours and wears a diaper. He may need to be strapped into his chair.

At first, doctors tried to treat Koa with traditional anti-seizure drugs, which his parents say only made things worse. Seizures skyrocketed from a few a week to more than 100 a day. After several months of failed drug combinations, Kim and her husband Bobby decided the side effects were too dangerous. They took him off the medication.

Kim Kalua juggles several tincture bottles for high-cannabidiol marijuana extract oil that the family has used to treat Koa's epilepsy.

But eight years later, as his symptoms worsened, the family admitted him to Seattle Children's Hospital, where doctors recommended Lamictal, the same anti-seizure drug as before. Kim says she could not believe it: "We're back to the exact same spot."

In August of 2013, having reluctantly filled a prescription for Lamictal, Kim happened to come across a family successfully managing Doose Syndrome with marijuana extract. It seemed absurd and confusing. But short of options, the Kaluas, like many other Washington parents, turned to a substance they previously considered unthinkable.

"When we started him on the marijuana," Kim says, "what I noticed was his good days got better and his bad days got better."

While much of the public debate on marijuana legalization has focused on taxes, law enforcement or stoner puns, some families increasingly view marijuana regulation as a matter of life or death. Local marijuana advocates estimate more than 70 families across Washington use cannabis to treat a child with a serious medical condition such as epilepsy or cancer.

Those families have watched nervously as Washington lawmakers move to fold medical marijuana into the new recreational retail framework, leading officials to consider tighter restrictions on private growing and possession of medical marijuana. The legislature recently failed to pass any new bill (SB 5887) this session, extending the uncertainty another year.

In the absence of consistent law or medical expertise, parents turn to each other, either in-person or online, for help navigating a brave new world. Kim found families in California and Colorado struggling with many of the same challenges. They trade research on marijuana strains, extract recipes and legal roadblocks.

"We have no experience with the usage of marijuana in either of our pasts," Bobby says, adding, "Our background is marijuana's in the same bucket as cocaine. [It] belongs in the absolutely illegal, go-to-jail zone. Just to bring it in the conversation, it's a bit of a head twist for us."

To treat children, families seek out specially cultivated plant strains containing low concentrations of the psychoactive THC, combined with high amounts of non-intoxicating cannabidiol, or CBD, which research links to the plant's legitimate medical benefits. Kim says the purest medical strains have a CBD-THC ratio of 34 to 1.

The Kaluas went to the Pacific Northwest Medical dispensary in Spokane to make their initial purchases for Koa. Owner Sean Green, who received the state's first processing license earlier this month, says providing cannabis to minors is a "very delicate" process that he only considers on rare, case-by-case terms after vetting physicians and medical records.

But Green says he's seen enough success stories to justify any risks.

"Seeing people have a better standard of life is a reward in and of itself," he says. "These are just families trying to take care of their children."

Kim holds up a handful of small eye-dropper bottles of marijuana tincture, a highly concentrated CBD extract oil. Six months ago, she hadn't known what tincture was, but in that time—with the help of online tutors and chat rooms—she has learned how to process loose marijuana by boiling it down in alcohol and infusing it into olive oil.

They mix the extract into Koa's oatmeal or spread it into his sandwiches. Koa responded well, they say, but they quickly determined it would take an ounce of loose marijuana a week to cook down to the dosages he needed. At more than $300 an ounce, they needed to make it affordable. They reached out to Ryan Day in Thurston County.

A U.S. Marine Corps veteran now working as a children's health advocate, Day grows his own marijuana to treat his son Haiden. The 5-year-old suffers from Dravet syndrome, another form of epilepsy that causes dozens of seizures a day and leaves him cognitively delayed, similar to Koa. Day passes along much of what he has learned to other families.

"I am not ashamed of what I'm doing for my son," Day says. "It has dramatically improved his quality of life."

As he has lobbied in Olympia for improved medical marijuana policy, Day has also served as an informal consultant or sounding board for many regional families trying to get their arms around the shifting legal landscape. Having just found new hope, many families fear authorities could choke off access, impose impossible fees or criminalize their medication inventories.

"At any moment, the rug could get pulled out from under these families," Day says. "It's a very precarious situation right now. . . . It's really a scary time."

While Day would like some clear and consistent regulations at the state level, he says the federal government continues to pose a huge obstacle to treating children. Because of marijuana's classification as a Schedule I narcotic, few agencies can legally offer medical support or guidance. Families cannot seek out specialized or less expensive strains across state lines. And they often pay thousands of dollars a year out of pocket because insurance won't cover it.

"It's a little ridiculous," he says. "We're mostly people who have no other options. We're trying to save our kids' lives."

With some guidance from Day and reduced marijuana costs through Pacific Northwest Medical, the Kaluas succeeded earlier this year in getting Koa on a stable regimen of CBD extract for about six weeks. After so many failed drugs and terrifying side effects, they say the marijuana results have been amazing. Koa became happier and more focused. He walks more. He talks more.

"His school attendance went up," Kim says. "That's something you can quantify. His speech went up. We noticed him using words we hadn't heard him use in a long time. He visibly had fewer seizures. Several people who he interacts with said, 'Oh my goodness. He's got his sparkle back.' And he does."

Those six weeks have them convinced that they can get their little boy back.

But they had to halt the treatment in February. At close to $1,500 a month, they could no longer afford to keep up with his dosages. They believe they will have to grow it themselves to make it feasible. Kim says they're putting together a long-term plan now, but wish lawmakers would stop threatening to change the rules.

"We're sort of at this juncture," she says.

Sitting nearby, Koa's head slumps to the right and his body goes limp. His eyes glaze over as Kim leans in to comfort him.

"He's having a seizure right now," she says. "He just blanks out."

In a patient and reassuring voice, she beckons him back, waving her hand in front of his face.

"Koa," she calls quietly. "Koa. Hey, buddy."

Marijuana Raid in Bates County Illustrates the Evolution of an Issue

By Donald Bradley
The Kansas City Star, March 29, 2014

As usual, Gene Halbin rolled a fat one after lunch.

He'd taken a couple of hits when two strangers appeared at the front door. Halbin's place sits way out of town, off the blacktop, down a dirt road, round a bend, over a bridge and deep into some woods in northwestern Bates County.

Good bet they weren't solicitors working the neighborhood.

But they did come with purpose and the first words out of one of their mouths stated it clearly:

"I can smell marijuana right now."

For the rest of the day, Halbin, 60, a retired air conditioning serviceman with a rare and severe form of glaucoma, sat quietly as officers carted out 41 pot plants, growing lights, a dozen or so guns and his grandfather's pipe collection.

Sometime during all this, Halbin's wife, Dolores, a registered nurse, came home and saw all the cars. She figured what was happening, got scared and drove on past. She drove around until she ran out of gas.

Now these two are waiting to see whether Gene or both of them will be charged, and Dolores, formerly the school nurse at University Academy in Kansas City, has lost her job at a hospital—all for something that likely would be legal in the 20 states that allow medical marijuana.

Several proposed bills are being considered in the Missouri General Assembly, but none might come soon enough to help the Halbins with what was known in the family as "Grampa's medicine."

The case, which comes as some health organizations pull back from earlier opposition to medical marijuana, shows how weed has evolved on the American landscape.

The Halbins belong to a shooting club. They display Old Glory in their house. A 79-year-old farmer up the road says they're fine neighbors.

"She (Dolores) brought me a hot meal several days there when I was down sick last winter," Dave Riaman, who has lived alone since his wife died, said one day last week while airing up a truck tire.

He put his boot up on the fence and said he didn't know much about marijuana.

"But he wasn't selling it and he wasn't bothering anybody, so I think they over-done it," Riaman said. "If it made him feel better, what's the problem?"

The couple's pharmacist in the nearby town of Drexel, Mo., thinks the whole thing is ridiculous.

"They are good people and he found a treatment that works for him," said Mark Finke at Drexel Pharmacy. "I fully support them. He has tried things I have here, but nothing works for glaucoma like marijuana and you would be hard-pressed to find a doctor to say otherwise.

"He wasn't hurting anyone. I have drugs in here like OxyContin that are legal and they kill someone every day."

After Dolores got over her initial despair, she decided she's too Irish to take all this quietly, especially with her belief that Missouri soon will join the ranks of medi-cal marijuana states. She blames President Barack Obama for not backing off the country's long-held classification of marijuana as a Schedule I drug—the same as heroin and LSD.

Gene's crop included mostly small plants and took up a corner of their basement.

"I've lost my job and I could lose my nursing license," Dolores said last week at the dining table. "My husband has lost his medication, and it's the only thing that lets him have anything close to a normal life.

"The only thing I have left is to fight. I want it all back—my job, our guns, the lights, Gene's dad's pipe collection. Even the medication."

Gene turned and looked at his wife.

"I doubt seriously they're going to give back the marijuana."

Evidence shows that marijuana can lower the painful high intraocular pressure caused by glaucoma and help with other medical issues as well, but that doesn't mean everybody favors legalization.

On Dec. 3 in *The Star*, Ravikumar Chockalingam and Dragan Svrakic, doctors at the Washington University School of Medicine in St. Louis, wrote: "The dangers of medical marijuana far exceed any therapeutic usefulness, particularly in the context of safer and more evidence-based alternate treatment. Legal cannabis is a bad drug trip the public should avoid."

More notably, the American Glaucoma Society's official position is against medi-cal marijuana.

"Although marijuana can lower the intraocular pressure, its side effects and short duration of action, coupled with a lack of evidence that its use alters the course of glaucoma, preclude recommending this drug in any form for the treatment of glau-coma at the present time."

But other medical groups have pulled back blanket opposition.

The American College of Physicians now supports research into the therapeutic powers of marijuana. The American Medical Association "calls for further adequate and well-controlled studies of marijuana."

The AMA's official position goes on to say that "effective patient care requires the free and unfettered exchange of information on treatment alternatives and that discussion of these alternatives between physicians and patients should not subject either party to criminal sanctions."

Last month, the Epilepsy Foundation announced it "supports the rights of patients and families living with seizures and epilepsy to access physician directed care, including medical marijuana."

A study released last week by the American Academy of Neurology said medical marijuana might be the most effective complementary or alternative medicine for relief of symptoms caused by multiple sclerosis.

A high-profile change of mind came last summer from one of the country's best-known doctors. Sanjay Gupta, a neurosurgeon and the chief medical correspondent for CNN, had long opposed medical marijuana because of studies that showed it had potential for great abuse and no medical benefit.

But Gupta did his own research and concluded neither of those to be true.

"We have been terribly and systematically misled for nearly 70 years in the United States, and I apologize for my own role in that," Gupta wrote August 8.

According to ProCon.org, a group that monitors controversial issues, the national momentum is clearly with medical marijuana.

A Maryland Senate panel last week approved changes to a bill that would remove a cap on the number of growers in the state and include a study on how to best provide medical marijuana to veterans.

In Illinois, legislation advanced that would expand the use of medical marijuana for severely epileptic children. The proposal, pushed by parents, would allow children with seizure disorders, including epilepsy, to take a derivative of medical cannabis.

Not too many years ago, the prospects for medical marijuana in Missouri were far-fetched.

But things have changed, said Missouri Senator Jason Holsman, a Kansas City Democrat who introduced legislation that is scheduled for a hearing this week. He said polling includes approval from 70 percent of AARP members and shows the state is ready.

Support also comes from Republican ranks. Representative Rob Schaaf, a family physician from St. Joseph, sponsored a previous medical marijuana proposal.

Final approval, though, probably will come through a voter initiative that Holsman's bill provides.

"In the end, the people of this state will decide," he said.

Then Holsman told why he was doing this. When he was campaigning, Holsman asked a member of his church if he could put a sign in his yard. The man declined because he was a Republican. A year later, the man had been diagnosed with cancer and was undergoing chemotherapy. He asked Holsman to try to get medical marijuana for Missouri.

The man said he got some pot from his sister but didn't want to be a criminal. Holsman said he would try.

"He died a month later," Holsman said. "He was a fine gentleman of conservative values and (was) made out to be a criminal because he used marijuana to improve his appetite."

Now Holsman and others in the General Assembly are getting emails, some from parents of children who have seizures. These families say they will move to Colorado or another state with medical marijuana.

That's what Ryan and Kathy Reed of Baldwin City, Kan., are doing. With little chance of legislation anytime soon in that state, Ryan, a teacher, plans to move in May to Colorado with the couple's toddler son, Otis, who has as many as 300 seizures a day.

Kathy will stay and work at her job at the University of Kansas because the family needs insurance.

No medication available to Otis has worked. So his parents are hoping something called Charlotte's Web, a marijuana extract that has proved to be successful in the treatment of child seizures, will help their son. It's applied as drops under the tongue and has almost no THC.

Ryan wrote on a blog about Otis: "It (Charlotte's Web) is saving lives right now and should be available to children and adults who, like Otis, are out of options regardless of their ZIP code."

Around the country, families like the Reeds headed to Colorado are known as "medical marijuana refugees."

Gene and Dolores Halbin aren't likely to move to Colorado.

They're dug in. The woods around here are home, for themselves and their four dogs.

Life's not perfect. They think a relative turned them in. But they hadn't been in trouble and neighbors speak highly of them.

"When I saw a picture on a website of all the plants and lights, it was like they were really trying to make them out to be criminals," said Dana Robertson, a nurse who lives nearby. "I know what they did is illegal, but it wasn't anything malicious and they are great neighbors. She brings me strawberry jam."

The Halbins don't hold anything against the officers who came to their house.

"They were just doing their job," Dolores said.

"They were nice guys," Gene added.

Dolores makes clear, too, that she wasn't fired from her job at Bates County Memorial Hospital. She was allowed to resign.

"They were very nice about it," she said.

For now, Gene is back to treating his glaucoma with prescription eyedrops that he described as expensive and fairly ineffective.

"Oh, they help a little, I guess," he said. "But nothing like smoking a joint."

The Top 10 Studies of 2013 Proving the Medicinal Power of Cannabis

By Arjun Walia

Collective Evolution (CE), January 5, 2014

Just because a substance is illegal does not mean it is bad. In fact, many legal substances are responsible for a variety of ailments; prescription drugs alone are responsible for killing over 100,000 people each year. Cannabis was considered a harmful drug for many years despite the fact that scientific evidence to prove it is greatly lacking. All of the evidence points to this plant having great benefits for the human body. It's 2014 now, and more people are becoming aware of the fact that our body actually produces compounds called endocannabinoids, and they play an important role in many processes within the body that help to create a healthy environment. Cannabis activates the cannabinoid receptors in the body. It's important to note that the best method of ingestion is not through smoke, because this changes the chemical structure of the plant. Cannabis is a powerful key to good health when we eat it versus smoking it.

1. Cannabis May Grow Stem Cells and Repair the Brain after Injury.

A new study published in the journal *Biochemical Society Transactions* found that the brain's endocannabinoid system, which is activated through cannabis use, has neuroprotective and immunomodulatory capabilities which might lead to the growth of stem cells. This study coincides with [others], such as the study which demonstrated that cannabinoids improve the efficiency of mitochondria and remove damaged brain cells. Scientists discovered that cannabis may reduce brain damage caused by alcohol. There are many studies which show the potential benefits of cannabis on the brain. Not long ago, the very first human trials started to study the benefits of cannabis on brain cancer.

According to this study "activation of cannabinoid receptors suppresses chronic inflammatory responses through the attenuation of pro-inflammatory mediators." Moreover, the endocannabinoid system directs cell fat specification of the NSCs (neural stem cells) in the CNS (central nervous system). This study concluded that "the endocannabinoid system, which has neuroprotective and immunomodulatory actions mediated by IL-1 signalling cascades in the brain, and that this could assist the process of proliferation and differentiation of embryonic of adult NSC's, and this may be of therapeutic interest in the emerging field of brain repair."

2. THC May Treat Inflammatory Diseases and Cancer by Altering Genes

A new government funded study that was published in the *Journal of Biological Chemistry* has found that THC may actually alter certain genes in our body. This could result in a positive effect on a number of conditions, especially cancers and inflammatory diseases. Cannabis is currently used to help with the side effects of chemotherapy; there have also been a number of studies that confirm it can be an effective treatment and cure for multiple cancers.

In this study, researchers using rat models found that THC positively altered 13 different microRNAs, which are linked to inflammatory responses. As the study states, "select miRNA such as mir-690 targeting genes involved in myeloid expansion and differentiation likely play crucial roles in this process and therefore in cannabis-induced immunosuppression."

3. Cannabinoids Found to Reduce Skin Cancer in Just 20 Weeks

A new study published in the *Journal of Pharmacy and Pharmacology*, conducted by the Tokyo Metropolitan Institute of Public Health has found that cannabinoids can reduce skin cancer in just 20 weeks. In this study, researchers used the synthetic cannabinoids on mice with skin cancer in a 20 week study, and found that the cannabinoids had a very positive effect through "inhibiting tumor promotion." We do not support animal testing, and feel it is unnecessary, that it's time to move past all of this proof and just acknowledge cannabis as a natural medicine, if used correctly, with the correct intake method.

4. Cannabinoids May Be Helpful in Combating HIV

A new study published in the *Journal of Leukocyte Biology* indicates that the activation of the cannabinoid system may offer a means to limit HIV infection. The research was conducted by the Temple University School of medicine in Philadelphia. Researchers infected a type of white blood cell in our body that fights infections with the HIV virus, before exposing it to cannabis. After seven days against a control group, the results revealed a decrease in the rate of HIV infection, the blood cells became stronger at keeping the HIV virus out. "The synthetic compounds we used in our study may show promise in helping the body fight HIV infection. As compounds like these are improved further and made widely available, we will continue to explore their potential to fight other viral diseases that are notoriously difficult to treat."

5. THC Can Provide Protection from Cardiac Arrest

A new study that was released in the journal of *Biochemical Pharmacology* determined that even a small, "ultra low" does of THC before ischemia is a safe and effective treatment that "reduced myocardial ischemic damage." Basically, THC can provide protection from heart attacks, as well as reduce the potential cardiovascular damage associated with suffering one.

6. Cannabis Can Stop Seizures.

A new study published in the *British Journal of Pharmacology* has found that cannabis can stop seizures due to its "significant anticonvulsant effects." The findings of the study "strongly support the further clinical development of cannabis for the treatment of epilepsy." There are many examples of people who use cannabis for treatment to stop seizures. This isn't the only study that proves it, but it's the first one to study the effect of the entire cannabis plant.

7. Cannabis Combats Brain Degeneration and Increases Stamina

A new study published in *Philosophical Transactions of The Royal Society, B*, conducted at the institute of Molecular Psychiatry at the University of Bonn in Germany suggests that the activation of the brain's cannabinoid system triggers the release of antioxidants, which act as a cleansing mechanism, improving the efficiency of mitochondria and removing damaged brain cells. This is on par with the first study in this list, as well as many others.

8. Cannabinoids May Be the Best Medication for Those with PTSD

A new study published in the *Journal Molecular Psychiatry*, conducted by researchers at the New York University School of Medicine found a connection between the number of cannabinoid receptors in the brain and the effects of post traumatic stress disorder (PTSD). They used brain imaging to show that PTSD sufferers have lower concentrations of anandamide that the average person, these are endocannabinoids that bind to the CB1 receptors. Many people use marijuana to assist them with relaxation and stress.

9. Cannabis Can Treat Osteoarthritis

According to a new study published in the journal *PLOS One*, as well as the National Institute of Health found strong evidence that cannabis can treat osteoarthritis. "These data provide new clinically relevant evidence that joint damage and spinal CB2 receptor expression are correlated combined with converging preclinical evidence that activation of CB2 receptors inhibits central sensitization and its contribution to the manifestation of chronic OA pain." This study was funded by Arthritis Research U.K., as well as the National Institute of Health.

10. Cannabis May Prevent Organ Transplants from Being Rejected

A new study published in the journal *Biochemical Society Transactions*, and the *Journal of Neuroimmune Pharmacology* found that cannabis may prevent organs from being rejected during transplant, which usually leads to death.

These are 10 studies out of a very large amount that are available within the public domain. Cannabis is a gift from nature, it's an extremely powerful medicinal plant that has proven to be effective in treating a wide range of ailments. If you were unaware of this, hopefully these ten studies encourage you to further your research on the medicinal power of cannabis, which can no longer be denied.

Medical Use of Marijuana in Palliative Care

By Suzanne Johannigman and Valerie Eschiti
Clinical Journal of Oncology Nursing, August 2013

Marijuana has been documented to provide relief to patients in palliative care. How-ever, healthcare providers should use caution when discussing medical marijuana use with patients. This article features a case study that reveals the complexity of medical marijuana use. For oncology nurses to offer high-quality care, examining the pros and cons of medical marijuana use in the palliative care setting is important.

Historically, marijuana has been used as a natural remedy for various ailments. Ex-amining the pros and cons of the medical use of marijuana in the palliative care set-ting is important for oncology nurses and advanced practice nurses (APNs).

Marijuana History and Use

Cannabis, or marijuana, is an herb used by humans for centuries and is the most commonly used drug in the world (United Nations Office on Drugs and Crime [UNODC], 2011). Early prescribers for cannabis recommended eating the seeds for nutritional value and smoking the plant to relieve pain, vomiting, convulsions, and spasticity (Bostwick, 2012).

Studies have shown that delta-9 tetrahydrocannabinol (THC) is the principle psychoactive, or hallucinogenic, component in cannabis (UNODC, 2011). Smok-ing marijuana allows for maximum rapid absorption into the lungs, whereas oral ingestion provides erratic absorption (Green & de Vries, 2010). Once THC binds to cannabinoid receptors in the brain, side effects may include appetite stimulation, decreased anxiety, relief of nausea and vomiting, diminished spasticity, relief from pain (neurogenic in nature), and decreased intraocular pressure (Joffe & Yancy, 2004).

Cancer is a qualifying indication for medical marijuana use in states that have legalized it (Bowles, O'Bryant, Camidge, & Jimeno, 2012) (see Table 1). For oncol-ogy palliative care use, marijuana may control pain, increase appetite, and decrease nausea and vomiting. However, antiemetic guidelines do not support THC, syn-thetic or inhaled, as first-line therapy (Bowles et al., 2012).

Table 1: Legalized Medical Marijuana Use by State

State	Year Legalized
Alaska	1998
Arizona	2010
California	1996
Colorado	2000
Connecticut	2012
Delaware	2011
District of Columbia	2010
Hawaii	2000
Maine	1999
Massachusetts	2012
Michigan	2008
Montana	2004
Nevada	2000
New Jersey	2010
New Mexico	2007
Oregon	1998
Rhode Island	2006
Vermont	2004
Washington	1998

Note. Based on information from the National Conference of State Legislatures, 2013.

Marijuana and the Legal System

Prior to 1937, marijuana in the United States was frequently prescribed for an array of ailments. However, when cannabis was outlawed in 1937, marijuana began to be portrayed negatively (Millhorn et al., 2009). Since then, society has not fully accepted marijuana for medicinal use.

The Drug Enforcement Agency (DEA) continues to maintain a conservative stance on cannabis use, calling for it to be classified as a schedule I drug. Rescheduling it to a schedule II drug would reflect the "known medicinal value of marijuana while acknowledging the importance of proper medical supervision and accepting that more research is necessary into the side effects and possible dangers of medical marijuana use" (Rendall, 2012, p. 338).

Federal policy states cannabis possession is a criminal offense (DEA, 2011). The American Medical Association notes it would support marijuana rescheduling if doing so would facilitate research and development of cannabinoid-based medicine (Hoffman & Weber, 2010). Physicians and APNs may recommend marijuana use, but if officially prescribed or dispensed, practitioners may be federally charged with aiding and abetting (Hoffman & Weber, 2010). Rescheduling marijuana would enable oncology APNs to prescribe the drug, allowing for regulation and appropriate dispensing techniques.

Legal use of marijuana is a state-level decision. Because federal law prohibits possession of marijuana, patients who possess marijuana are still subject to federal criminal charges (Hoffmann & Weber, 2010). In the United States, 18 states and the District of Columbia have legalized marijuana so far (National Conference of State Legislatures, 2013). In those states, patients are allowed to use and possess small quantities of marijuana for medical purposes (Hoffman & Weber, 2010). State laws, however, do not regulate marijuana's quality or potency, and most do not address how to obtain the drug (Hoffman & Weber, 2010).

Millhorn et al. (2009) reported that public opinion regarding marijuana legalization was influenced by the current debate of how to use it medicinally. States with legalized marijuana use for medical purposes have a significantly higher rate of marijuana use, abuse, and dependence. Marijuana dependence has been doubted in the past; however, marijuana has a documented withdrawal syndrome that produces side effects similar to other drug withdrawal syndromes (Budney, Roffman, Stephens, & Walker, 2007). The National Institute on Drug Abuse (2011) also cites that long-term marijuana use leads to an addiction that interferes with family, school, work, and recreational activities. Often, symptoms of withdrawal include irritability, anger, depression, difficulty sleeping, craving, and decreased appetite (Budney et al., 2007). Many marijuana users cite these physiologic symptoms as the reason to continue using the drug (Budney et al., 2007). The symptoms begin 24–48 hours after the last inhalation, peak within 4–6 days, and may last up to 3 weeks (Budney et al., 2007).

Case Study

E.W., a 55-year-old woman residing in urban California, was diagnosed with ovarian cancer. At initial presentation to her primary care provider, she complained of diffuse, non-specific abdominal pain with intermittent constipation. Subsequent computed tomography scans showed a mass adjacent to the right ovary with metastatic mesenteric and hepatic lesions noted, as well as an extremely elevated cancer antigen (CA) 125 at 6,523. Normal range for the common ovarian cancer tumor marker, CA125, is laboratory site specific, but mostly noted to be below 25 units per ml (Alagoz et al., 1994). Therefore, E.W. was referred to a gynecologic oncology clinic for surgical and treatment options. After the initial surgical treatment, which consisted of a total abdominal hysterectomy with bilateral salpingo-oophorectomy, pathology revealed a high-grade ovarian clear cell carcinoma in an advanced state.

E.W. underwent eight cycles of taxane/carboplatin-based adjuvant chemotherapy with relatively no delays and only chemotherapy-induced nausea and vomiting

(CINV) as a major side effect. At the end of the initial therapy, E.W. was found to have persistent disease, with referral to an ongoing phase I clinical trial at the suggestion of her oncology APN. Per the clinical trial, E.W. had an experimental treatment once a week. Throughout her diagnosis and treatment, E.W. relied on many alternative therapies, including acupuncture, Reiki, massage, and herbal therapy (turmeric and green tea preparations).

E.W. experienced high levels of anxiety related to her weekly infusions, as well as frequent CINV episodes. She took many combinations of antiemetic medications, including 5-HT3, neurokinin-1 antagonists, corticosteroids, dopamine receptor antagonists, and benzodiazepines. At best, E.W. experienced moderate relief from unrelenting nausea. When E.W. inquired about use of medical marijuana, the APN referred E.W. to her oncologist, explaining that it must be a physician who formally recommends a patient for medical marijuana. Once the recommendation was obtained, E.W. was issued a patient registry card and legally obtained her medical marijuana through a local reputable dispensary known to assist patients in palliative care.

Support for Legalizing Medical Marijuana

Kleber and DuPont (2012) listed indications with maximum benefit achieved by smoking marijuana as CINV, cachexia, spasticity, pain, and relief from rheumatoid arthritis.

A national Gallup® poll revealed that 50% of Americans support cannabis legalization (Newport, 2011). Millhorn et al. (2009) reported an overall increase in positive attitudes toward allowing marijuana legalization in North America. Attempts to restrict cannabis for medical use have been expensive, ineffective, and usually counterproductive; therefore, proponents for decriminalizing cannabis for medical use argue that fiscal resources would be conserved (Wodak, Reinarman, Cohen, & Drummond, 2002).

Opposition to Legalizing Medical Marijuana

No U.S. Food and Drug Administration (FDA)-approved medication is administered by smoking, which is the most effective route of administration (Kleber & DuPont, 2012). Smoking of any substance has been linked to lung cancer, which carries the highest mortality rate of any cancer type in the United States (Weiss, 2008).

Decriminalizing or legalizing marijuana could result in advertisement for its use, some of which may be directed to youth (Joffe & Yancy, 2004). Control measures to prevent youth advertising may be difficult to implement. Legalization could decrease adolescents' perceptions of the risks of marijuana, causing a negative effect (Joffe & Yancy, 2004).

Another concern regarding legalization is dependence; 9% of users may become dependent (Kleber & DuPont, 2012). In efforts to sidestep potentially harmful effects of smoking marijuana, pharmaceutical companies have attempted to develop drugs that can be taken by other routes that target cannabinoid receptors in the brain. Only two options are currently available in the United States, dronabinol and nabilone, synthetic THC that target the cannabinoid receptor in the brain (Bostwick, 2012). However, their use is strictly limited by the narrow gap between effective therapeutic dosage and adverse effects such as euphoria, cognitive clouding, and drowsiness (Bostwick, 2012).

Implications for Practice

Oncology APNs must be aware of laws regarding marijuana use in regard to malpractice or liability issues (Kleber & Du.Pont, 2012). Therefore, APNs may clearly explain to patients that medical marijuana is not approved by the FDA, nor is it a standardized product; however, they may refer patients to proper marijuana dispensaries as appropriate after recommendation by an oncologist (Kleber & DuPont, 2012).

When managing patients who use medical marijuana, de Vries and Green (2012) listed five key points the APN must be aware of:

- Be well-informed about current research regarding all pharmaceuticals.

- Educate patients on the physical and psychological effects of medical marijuana, and how to interact with legally prescribed medications.

- Document medical marijuana use as reported by the patient as well as reported effects.

- Educate the patient on state and federal penalties regarding medical marijuana.

- Do not supply, fund, obtain, or in any other way prepare medical marijuana for patient consumption.

Conclusion

Although used safely throughout history, marijuana remains illegal under current federal law. Therapeutic effects of THC are sought by patients with cancer receiving palliative care. For patients with cancer to use marijuana, it must be decriminalized at the state level. Opponents cite smoking risks and potential abuse by teens as primary concerns. As evidenced in the case study presentation, oncology nurses must recognize liability risks as well as potential benefits of medical marijuana use in patients with cancer receiving palliative care.

Bibliography

Alagoz, T., Buller, R., Berman, M., Anderson, B., Manetta, A., & DiSaia, P. (1994). What is a normal CA125 level? *Gynecologic Oncology, 53*, 93–97.

Bostwick, J. M. (2012). Blurred boundaries: The therapeutics and politics of medical marijuana. *Mayo Clinic Proceedings, 87*, 172–186.

Bowles, D. W., O'Bryant, C. L., Camidge, D. R., & Jimeno, A. (2012). The intersection between cannabis and cancer in the United States. *Critical Reviews in Oncology/ Hematology, 83*, 1–10.

Budney, A., Roffman, R., Stephens, R., & Walker, D. (2007). Marijuana dependence and its treatment. *Addiction Science and Clinical Practice*, 4(1), 4–16.

de Vries, K., & Green, A. J. (2012). Therapeutic use of cannabis. *Nursing Times*, 108(9), 12–15.

Drug Enforcement Agency. (2011). *The DEA position on marijuana*. Retrieved from http://www.justice.gov/dea/docs/ marijuana_position_2011.pdf

Green, A. J., & de Vries, K. (2010). Cannabis use in palliative care—An examination of the evidence and the implications for nurses. *Journal of Clinical Nursing*, 19, 2454–2462.

Hoffmann, D. E., & Weber, E. (2010). Medical marijuana and the law. *New England Journal of Medicine*, 362, 1453–1457.

Joffe, A., & Yancy, W. S. (2004). Technical report. Legalization of marijuana: Potential impact on youth. *Pediatrics*, 113, e632–e638. doi:10.1542/peds.113.6.e632

Kleber, H. D., & DuPont, R. L. (2012). Physicians and medical marijuana. *American Journal of Psychiatry*, 169, 564–568.

Millhorn, M., Monaghan, M., Montero, D., Reyes, M., Roman, T., Tollasken, R., & Walls, B. (2009). North Americans' attitudes toward illegal drugs. *Journal of Human Behavior in the Social Environment*, 19, 125–141.

National Conference of State Legislatures. (2013). State medical marijuana laws. Retrieved from http://www.ncsl.org/ issues-research/health/state-medical -marijuana-laws.aspx

National Institute on Drug Abuse. (2011). *Topics in brief: Marijuana*. Retrieved from http://www.drugabuse.gov/sites/ default/files/marijuana_3.pdf

Newport, F. (2011). Record-high 50% of Americans favor legalizing marijuana use. Retrieved from http://www.gallup .com/poll/150149/record-high-americans-favor-legalizing-marijuana.aspx

Rendall, R. (2012). Medical marijuana and the ADA: Removing barriers to employment for disabled individuals. *Health Matrix*, 22, 315–343.

United Nations Office on Drugs and Crime. (2011). *World drug report 2011*. Retrieved from http://www.unodc.org/documents/ data-and-analysis/WDR2011/World_ Drug_Report_2011_ebook.pdf

Weiss, P. A. (2008). Does smoking marijuana contribute to the risk of developing lung cancer? *Clinical Journal of Oncology Nursing*, 12, 517–518.

Wodak, A., Reinarman, C., Cohen, P. D., & Drummond, C. (2002). Cannabis control: Costs outweigh the benefits. *BMJ*, 324, 105–108. doi:10.1136/bmj.324.7329.105

A Boost for Medical Marijuana?

By Leonie Welberg
Nature Reviews Neuroscience, January 2014

Marijuana is used to treat pain and other clinical conditions, but its use can lead to unwanted side effects, including cognitive impairment. A study in *Cell* now shows that marijuana use increases cyclooxygenase 2 (COX2; also known as PTGS2) signalling in the hippocampus and that this effect is linked to memory impairment, suggesting that COX2 inhibitors may enhance the medical utility of marijuana by reducing its side effects.

The main psychoactive ingredient of marijuana is Δ^9-tetrahydrocannabinol (Δ^9-THC), and Chen *et al.* set out to identify the mechanisms by which it impairs memory function. They focused on COX2 as a potential mediator because the endocannabinoid 2-arachidonyl-glycerol (2-AG) has been shown to inhibit COX2 signalling. The authors were therefore surprised to find that repeated intraperitoneal injections of Δ^9-THC in mice caused a sustained increase in hippocampal levels of COX2 and its product prostaglandin E2 (PGE2). Administration of a COX2 inhibitor prevented the Δ^9-THC-induced increase in PGE2 levels. Moreover, they showed that the contrasting effects of Δ^9-THC and 2-AG on COX2 activity both involve the $G_{i/o}$ protein-coupled cannabinoid1 receptor (CB1R) but that different G protein subunits mediate these opposing effects: specifically, $G\beta\gamma$ subunits mediate the effect of Δ^9-THC, and the $G\alpha_i$ subunit that of 2-AG.

As shown previously, daily injections with Δ^9-THC reduced both hippocampal long-term potentiation and performance on hippocampus-dependent memory tasks in mice. These effects were prevented by concurrent administration of a COX2 inhibitor and did not occur in transgenic mice lacking COX2. Δ^9-THC injections also caused morphological changes in the hippocampus that have been associated with such impairments in synaptic plasticity and memory, including a reduced density of dendritic mushroom spines containing AMPA and NMDA receptors in CA1 neurons. Moreover, Δ^9-THC decreased the expression of the postsynaptic scaffolding protein PSD95 (also known as DLG4) and the expression of several synaptic and extrasynaptic glutamate receptor subunits. Administration of a COX2 inhibitor prevented all of these effects.

To determine whether administration of a COX2 inhibitor interferes with any of the medically beneficial effects of marijuana, the authors examined a transgenic mouse model of Alzheimer's disease. They found that daily Δ^9-THC injections for 4 weeks reduced levels of both amyloid-β and neurode-generation (by increasing levels of the enzyme neprilysin, which can degrade amyloid-β), regardless of whether the injections were accompanied by administration of a COX2 inhibitor. This suggests that COX2 inhibition does not affect this particular beneficial effect of Δ^9-THC.

Together, these findings point to the possibility that COX2 inhibitors, including widely available non-steroidal anti-inflammatory drugs such as ibuprofen, could be used to prevent at least some of the unwanted side effects of the marijuana component Δ^9-THC without impairing its beneficial properties.

Bibliography

Chen, R. *et al.* Δ^9-THC-caused synaptic and memory impairments are mediated through COX-2 signaling. *Cell* 155, 1154–1165 (2013).

Is Pot Getting More Potent?

By William Brangham
PBS NewsHour, April 2, 2014

The average potency of pot has more than tripled in the past two decades, according to testing done for the federal government. This comes just over a year after Colorado and Washington legalized the drug and as many other states consider making it legal for medical or recreational use.

Scientists determine potency by measuring levels of THC, or delta-9-tetrahydrocannabinol, the main psychoactive ingredient that gives marijuana its "high." And data from the University of Mississippi's Potency Monitoring program found that the average potency of marijuana has jumped from 3.4 percent THC in 1993 to 12.3 percent THC in 2012. Scientists at the lab say they've seen samples as high as 36 percent.

This month's *High Times* magazine, with a cover promoting "The Strongest Strains on Earth," claims to have analyzed 15 strains of pot with potencies ranging between 25 to 28 percent THC. Marijuana near that strength can be bought at many legal retail shops and medical dispensaries across the U.S.

A quick bit of botany: The two main species of the Cannabis plant, Cannabis indica and Cannibas sativa, produce different kinds of highs. Most varieties of pot sold today are hybrids of both. Effects of either can include "altered perceptions and mood, impaired coordination, difficulty with thinking and problem solving, and disrupted learning and memory," according to the National Institute on Drug Abuse. Newer strains of marijuana have different effects than those of the 1970s and 1980s, when THC averaged roughly 3 percent.

Indica is described as having a calming, relaxing, and narcotic effect, while sativa is said to have a more uplifting, stimulating, or "cerebral" effect.

Increasing the potency of the THC in marijuana plants means an increasing intensity of those effects.

So what explains the rise in potency? Consumer demand is clearly one driver.

"I see people walk in all the time saying, 'Give me the strongest thing you have,'" says Tim Cullen, co-owner of Evergreen Apothecary, which runs two retail marijuana stores in Colorado. "It's bizarre. . . . Can you imagine being in a liquor store and having someone say, 'Just give me your strongest stuff?' But for now, that's what a lot of people seem to want."

And marijuana growers have clearly been working to meet the demand. Robert MacCoun, a behavioral scientist at U.C. Berkeley who has studied drug policy here and abroad, calls it an "arms race," in which growers strive to create the highest-octane varieties, and then bestow awards on themselves at the annual Cannabis Cup competition.

"The unfortunate aspect of this arms race is that they're finally turning the drug into everything the U.S. government once said it was," MacCoun says. "It used to be we could say the government exaggerated the threat of this 'crazy weed,' but these new potent strains belie that."

Others say the U.S. government's war on drugs has had the unintended effect of driving up potency.

"This is a problem of our drug policies, not a problem of the drug," says Julie Holland, a psychiatrist, drug researcher, and editor of *The Pot Book: A Complete Guide to Cannabis*. Because marijuana is still considered illegal by the federal government, she says, growers and sellers have an incentive to pack more potency into a smaller volume. And that's a problem, she adds: "Because it's illegal, you have no idea what you're getting. If it were legal and could be taxed and regulated, it would be safer."

While many consider pot far less harmful than legal drugs like tobacco and alcohol, it can pose risks to adolescents, pregnant women, and those with the potential for certain mental disorders like schizophrenia, according to the National Institute on Drug Abuse.

NIDA Director Dr. Nora Volkow believes higher potencies may exacerbate some of marijuana's harms, triggering more feelings of paranoia and panic attacks in certain users.

"You become paranoid, you think that people are persecuting you and you get very, very anxious and you end up in the emergency room," Dr. Volkow says. "[But] that usually resolves pretty rapidly."

Of greater concern, says Volkow, is rising admissions to drug treatment programs where marijuana is cited as the main problem. This too she attributes to the drug's potency.

"There really hasn't been an increase in the number of people smoking marijuana," Dr. Volkow says. "What has changed is the potency of the marijuana that individuals are exposed to."

Critics of this argument, like the Drug Policy Alliance, argue that the growing number of treatment admissions have nothing to do with potency, and are instead a by-product of the war on drugs where those arrested for marijuana possession are diverted into treatment by the courts. The Alliance writes: "increasing admissions for treatment are a reflection of the criminal justice system's predominant role, rather than increasing rates of clinical dependence."

As to whether higher potency mean it's more addictive, that's unclear.

NIDA states that 9 percent of people who are exposed to marijuana will become addicted to it. While that's a much lower rate than that of drugs like cocaine, which has a 17 percent addiction rate, or heroin at 23 percent, Dr. Volkow believes that more potency may be linked to higher addiction rates, though she admits there's no good evidence connecting the two.

"[It's] indirect evidence that there may be a linkage between the potency and its addictiveness," she says.

A recent small study conducted in the Netherlands indicates that the way a user smokes marijuana—how frequently they take puffs, and how much of a cigarette they consume—might be a better predictor of marijuana dependence than potency, though these results haven't been replicated elsewhere.

"What you worry about with dependence is, what does it look like if you abruptly stop?" Holland says. And withdrawing from marijuana, she says, is not nearly as difficult, or dangerous, as withdrawing from heroin or alcohol. "Abrupt cessation of alcohol is potentially lethal. Abrupt cessation of cannabis? . . . If you use pot every night to put yourself to sleep and then you don't have any pot, then you may have trouble falling asleep. If you use pot every day to treat your nausea or your pain and you don't have any pot, you're going to be nauseous and in pain."

But if marijuana is stronger, won't users just consume less of it?

That's what Columbia University neuroscientist Carl Hart says he's documented in his work. Hart (also an author who has been critical of U.S. drug policy) has performed numerous cognitive experiments with marijuana. He believes that when experienced users are given stronger pot, they simply smoke less.

Hart says when marijuana is smoked, the drug's effects are felt almost immediately, so users know when they've had enough. When test subjects in his lab are given marijuana cigarettes with relatively low THC levels, they'll smoke the entire cigarette. "But when you increase the THC, half the cigarette comes back," says Hart. "They don't smoke it all."

In fact, Hart believes there might even be a health benefit to stronger marijuana. "If you inhale less, it might reduce toxicity in the lungs," he says.

But Volkow says not all users are able to 'titrate'—or modulate—their intake. "If you are a regular user and an expert on how you're expected to feel with marijuana, you may be able to titrate," she says. "But if you are not such an expert, how are you going to?"

Plus, modulating your intake of THC is also much harder if you're eating rather than smoking it.

In Colorado, where retail shops have been selling legal pot for several months, edible marijuana products have become hugely popular. In these 'edibles'—which can feature marijuana-laced cookies or chocolates or gum drops—the entire dose of THC is contained in just a few bites, and when eaten, the drug's effects take longer to register on the user. So even though it's virtually impossible to overdose on marijuana, someone eating THC could end up consuming far more of the drug than intended.

In fact, a recent investigation by the *Denver Post* found "blatant misstatements" about the actual levels of THC in a range of edible products being sold presently in Colorado. Many of the products were far weaker than their labels claimed, but alarmingly, several of the products had THC levels almost 50 percent higher than advertised.

4

Marijuana Reclassification:
The Next Debate

Lt. Kevin Stevens shows off 47 seized marijuana plants in the bed of a pickup truck in Saginaw, Michigan. Deputies seized the plants, worth about $23,000, from fields during a marijuana eradication operation.

The Reclassification Quagmire

Under US federal law, it is a crime to grow, sell, or possess marijuana. However, as of August 2014, nearly half of US states have legalized marijuana for medical use. Several more states have decriminalized marijuana for recreational purposes, and two, Colorado and Washington, have legalized it altogether. This discrepancy between federal and state law creates a confusing and politically charged landscape for marijuana law enforcement. One significant issue in the legalization debate is whether federal law should change to permit medical marijuana use, or if states should be allowed to legalize medical marijuana within their own borders. At the heart of that debate is whether marijuana has any legitimate medical use, and whether it can be prescribed in a safe, consistent manner.

The Controlled Substances Act

One of the main documents controlling federal drug policy in the United States is the Comprehensive Drug Abuse Prevention and Control Act of 1970, commonly called the Controlled Substances Act. The act places certain drugs into "schedules" based on their physical and psychological dangers, likelihood of addiction, and usefulness for medical purposes. How a drug is regulated depends on the schedule in which the drug is placed. For example, Schedule I drugs are those which have a high potential for abuse and no currently accepted medical use in the United States. This includes heroin, LSD, and ecstasy. These drugs are always illegal to sell and possess. Schedule II includes drugs that have a high potential for abuse but known medical applications. This includes narcotic drugs such as Oxycontin and amphetamines such as Adderall. These drugs can be legally prescribed by doctors and used under medical supervision, but their production is regulated by the government. Schedules III, IV, and V are for progressively smaller risks of addiction, and have correspondingly lower levels of regulation.

As of 2014, marijuana is classified under Schedule I, as it has been since the law was passed, despite the lack of evidence of high potential for abuse, and despite studies that suggest it has valid medical applications. As a result, it is a federal criminal offense to possess or sell marijuana, even in states where its use has been decriminalized or legalized. This creates a challenging situation: while most states have drug laws that mirror the federal prohibitions against marijuana, some states address issues of trafficking and abuse through regulation rather than prohibition. Section 873 of the act states that the attorney general must "cooperate with local, State, tribal and Federal agencies concerning traffic in controlled substances and in suppressing the abuse of controlled substances." However, lawmakers debate whether this language requires the federal government to respect the laws of states that decriminalize marijuana use, or whether the federal government can continue to enforce criminal penalties if it believes that state regulations are insufficient to control drug trafficking and substance abuse.

Resolving State and Federal Laws

This debate is vital as more states pass laws that conflict with the federal prohibition. In the 2009 Ogden Memo, the US Justice Department, Attorney General Eric Holder, and Deputy Attorney General David W. Ogden stated that, while enforcement of federal drug laws is important, it is "unlikely to be an efficient use of limited federal resources" to prosecute "individuals with cancer or other serious illnesses who use marijuana as part of a recommended treatment regimen consistent with applicable state law, or those caregivers in clear and unambiguous compliance with existing state law who provide such individuals with marijuana." While the memo did not legalize medical marijuana use, it recommended to other attorneys general that seeking out, prosecuting, and incarcerating individuals who use small amounts of marijuana for medical purposes in compliance with state laws should not be the focus of law enforcement efforts. Instead, it notes that "prosecution of commercial enterprises that unlawfully market and sell marijuana for profit continues to be an enforcement priority of the Department."

The memo received mixed reviews: some welcomed it as an important step toward recognizing the legitimacy of medical marijuana use, and a victory for states' rights to create and enforce their own laws. Others criticized it for circumventing the legislative process and encouraging inconsistent enforcement of federal law. In either case, it marked a significant departure from enforcement policies under the administration of President George W. Bush, where the Drug Enforcement Administration (DEA) authorized raids on medical marijuana dispensaries even when they appeared to be in compliance with state laws.

However, the enforcement landscape has not changed significantly under the administration of President Barack Obama, despite the memo's apparent assurance to the contrary. According to Kris Hermes, a spokesperson for the pro-legalization advocacy group Americans for Safe Access, the number of marijuana dispensaries doubled from about 1,000 to somewhere between 2,000 and 2,500 between 2009 and 2013. During this same period, hundreds of dispensaries were raided by federal law enforcement officers, while banks and landlords who do business with dispensaries were allegedly targeted by the Internal Revenue Service. Some dispensary owners argued entrapment, saying they opened their businesses legally under state law because the Ogden Memo said they would not be prosecuted; they felt the federal government published the memo to entice people to open dispensaries, just so they could conduct more raids. But others, including the DEA, note that the memo is not law: selling marijuana remains a federal offense, and the Justice Department's suggestion not to prioritize the prosecution of medical marijuana users does not change its illegality under federal law.

Additionally, federal agencies—including the Justice Department, the DEA, and the National Institute on Drug Abuse (NIDA)—disagree about enforcement strategies. This leads to further inconsistency, and accusations that agencies intentionally time raids to achieve political gains. For example, federal agents raided Montana dispensaries in March 2011, shortly before the state legislature was scheduled to vote on the future of its medical marijuana laws. The images of drugs and guns that flooded the nightly news made medical marijuana use appear dangerous and criminal, despite being legal under state law, and swayed the legislature to repeal the legalization. Governor Brian Schweitzer vetoed the repeal, but the law that eventually passed was more restrictive than the original law, and did not permit dispensaries.

In April 2013, Republican representative Dana Rohrbacher of California introduced the bipartisan Respect State Marijuana Laws Act, designed to protect medical and recreational marijuana users from federal prosecution in states that legalized or decriminalized the drug. However, as of August 2014, the bill remains languishing in the House Subcommittee on Crime, Terrorism, Homeland Security, and Investigations. California was one of the first states to legalize medical marijuana, and Rohrbacher previously sponsored legislation to have marijuana reclassified as a drug with accepted medical uses.

Reclassifying

Reclassification of marijuana from a Schedule 1 controlled substance to at least Schedule II or III is a key step in changing federal drug policy. However, this is a complicated process. A drug cannot be classified under Schedule II or III until research studies fully identify its potential health effects—both helpful and harmful—and establish safe, effective doses for its use in medical treatment. However, there are several challenges to conducting marijuana research. One persistent challenge is that, because marijuana is a plant that can be grown in many settings, its production is not regulated. A drug manufactured according to specifications by a pharmaceutical company can be tested for effectiveness and potential dangers, and classified accordingly. This is complicated in the case of marijuana because, while many agree that its chemical compounds—including delta-9 tetrahydrocannabinol (9-THC) and cannabidiol (CBD) – have medicinal value, there are numerous different strains of the plant. These strains do not have identical chemical makeup, and there is no regulated dosage or method of administration to test for safety and efficacy. As a result, it is difficult to perform the kind of highly regulated clinical testing required by the federal Food and Drug Administration (FDA) to prove that a drug has a low potential for abuse and valid medical use.

Additionally, while marijuana remains classified as Schedule I, it is extremely difficult for teams to obtain legally sufficient quantities to be able to conduct the necessary research. This is made even more difficult because the University of Mississippi has a monopoly on the production of marijuana that can be used for FDA-approved research. While this does help ensure that the research results are experimentally valid (since all studies are conducted on the same strain of marijuana, with the same chemical properties), researchers argue that it gives the federal government too much control over which studies are allowed to proceed. Research projects must obtain clearance to study marijuana, and then make a special application to the DEA and NIDA in order to receive several grams of the drug. This requirement does not apply to any other controlled substance and is widely criticized, in part because more than 90 percent of federally approved projects study the potential harms of marijuana, while fewer than 10 percent study its potential medical applications.

Medical Use Exceptions

Legalization advocates are split between those who support full legalization regardless of use, and those who support medical use exceptions only. Several research studies and much anecdotal evidence exists to show that marijuana can help individuals who suffer from serious medical ailments control pain, stimulate appetite, and reduce nausea. But in states where medical marijuana use is permitted, the approval processes required to obtain clearance for lawful possession are often criticized for being highly subjective.

For example, most states require that medical marijuana be administered by a medical professional or other licensed caregiver. But this raises questions about who qualifies as a caregiver, and what role these caregivers play in who receives medical marijuana and how much. Due to the lack of medical studies and the widely varied content of active ingredients such as THC and CBD in any given plant, it is difficult to determine the appropriate dosage of marijuana for any given ailment.

Additionally, the ailments most likely to be helped by medical marijuana use, such as chronic pain, cannot be objectively tested. As a result, recreational users can obtain medical marijuana licenses with relative ease. For example, Colorado estimates that only about 20 percent of marijuana sales made under its medical use laws are to individuals who have a legitimate medical condition. To combat this, some places, such as Washington, DC, removed chronic pain from the list of ailments that qualify for medical marijuana use. Unfortunately, this rules out a potentially valuable treatment option for many individuals. Advocates such as Allen St. Pierre, the executive director of the National Organization for the Reform of Marijuana Laws (NORML), question the intellectual honesty of making these types of subjective medical judgments subject to federal regulation, and believes that limiting access in this way can cause further stress and harm to the individuals that the exceptions are meant to be helping.

Conclusion

Unfortunately, the potential reclassification of marijuana is caught in a legal quagmire. It is unlikely to be reclassified from Schedule I to a less-restrictive Schedule II or III until research studies can prove legitimate medical uses, and safe and effective doses can be determined. However, until it is reclassified, it will be difficult for research groups to obtain enough marijuana from the federal government's repository to conduct the necessary FDA-approved studies. And while the federal government retains the authority to grant or deny access to the drug, the approved studies risk reflecting the federal government's agenda on drug policy, rather than the needs and will of the public.

—Tracey M. DiLascio

Bibliography

Halper, Evan. "Mississippi, Home to the Federal Government's Official Stash of Marijuana." *Los Angeles Times*. Los Angeles Times, 28 May 2014. Web. 15 Aug. 2014.

"H.R. 1523—Respect State Marijuana Laws Act of 2013." *Congress.gov*. Lib. of Cong., 2013. Web. 15 Aug. 2014.

Kleiman, Mark A. "Confused about Pot? So's the Law." *Bloomberg View*. Bloomberg, 14 Feb. 2014. Web. 15 Aug. 2014.

Leon, Harmon. "Pot Block! Trapped in the Marijuana Rescheduling Maze." *Nation*. Nation, 30 Oct. 2013. Web. 15 Aug. 2014.

Ogden, David W. "Memorandum for Selected United States Attorneys." *Justice Blog*. US Dept. of Justice, 19 Oct. 2009. Web. 15 Aug. 2014.

Reilly, Ryan J. "Obama's Drug War: After Medical Marijuana Mess, Feds Face Big Decision on Pot." *Huffington Post*. TheHuffingtonPost.com, 8 Feb. 2013. Web. 15 Aug. 2014.

Stout, David, and Solomon Moore. "US Won't Prosecute in States That Allow Medical Marijuana." *New York Times*. New York Times, 19 Oct. 2009. Web. 15 Aug. 2014.

Sullum, Jacob. "When Holder Says Congress Can Reclassify Marijuana if It Wants, Is He Taking a 'Big Step' toward Legalization?" *Reason*. Reason Foundation, 7 Apr 2014. Web. 15 Aug. 2014.

The Politics of Cannabis Psychosis

By Jason Reed
The Huffington Post, July 17, 2013

It has become an indelible etching on the national psyche; cannabis and psychosis dovetail like fish and chips. The impact of cannabis on the mind has been well documented in the British press, but it remains an unfortunate muddle as the link is as far from clear as one is led to believe.

In a recently published time series analysis, The Effect of Reclassification of cannabis on hospital admissions for cannabis psychosis, the relationship between laws and mental health have been assessed with the data analyzed from 1999 through 2010. The Gordon Brown Labour government used the emerging concerns of cannabis related psychosis as ardent justification to reclassify cannabis from Class C to a stricter Class B. This move was firmly against the ACMD's advice and gave rise to the now infamous incident that saw Professor David Nutt, the then Chair of the ACMD, lose his position. It's also noteworthy that a similar situation has occurred in recent weeks with the arbitrary banning of khat; once again this decision was made by the Home Secretary without the backing of the ACMD's advice or evidence.

Cannabis was downgraded to Class C in 2004 under Tony Blair, it was then put back to Class B in 2009. So what can we learn from the psychosis related hospital admissions during this time? Logic would tell us that an appropriate impact would have been made, but surprisingly, cannabis psychosis actually fell when it was Class C, and had no impact when it was in Class B. On one hand, this is widely in keeping with the projections made by those in criminology and science, but the reduction under Class C was unexpected. The new findings quickly went viral. Alex Stevens, Professor of Criminal Justice at the University of Kent, said "Told you so—that the move up to Class B would not reduce psychosis." But Professor Stevens was: "Surprised that it was followed by a reduction."

The debate around harsher laws and how they relate to proposed reductions in substance harms has raged for some time. The complex relationship of drug harms from a socio-economic view versus a pharmacological standpoint is an area in much need of a discussion, it should be free from emotional investment, and based on hard empirical evidence: *there is no evidence to support the logic underpinning the 2009 move to Class B*.

The relationship between our daily lives and mental health is clearly as complex as the very essence of life itself. Professor Robin Murray has worked in the field of cannabis and mental health and is quite clear that he has changed his mind on the issue of schizophrenia on many occasions. He also points out the ingrained complexity of environmental factors. For example, you are 6 times more likely to suffer psychotic episodes if you're a migrant, and the increase risk to mental health is far greater if you live in a city, and the risk increases to the size of the city you live in. What this can tell us is that set and setting are paramount to our mental well-being, so it's not a big leap to explore the possibilities of how law enforcement and classifications of substances affect the mental health of their users. A paper by Dr. Richard Bunce also delves into this realm: "Social and Political Sources of Drug Effects: The Case of Bad Trips on Psychedelics."

For many years, there has been the necessitous disclaimer of *correlation is not causation* and this needs firm reiteration whenever we teeter on the wire of substance harms and their pharmacology. In a recent talk for *Reason TV*, neuropsychopharmacologist Dr. Carl Hart made the eminent case for evidence over perception. Using the example of crystal meth, he found that the harms that society projects often don't live up to the pharmacological realities; popular myths and folklore on drug harms are ever circular, and as a result education is the true casualty.

Fellow neuropsychopharmacologist Professor David Nutt, has written what is perhaps the definitive book on drug education: *Drugs Without the Hot Air*. This must-have book for parents and teachers gives a non-excluding summary on the evidence of drug harms. Professor Nutt's previous work within the ACMD showed that to stop one case of cannabis related psychosis we need to prevent 5000 young men from using the substance, and 7000 young women. The risk remains statistically very low, but of course worthy of concern.

The hyperbolic version of events would lead us to believe that just one cannabis joint can irreparably damage the brain. The *Daily Mail* has actually won awards for the misinterpretation of drug science and their willful projection of myth. A rather brilliant analysis of the somewhat infamous "Just ONE cannabis joint 'can bring on schizophrenia' as well as damaging memory" can be found on the Neurobonkers site. A catastrophic amount of errors were found in the *Daily Mail*'s report, and with a rather lethargic, begrudging correction subsequently following. Consequently, The *Daily Mail* won the Orwellian Prize for Journalistic Misrepresentation, a prize founded by Oxford University neuroscientist, Professor Dorothy Bishop.

We need to ask ourselves: does the risk of cannabis related psychosis give us enough reason to arrest and punish by law? Professor David Nutt goes on to say in his book: a prisoner is 10 times more likely than the general population to commit suicide, and around 40% of men and 60% of women will have some form of neurotic disorder. It's quite apparent that our drug laws are not making much sense, and they certainly don't correspond to the nuanced subject of mental health. Our drug laws are designed to protect society from potential harms but are actually predicating just as many by placing them under the control of law enforcement and punishment. The debate needs to be had on how best to minimize *all* harms of *all* drugs. If the law and socio-economic factors are playing a part in those harms, then we need to appropriately address and reform as we're mandated to do. What we don't need is a bolstering of political rhetoric; we must allow the evidence to lead our policy makers.

Pot Block! Trapped in the Marijuana Rescheduling Maze

By Harmon Leon
The Nation, October 30, 2013

Under the Controlled Substances Act, marijuana is classified as a Schedule 1 drug in America. According to the Drug Enforcement Administration, *Cannabis sativa* is as dangerous as heroin. (You know . . . as in *heroin*!) To justify this ranking, the DEA has declared that the plant has absolutely no medical value. Zero. Nada. Zip. The federal government has determined that this position is backed by science.

Marijuana's current status as *one of the most dangerous drugs in America* became official in 1970, during the Nixon administration. (Putting matters in ludicrous perspective, cocaine and even *Breaking Bad* meth are Schedule II.) Every administration since then has treated marijuana as mad, bad and dangerous to know, with virtually no attempt made to reclassify it. And that list includes the current one.

"It's a bit of an *Alice in Wonderland* scenario with the Obama administration," explains Kris Hermes of Americans for Safe Access (ASA). "He made statements prior to being elected about changing the policy on marijuana, but in reality the opposite has happened."

Not only have there been more medical marijuana arrests during Obama's administration than the entire Bush regime, but even in states like California and Washington, there's been a steady rise in the number of people being raided even though they're in full compliance with state law. The federal government has threatened landlords and financial institutions working with medical marijuana businesses; the IRS has been involved with audits; pro-pot lawmakers have been bullied; and veterans using marijuana for conditions like post-traumatic stress disorder have been denied medical benefits by the Veterans Administration—all because of marijuana's Schedule I status.

On the other hand, dropping pot down a notch to Schedule II (let alone III, IV or V, or removing it from the Controlled Substances Act completely) would be a big step in resolving the clash between state and federal law, since such a move would at least acknowledge marijuana's medical utility and allow doctors to legally prescribe it.

So what can be done to reschedule marijuana in a country where the "drug czar" is required by law to *oppose* any attempt to legalize the use of a Schedule I substance—in any form?

Time to put on our trusty journalist-provocateur's hat and go through the looking glass into the bizarre legal labyrinth of the rescheduling process. Kris Hermes warned that it wouldn't be easy: "Bureaucrats shut down and refuse to talk when it's convenient for them not to talk . . . when it suits their purpose!"

I Contact the DEA

Phoning the DEA is an unnerving experience—a sensation similar to being in high school and calling your dad at 2 a.m. to inform him that you've crashed the family car (though now safe in the knowledge that the NSA will keep tabs on me).

I get a DEA representative on the phone. He goes by the name Rusty. (Perhaps because of his employer's corroded views on ending the drug war?)

"Could I get any information regarding the rescheduling of medical marijuana?"

"I don't want to spark a debate," Rusty from the DEA replies. "I don't know if that's something we'd weigh in on. I don't know what the point would be—our stance is pretty much on our website."

Rusty from the DEA informs me that the agency's position on medical marijuana can be found under the tab astutely labeled "The Dangers and Consequences of Marijuana Abuse." (The thirty-page PDF reads like some bureaucrat's idea for a remake of *Reefer Madness*.)

The key words in this manifesto: *dangers, consequences, abuse*. That doesn't seem to indicate much willingness to consider pot's medical value. Apparently, the DEA is still convinced that cancer victims are merely "abusing" marijuana to alleviate their chemotherapy-induced vomiting and nausea.

Rusty from the DEA adds: "You know, Congress can change this at any point—which people seem to forget."

Perfect. That would be the same body that recently shut down the federal government and threatened the United States with default. But while the DEA might say that rescheduling is up to Congress, according to the ASA, that's not exactly the case. The DEA actually delays the process—with no time limit imposed for answering rescheduling petitions, the agency takes the longest possible time before reaching a decision. (And then it says no.) To get around to denying the ASA's rescheduling petition, it took the federal government a whopping *nine years*.

I Contact the FDA

According to a memorandum of understanding between the DEA and the Food and Drug Administration, a rescheduling petition has to go through the FDA. (Despite the fact that the DEA is under no obligation to recognize the conclusions of that agency.) Meanwhile, roughly every nineteen minutes, an American dies of accidental prescription-drug overdose—and these are pills approved by the FDA. ("Approved!") Since the big pharmaceutical companies can't make money off homegrown medical marijuana, might that be swaying the FDA's recommendation?

"Can I ask a few questions about the rescheduling of medical marijuana?" I ask an unnamed FDA representative.

"I'm looking into this for you," she replies.

Moments later . . .

"We cannot comment on this topic due to pending citizen petitions, other than to say our analyses and decision-making processes are ongoing."

Not much to work with there, though I'm intrigued by the mention of "pending citizen petitions." I press on: "What would be the process needed for medical marijuana to be approved by the FDA?"

"As you are aware, Schedule 1 drugs have no currently accepted medical use in treatment in the United States, and as I indicated before, we cannot comment on this topic of rescheduling due to pending citizen petitions."

My information parade has been rained out. Why so cagey? After all, the FDA approved Marinol, whose active ingredient is *100 percent* synthetic THC (i.e., the stuff that makes pot so dangerous and addictive that it has to be classified as Schedule I). And Marinol, strangely enough, is Schedule *III*—even though no pot plant in the history of marijuana has tested at 100 percent THC. (Even the strongest pot these days clocks in at under 40 percent.)

So my basic question goes unanswered, though the FDA representative does grant me an open invitation to check out the agency's website—anytime I please!

My inquiry at the Justice Department yields similar results: "Hi Harmon—DOJ's enforcement policy on marijuana is in the attached. Thanks."

My attempt at securing a comment from the DC Circuit Court of Appeals—which threw out the ASA's appeal on its rescheduling petition—doesn't go much better: "I'm sorry. I don't know the answer to your question. I am sure there must be subject matter experts out there who would know. . . . Good luck!"

Down and down the Rabbit Hole . . .

At the heart of the approval process is the National Institute on Drug Abuse. Ironically—or maybe not—the organization is funded by the federal government. Catch-22: for the DEA to reschedule marijuana, scientific studies authorized by NIDA have to prove its medical benefits. This is basically like putting the mice in charge of the mousey snacks. In his now-famous about-face on medical marijuana, Dr. Sanjay Gupta pointed out how many of NIDA's studies are actually designed to find detrimental effects—with only about 6 percent, he estimates, looking into medical benefits. The end result of NIDA's efforts: the almost-complete suppression of research into the therapeutic value of marijuana.

"Will Dr. Sanjay Gupta's statement have any impact on rescheduling medical marijuana?" I ask the NIDA rep.

NIDA's response: "The best resource for questions about rescheduling is the Drug Enforcement Administration." (A phone number is provided.)

Reaching deep into my journalist-provocateur's bag of tricks, I try a more straightforward approach: "What would it take to have medical marijuana rescheduled? Clearly we're at a crossroads where public opinion is changing, yet the federal government doesn't want to change its stance. Is it left to further scientific studies or any other factors?"

"You'll need to contact the DEA for questions about rescheduling."

And so I'm back at square one. It turns out that getting an answer from the federal government on rescheduling marijuana is a lot like contacting the local Scientology center and asking them to go on record about the planet Xenu. In the meantime, the Supreme Court recently declined to hear ASA's appeal on its rescheduling petition—the one that the DEA waited nine years to reject, and that the DC Circuit Court turned down on appeal, declaring that only Congress has the power to amend the Controlled Substances Act.

If the federal government is determined to maintain marijuana as a highly illegal Schedule 1 substance—despite overwhelming scientific evidence to the contrary and an ongoing sea change in public opinion—then perhaps its best ploy at this point would be to sit on its hands and do absolutely nothing.

Mission accomplished.

Rescheduling Marijuana

My 17-Year Battle against Marijuana's Prohibition

By Jon Gettman
High Times, October 17, 2012

The proper scheduling of marijuana under the provisions of the federal Controlled Substances Act (CSA) is under review by the US Court of Appeals for the District of Columbia, and the Court began hearing oral arguments on this issue October 16, 2012.

This review is in response to an administrative petition filed in 2002 by the Coalition for Rescheduling Cannabis (CRC), a collection of advocacy groups and medical cannabis patients including Americans for Safe Access, Patients Out of Time, NORML, HIGH TIMES, and patient advocacy groups in California, New Mexico, and Texas. HIGH TIMES has provided legal counsel and additional support for this project since my original rescheduling petition was filed in 1995.

The petition sought a change in marijuana regulatory status under the CSA and argued that under the criteria of the CSA marijuana should be reclassified and placed in a less restrictive schedule in the regulatory scheme established by the statute.

After several years of delay and facing the prospect of a federal court order to take action, the Drug Enforcement Administration (DEA) formally rejected the petition in July of 2011. The current court action consists of a judicial review of the DEA's rejection of the petition. The history of this administrative petition is summarized below in Table 1.

Table 1: The History of the CRC Petition to Reschedule Marijuana under Review by the US Court of Apeals.

Coalition for Rescheduling Cannabis (CRC) files administrative petition	October 9, 2002
Referred by DEA to HHS for review	July 2004
HHS review provided to DEA	December 6, 2006
CRC requests federal court order to compel final action on petition	May 23, 2011
Petition denied by DEA	July 8, 2011
Request for judicial review filed with the US Court of Appeals	July 21, 2011
Petition's brief filed with the US Court of Appeals	January 26, 2012
Oral Arguments before the US Court of Appeals	October 16, 2012

Rescheduling marijuana is a complex subject with a long history and profound relevance to the medical use of marijuana in the United States. Despite the technical complexity of this issue, its relevance is fairly straightforward. Rescheduling has both practical and instructive significance with respect to federal policy and law regarding marijuana.

First, scheduling under the CSA determines specific regulatory requirements regarding the manufacture and distribution of listed substances for both research and commercial purposes. Rescheduling marijuana would move it from the most restrictive schedule under law to a less restrictive schedule, which would expedite additional research and make it easier for states that have authorized medical marijuana use to comply with federal law.

Second, rescheduling would acknowledge the scientific accomplishments that have taken place since marijuana was originally scheduled in 1970 and make marijuana's legal status under federal law consistent with contemporary scientific knowledge about the drug. This would require the federal government to acknowledge that marijuana is not similar, scientifically, to drugs like heroin, cocaine, and methamphetamine in terms of safety, abuse potential, and dependence liability.

Most important, rescheduling requires the federal government to recognize that marijuana has an accepted medical use in the United States.

The nation's drug laws were overhauled in the late 1960s, resulting in the passage of the Controlled Substances Act in 1970. One of the introductory provisions of this Act was a congressional finding that "many of the drugs included within this subchapter have a useful and legitimate medical purpose and are necessary to maintain the health and general welfare of the American people." The purpose of the CSA was to balance the need to produce effective controls on the manufacture and distribution of substances that have a potential for abuse in order to reduce their availability for illegal sales and use. The goal was to create a closed system of manufacture and distribution for these substances in order to prevent non-medical access.

The result was a system of five schedules with varying degrees of regulatory scrutiny. Schedule I provided the strictest regulatory provisions, with access severely limited to research under the strictest conditions. Schedule V has the least restrictive requirements. Placement in the schedules is determined by a set of scientific criteria. The scientific branch of the federal government (at the time, the Department of Health, Education, and Welfare, now the Department of Health and Human Services) would make scientific determinations relevant to the scheduling of a drug or substance, and the Drug Enforcement Administration would make the final decision about scheduling and enforce the regulatory provisions.

There are two sets of criteria relevant to scheduling. First, in order to determine a drug's placement in the schedules the following topics would be assessed: accepted medical use, safety for use, abuse potential, and dependence liability.

Schedule I drugs are characterized by a high potential for abuse and a lack of accepted medical use. Schedule II drugs have a high potential for abuse but also have an accepted medical use. The remaining schedules all acknowledge medical use, but varying degrees of lower dependency liabilities.

The following criteria would be used to assess the topics used to determine placement in the five schedules:

1. Its actual or relative potential for abuse.
2. Scientific evidence of its pharmacological effect, if known.
3. The state of current scientific knowledge regarding the drug or substance.
4. Its history and current pattern of abuse.
5. The scope, duration, and significance of abuse.
6. What, if any, risk there is to the public health.
7. Its psychological or physiological dependence liability.
8. Whether the substance is an immediate precursor of a controlled substance.

The key question, thus, is where does marijuana belong in this scheduling scheme? The rescheduling petition filed by the CRC argues that marijuana does not belong in Schedule I because it a) has an accepted medical use in the United States and b) does not have the high potential for abuse required for this category. Interestingly enough, this was also the opinion advanced by Nixon Administration officials when the CSA was being created by Congress.

According to the legislative history, "The extent to which marijuana should be controlled is a subject upon which opinions diverge widely. . . . During the hearings, Dr. Stanley F. Yolles, who was the Director of the National Institute of Mental Health, submitted a chart of fable and fact concerning marijuana. . . . In the bill as recommended by the administration and as reported to committee, marihuana [sic] is listed under schedule I, as subject to the most stringent controls under the bill, except that the criminal penalties applicable to marijuana offenses are those for offenses involving non-narcotic controlled substances.

"The committee requested recommendations from the Department of Health, Education, and Welfare concerning the appropriate location of marijuana in the schedules of the bill . . . and by letter of August 14th, 1970" the assistant secretary for Health and Scientific Affairs recommended "that marijuana be retained within Schedule I at least until after the completion of certain studies now underway."

This important letter from Roger Egeberg of the Department of Health, Education, and Welfare to Congress regarding the scheduling of cannabis. This August 14, 1970 letter states:

> Some question has been raised whether the use of the plant itself produces "severe psychological or physical dependence" as required by a schedule I or even schedule II criterion. Since there is still a considerable void in our knowledge of the plant and effects of the active drug contained in it, our recommendation is that marihuana be retained in schedule I at least until the completion of certain studies now underway to resolve this issue. If those studies make it appropriate for the Attorney General to change the placement of marihuana to a different schedule, he may do so in accordance with the authority provided under section 201 of the bill.

That was 1970. There have been numerous studies completed since then, but every administration since has declined to avail itself of the ever-increasing scientific record regarding marijuana's incompatibility with the legal requirements of its continuing Schedule I status.

There have been two prior efforts to have marijuana rescheduled. The first rescheduling petition was filed by NORML in 1972. The administration refused to process it according to the provisions of the CSA, and was subject to orders from the US Court of Appeals in 1974, 1977, and 1980 to fulfill the procedural requirements of the statute. After denial of the petition and a recommendation from an administrative law judge to reconsider, the DEA's decision not to reschedule was upheld under judicial review by the Court of Appeals in 1994.

I filed a second rescheduling petition in 1995. It was also denied by the DEA, and this decision was upheld by the Court of Appeals in 2002 on the basis that I was not a medical marijuana patient and did not have standing to take the case to the federal courts. In response to that decision, I organized the CRC and submitted a new petition to the DEA in October 2002.

One of the key scientific developments since marijuana's original placement in Schedule I by Congress was the discovery of the cannabinoid receptor system in 1988. In effect, scientists discovered how marijuana produces its effects on the human body, and this discovery revolutionized research on marijuana.

Prior to this discovery research sought to explain how marijuana affected the body and to confirm concerns that it was a harmful and dangerous drug. Subsequent research, however, has established the opposite—that marijuana is a relatively safe drug with tremendous medical potential. This discovery has produced considerable scientific research in the last two decades—research that fulfills the requirements for marijuana's rescheduling.

Marijuana does not have a high potential for abuse, it is safe for use under medical supervision, and has accepted medical use in the United States. Indeed, 17 states have recognized marijuana's medical use, creating conflicts between state and federal law throughout the country. The CRC petition summarized the scientific record in support of rescheduling as of 2001. That record has continued to expand since then and was largely ignored by the HHS and DEA during their review of the CRC petition over the past decade.

The Court has several legal issues to address. These include the following key questions:

- Can a drug without a high potential for abuse remain in Schedule I?
- Does recognition by 17 states qualify as accepted medical use in the United States?
- And, as significantly, can the administration choose to ignore the spirit and letter of the law when it conflicts with their own policy preference?

Since its passage in 1970 every administration has resisted efforts to be held accountable to the provisions of the Controlled Substance Act, insisting on subjecting marijuana to a policy of prohibition when other, more practicable, less costly, more effective, and less restrictive options are required by law.

Confused about Pot? So's the Law

By Mark A. Kleiman
Bloomberg View, February 14, 2014

Federal law makes it a crime to grow, sell or possess cannabis. New state laws in Colorado and Washington state permit those activities, and officials there are issuing licenses to local companies to commit what remain federal felonies.

The U.S. Department of Justice announced in August that it would give a low priority to enforcement efforts against state-licensed growers and sellers in states with "strong and vigorous" regulations, except where they involve other activities such as violence or interstate sales.

President Barack Obama has spoken out about the harm done by the 650,000 arrests a year for cannabis possession (disproportionately among young minority men). He recently said that marijuana is no more dangerous than alcohol, and that he's willing to let the legalization experiments in Colorado and Washington go forward, though he shied away from an endorsement of legalization nationally.

Critics, including Representative John Mica, a Florida Republican, have attacked both the president and Attorney General Eric Holder for sending "mixed messages," with Mica using the term "schizophrenic." Some Republicans, and some pundits, have charged Holder with having a "pot problem," and with disregarding "the rule of law" by choosing which laws to enforce. Those criticisms are badly wide of the mark.

While there is much to criticize in both the actions and the inactions of the administration on cannabis policy—especially its failure to tear down the unnecessary bureaucratic barriers to research—critics of the Justice Department decision to let Colorado and Washington state go forward with their tax-and-regulation systems seem uninformed both about the facts and the law.

As a matter of law, Section 873 of the Controlled Substances Act orders the attorney general to "cooperate with local, State, tribal and Federal agencies concerning traffic in controlled substances and in suppressing the abuse of controlled substances." Most states have drug laws that track federal prohibitions. But the voters in Washington state and Colorado chose regulation over prohibition as a means of dealing with cannabis abuse; if the state regulatory systems succeed, there will be less drug abuse than if they fail.

A straightforward reading of the law would therefore seem to require the attorney general to cooperate with those state efforts rather than trying to disrupt them, if in his judgment doing so promotes the purposes of the law in controlling drug trafficking and drug abuse. It is Holder's critics who seem to be selective about which laws they want to pay attention to.

As a matter of fact, federal drug law enforcement is a relatively small part of the national drug enforcement effort; about 80 percent of the 500,000 drug offenders behind bars in the U.S. are in state prisons and local jails. The Drug Enforcement Administration has fewer than 5,000 agents worldwide; Colorado and Washington state between them have more than 22,000 state and local police.

The Justice Department could easily have shut down the licensed growers and sellers in Washington and Colorado, but it would simply not have had the capacity to control strictly illegal production in those states without the help of state and local police. Letting the reasonably regulated Colorado and Washington systems operate while going after participants in California's virtually unregulated "medical marijuana" business creates the right incentives for state officials and industry participants; if you don't want federal attention, keep things under control.

The attorney general could reasonably be criticized for not driving a harder bargain with the authorities in Colorado and Washington.

He could have demanded effective measures to keep legal prices high to prevent increases in juvenile cannabis use and heavy use and to curb the risk that state-licensed cannabis will end up being sold across state lines. He could have (and still could) warn state-licensed cannabis sellers that the federal laws will be enforced strictly against any enterprise that engages in active marketing, as opposed to simply setting up a shop and a website and waiting for buyers to appear.

But the choice to work with the states rather than against them was both legally defensible and substantively reasonable.

Given the disproportion between the resources of the DEA and the size of the illicit drug markets, federal drug law enforcement is necessarily selective. Do Holder's critics propose to increase the DEA budget so it can take over all cannabis law enforcement in Colorado in Washington? If not, would they propose to reduce enforcement against cocaine? Methamphetamine? Heroin? Prescription drugs?

A serious argument can be made for cutting back on federal drug law enforcement generally—of the roughly 200,000 people in federal prison, about 100,000 are serving sentences for drug offenses. There's scant evidence that putting more and more dealers behind bars has resulted in higher drug prices or less drug availability. But that's not a case those now criticizing the administration seem interested in making.

Some people on the other side of the legalization debate criticize the administration for not "rescheduling" marijuana, claiming that it doesn't fit the criteria for Schedule I (which also includes heroin and LSD). Alas, Congress in its (somewhat limited) wisdom hasn't created a category for moderately dangerous but medically unapproved drugs. There's no legitimate doubt that some of the chemicals in cannabis have medical value. But "marijuana" doesn't name a medicine, if a medicine is a material of known chemical composition that clinical trials have shown, at some specific dosage and route of administration, to be safe and effective in the treatment of some specific ailment. The huge variations from strain to strain, and from one means of administration to another, mean that clinical trials would have to be done on specific cannabis preparations, not on "marijuana" as a general category. And it's only those specific preparations that would then qualify for "downscheduling."

Even an arbitrary decision to move the plant itself from Schedule I to Schedule II (or even Schedule III) would have mostly symbolic effects. It would still be a federal offense to grow, sell or possess cannabis except as a Food and Drug Administration-approved drug available by prescription. Downscheduling would be a consequence of clinical trials leading to FDA approval and prescription availability, not a substitute for them.

The administration deserves criticism for not tearing down the pointless bureaucratic barriers now obstructing clinical research. The University of Mississippi's monopoly on the production of cannabis for research should be broken, and research projects with appropriate clearances shouldn't have to make special application to the federal government for a "grant" of a few grams of cannabis: a requirement that applies to no other controlled substance, and that in effect enables federal censorship of research efforts that might lead to unwelcome results. But allowing research to go forward is one thing; making regulatory decisions unsupported by research is something else again.

Those demanding that the Justice Department shut down the Colorado and Washington experiments and those demanding rescheduling are alike in proposing national solutions to real problems. We need more coherent marijuana policies, but only changes in legislation—the province of the Congress, not the executive branch on its own—can bring them about.

Obama Just Took One Big Step towards Marijuana Legalization

By Matt Essert
PolicyMic, April 7, 2014

As the nation marches further down the long but seemingly inevitable road of marijuana decriminalization and legalization, President Barack Obama just made things a lot easier. On Friday, Attorney General Eric Holder said that the Obama administration is ready to work with Congress to take marijuana off the federal government's list of the most dangerous drugs.

"We'd be more than glad to work with Congress if there is a desire to look at and reexamine how the drug is scheduled, as I said there is a great degree of expertise that exists in Congress," Holder said during a House Appropriations Committee hearing. "It is something that ultimately Congress would have to change, and I think that our administration would be glad to work with Congress if such a proposal were made."

This is a strong affirmation from an administration that seems to be increasingly moving towards a more lenient, if not open stance on marijuana legislation reform. Under the federal Controlled Substances Act, the attorney general has the authority to "remove any drug or other substance from the schedules if he finds that the drug or other substance does not meet the requirements for inclusion in any schedule." However, Holder didn't say that he would utilize this power and seems more interested in working together with interested members of Congress.

Working together. Luckily for Holder, it shouldn't be too difficult to find interested members of Congress. Though there is still a lively debate on the issue, numerous congressmen have indicated an interest in rescheduling marijuana. In February, 18 congressmen went as far as to send Obama a formal letter indicating their strong desire to reevaluate how the federal government treats marijuana. This came shortly after Obama told David Remnick in the *New Yorker* that he believes pot is no more dangerous than alcohol.

Already opposition. However, not everyone is as thrilled with these changes. Last week, Drug Enforcement Administration chief Michele Leonhart even said that shifts in public opinion, state laws and the temper of the Obama administration have just motivated her to "fight harder" against the spread and acceptance of marijuana in America. But while Leonhart may believe this is her duty, a recent poll showed that an overwhelming majority of Americans feel strongly that the DEA's tactics have been fruitless and punishment should be replaced more often with treatment. Not only that, but an increasing number of Americans are also echoing Obama's sentiment and saying that alcohol is actually more harmful than marijuana.

Currently, marijuana is considered a Schedule I drug, meaning it has "no currently accepted medical use and a high potential for abuse." Schedule I drugs are considered "the most dangerous drugs . . . with potentially severe psychological or physical dependence." The other drugs in this category are heroin, LSD, ecstasy, Quaaludes and peyote—yeah, some pretty serious stuff. Not only would rescheduling marijuana open up the possibilities for much-needed scientific research, it would also allow marijuana-related businesses in states where medical or recreational marijuana is legal to take tax deductions and normalize many of their business practices. Many politicians who've voiced opposition to marijuana decriminalization or legalization point to the drug's current DEA classification as the cause of their concern: don't mess with Schedule I drugs. But if marijuana is rescheduled— as it arguably should be, the DEA considers both cocaine and crystal meth less dangerous—many Americans will likely have an easier time viewing marijuana in a less damning light.

When Holder Says Congress Can Reclassify Marijuana if It Wants, Is He Taking a "Big Step" toward Legalization?

By Jacob Sullum
Reason, April 7, 2014

On Friday, testifying before a subcommitttee of the House Appropriations Committee, Attorney General Eric Holder said he would be "be more than glad to . . . work with Congress if there is a desire to look at and re-examine how [marijuana] is scheduled." *PolicyMic*'s Matt Essert calls Holder's comment, which was first noted by Ryan Reilly at *The Huffington Post*, "one big step towards marijuana legalization." I'm not sure it's a step at all, since Holder, who has the power to reclassify marijuana administratively, essentially said the ball is in Congress' court. Furthermore, if you look at the context of his statement, you can see he mainly was trying to deflect criticism of the Justice Department's response to marijuana legalization in Colorado and Washington.

Holder was responding to a question from Representative Mario Diaz-Balart (R-Fla.), who argued that focusing Justice Department resources in those states on marijuana cases that implicate "federal enforcement priorities" amounts to treating cannabis differently from other drugs on Schedule I of the Controlled Substances Act (CSA). That category is supposedly reserved for drugs with "a high potential for abuse" that have "no currently accepted medical use" and are so dangerous that they cannot be used safely, even under medical supervision. If the Obama administration thinks marijuana does not belong on Schedule I, Diaz-Balart asked, "wouldn't it make sense to come to Congress with some recommendations, some changes . . . if nothing else, to give certainty and consistency, and the American people would understand that the law is applied with certainty and consistency?"

Holder rejected "the notion that we are selectively enforcing the law," saying the Justice Department is exercising appropriate prosecutorial discretion. "If you look at the kinds of marijuana cases that we will bring, or that we are bringing, and what was brought by the Justice Department previously," he said, "I'm not sure that you're going to see a huge difference." As for moving marijuana out of Schedule I, Holder said, "there is a great deal of expertise that exists in Congress," and "that is something that ultimately Congress would have to change." He added that "the administration would be glad to work with Congress if such a proposal were made." That answer did not satisfy Diaz-Balert. "Congress can do what it may," he said, "but

Congress is not the one who has decided to allow or to not go after folks in a couple of states who are . . . selling marijuana."

Diaz-Balert's line of questioning reflects the frequently heard Republican complaint that President Obama ignores the law when it proves to be inconvenient. There is considerable merit to this charge. But Republican presidents have been equally guilty of abusing executive power, and it's not true that the Obama administration's policy regarding state-licensed marijuana businesses violates federal law. The Justice Department has never prosecuted every violation of the CSA, and its priorities in Colorado and Washington are squarely within the executive branch's discretion.

You know what else is within the executive branch's discretion? Marijuana's classification under the CSA. Because of the CSA's reference to international treaty obligations, it is doubtful that Holder has the authority to remove marijuana from the schedules entirely. If that is what Diaz-Balert had in mind, Holder was correct to say "that is something that ultimately Congress would have to change." But the CSA does give the executive branch the authority to move marijuana to a less restrictive category.

Such rescheduling would not be tantamount to legalization—even for medical use, since the Food and Drug Administration still would have to approve any cannabis-based medicine before doctors could legally prescribe it. But rescheduling could have various benefits, such as loosening up some of the restrictions on research, legally freeing federal agencies to speak more candidly about marijuana, and allowing state-licensed marijuana suppliers to deduct their business expenses. Perhaps most important, rescheduling marijuana would advance a more honest discussion of drug policy by acknowledging the arbitrariness of the pharmacological distinctions drawn by the government.

Still, rescheduling, whether done by the administration or by Congress, would not accomplish nearly as much as, say, the Respect State Marijuana Laws Act, which would lift the federal ban on marijuana in the 20 states that have legalized it for medical or recreational use. I think the Drug Policy Alliance's response to Holder's testimony reflects about the right level of enthusiasm:

> Re-categorizing marijuana would not legalize the drug under federal law, but it could ease restrictions on research into marijuana's medical benefits and allow marijuana businesses to take tax deductions.

> "Rescheduling would be a modest step in the right direction, but would do nothing to stop marijuana arrests or prohibition-related violence," said Bill Piper, director of national affairs for the Drug Policy Alliance. "Now that the majority of the American public supports taxing and regulating marijuana, this debate about re-scheduling is a bit antiquated and not a real solution to the failures of marijuana prohibition."

The debate about rescheduling is illuminating to the extent that it focuses attention on how little sense the CSA's categories make. While marijuana surely does not meet the criteria for Schedule I, it's not clear that it meets the criteria for any other schedule either. A lot depends on how you define "currently accepted medical use." Putting marijuana aside, what should be done with a drug that has a low or medium potential for abuse (and therefore does not qualify for Schedule I) but is not a recognized medicine? There is no schedule for such drugs, which in practice end up either on Schedule I (where LSD, for example, is located) or on no schedule at all (currently the status of *Salvia divinorum*). Meanwhile, the CSA explicitly exempts from scheduling alcohol and tobacco, two widely consumed psychoactive substances with relatively high potentials for abuse and no accepted medical use. If Diaz-Balert is looking for "consistency," he will not find it in the CSA.

NIDA's Director Tells Us What We Know— and Need to Know—about Marijuana

By Bruce Barcott
National Geographic, March 4, 2014

Momentum toward public acceptance of marijuana is building. Last year Colorado and Washington became the first two states to legalize pot for recreational use. Alaska and Oregon may soon follow suit, and many other states are considering legislation to decriminalize use of the drug or make it legal for medical purposes. Earlier this year, President Obama himself noted that while he considered the drug a "bad habit and a vice," he did not think it any more dangerous than alcohol.

But how well do we really understand the health impacts of marijuana? At a private dinner party for journalists last week hosted by *National Geographic* and *USA Today*, NIH director Francis Collins voiced concerns: Studies have shown that prolonged use of the drug by teenagers can lead to permanent decline in cognitive ability, and the possible contribution of pot smoke to lung cancer is unknown. "We don't know a lot about the things we wish we did," Collins said.

To follow up on Collins's remarks, *National Geographic* interviewed Nora Volkow, director of the National Institute on Drug Abuse (NIDA).

What are your concerns about marijuana as legal sales begin in Colorado and Washington?

We're keeping an eye on a possible increase in use, particularly among young people. And there's concern about the fact that you're creating an industry whose purpose is to sell marijuana products. The more people who smoke, the more profit they generate. When you have a profit incentive to promote the use of a substance, that could increase the problems associated with it.

President Obama recently compared marijuana to tobacco and alcohol, two unhealthy but legally tolerated vices. Does marijuana belong in that category?

I don't like to say one drug is better or worse than another; each must be viewed within its own context. Tobacco is clearly the number one killer among drugs. On the other hand, when you smoke a cigarette, it doesn't impair your brain's cognitive capacity. That's very different from drinking alcohol or smoking marijuana.

Alcohol can disrupt your coordination; that's why it's so frequently associated with car accidents. It can also make you more impulsive. Marijuana, by contrast, drops your mental state; it makes you slower and interferes with your capacity to learn and memorize. For a young person, whose main responsibility is to learn and study, that can be very disruptive and have different consequences than cigarette smoking. That's why I say each [drug] has to be considered within its own context.

A number of studies have indicated that marijuana smoking holds far greater risks for teens than for adults, especially in terms of brain development. There's also concern over a possible connection between pot smoking and the onset of schizophrenia. But there are classic correlation-or-causation questions with these studies. What's your reading of the situation?

That's a difficult one. Establishing causality with mental illness is not clear cut. What the research seems to show—for schizophrenia, depression, and anxiety—is that if you have an underlying predilection for these illnesses, smoking marijuana may accelerate the disease's progress and exacerbate it. Studies have found that schizophrenics are more likely to smoke marijuana, but that doesn't mean that marijuana produced the schizophrenia.

In any normal person, if you give them high enough doses of 9-THC—delta-9 tetrahydrocannabinol, marijuana's major psychoactive ingredient—you may trigger paranoia. But it's generally short lived. In young people who have a vulnerability to schizophrenia, by contrast, marijuana can trigger a chronic psychosis, which is a much more serious condition. So there may be a connection there. It's a difficult question, because other factors may also be at work. Many people with schizophrenia may also have started smoking cigarettes at an early age, yet nobody suggests cigarettes trigger schizophrenia. In certain people who have genetic vulnerabilities, marijuana use might be a contributing factor for triggering a mental illness. I'm not completely ruling that out.

NIH Director Francis Collins recently touched on the need for more studies on marijuana smoking and lung cancer. What little research we have suggests a much lower risk of lung cancer among marijuana smokers as compared to tobacco smokers. What are the risks to a pot smoker's lungs?

The literature seems to indicate that if you're a heavy user of marijuana, that may be associated with an elevated risk of cancer of the lung. But it has to be very heavy use. For milder use, the risk seems to be much lower. There is some evidence of a heightened risk of testicular cancer, though, which is a fairly rare form of cancer.

The issue with marijuana and the lungs is that when you're smoking it, you're inhaling a wide variety of chemicals other than THC. Now, a tobacco smoker may smoke 20 cigarettes a day, whereas a very heavy marijuana smoker will smoke at most five joints a day. So the amount of exposure to all those chemicals is much greater in tobacco smoking than in marijuana smoking.

Medical marijuana advocates and federal officials do not agree on whether smoking the drug is a safe way to deliver its potential benefits. If THC and CBD have potential medical value, what are the risks of smoking the raw plant?

Some researchers are interested in the therapeutic value of THC and cannabidiol (CBD), another promising compound found in marijuana. But smoked marijuana is problematic as a medicine. You don't want to deliver cancer-causing compounds along with potentially therapeutic compounds.

One of the things technology and science allow us to do is investigate and isolate the active ingredients in a plant like marijuana, and then deliver them to the patient in a way that minimizes side effects. A doctor may have a patient for whom the dumbing-down effect of smoked marijuana may be very adverse. You want to give them the benefits without the harm. This is exactly why we develop medicine.

Heroin is a perfect example. It's a very potent narcotic. But when we're treating pain, we don't give heroin. We develop medications that can be just as effective but don't have the side effect of addiction.

Recently there have been calls to rethink marijuana's classification as a Schedule I drug. Is it time to consider rescheduling it?

Well, that's for another agency to decide. At NIDA, we do the research and provide the evidence that other agencies use to make their policy decisions. My view is that the cannabinoids are one of the most fascinating targets we have for the development of medicines. It's an extremely important area of research. As research starts to emerge showing the possible health benefits of specific compounds within marijuana, like 9-THC or cannabidiol, one could ask if it's appropriate. I think that ultimately the data will determine whether it should be reconsidered or not.

State regulators in Washington and Colorado have been frustrated with the lack of research into marijuana's effect on the body and mind. They're setting limits on THC content in edible products, but have little science to guide them. Should we be doing more research on the basic effects of marijuana on the body and brain?

I think we want that information. We need to do those studies and know more about the consequences of marijuana use. So many people want to polarize the issue: Marijuana is perfect, it cures everything; or it's evil and destroys everything. It's more complex than that. That's why we need science to come in and address these questions.

Are you optimistic or pessimistic about what might happen in Colorado and Washington state? What indicators are you watching?

My prediction is that state legalization will expose more people to marijuana. As a result you're going to have many more adverse consequences, just as we have with nicotine and alcohol—simply because so many more people will become exposed to it.

5

Taxing Marijuana:
Boon or Blunder?

Democratic Representative from Oregon Earl Blumenauer (center) delivers remarks beside Executive Director of the National Cannabis Industry Association Aaron Smith (second from right); Democratic Representative from Colorado Ed Perlmutter (right); and lawmakers, advocates and business owners during a news conference on marijuana tax and legislation reform, on Capitol Hill, June 2013.

Taxation

Marijuana as a Source of Revenue

In the early twenty-first century, much of the debate over marijuana use in the United States shifted away from the drug's status as an illicit narcotic toward the impact the drug would have on America were it to be legalized. This discussion began with a shift in focus from marijuana's recreational use to its apparent medicinal potential. Over time—and in reaction to state legislation legalizing recreational use in Colorado and Washington—the conversation regarding medical marijuana, has become a discussion about legalizing marijuana altogether.

Inherent in the debate is a question of economics. As with other illicit substances, the distribution and sale of marijuana has been illegal for some time and, therefore, offers no economic benefits to the community or for the government. The growing acceptance of medical marijuana and legal recreational use, however, has birthed a new industry—one that, if taxed by the government, could generate significant dollars for the economy. Still, widespread medical marijuana and the Colorado and Washington initiatives are relatively new, and it may still be too soon to determine the revenue potential of a regulated marijuana industry.

During periods of economic uncertainty or stagnation, legislators and other political leaders are often on the lookout for new sources of revenue. Some seek to maximize existing revenue sources by imposing new fees or surcharges for services. Others pursue applying tax codes to new products and services. The federal government has even attempted to tax criminal behavior, as was the case in the 1930s. Though states had taken individual legislative stands against marijuana for decades—Massachusetts was the first to criminalize the drug, doing so in 1911—federal action on the matter did not come until 1937, when Congress passed the Marihuana Tax Act. Congress, lacking the constitutional power to ban a substance officially, used the act to impose a prohibitive tax on the sale and use of marijuana. For importers, manufacturers, and cultivators, the tax would amount to about twenty-four dollars, while those who used the drug for medical and research purposes would pay one dollar. Such a tax would generate a large quantity of tax revenue while at the same time reducing use of the drug, the act's proponents believed.

Prohibitive taxation of marijuana became something of a moot point over the decades that followed. During the 1950s, more of an effort was made to halt marijuana use by imposing criminal sentences for those involved with the drug. During the 1950s, such measures as the Narcotics Control Act included mandatory sentencing guidelines for possession: a first-time violator of the law could receive two to ten years in jail and a fine of up to $20,000.

In the 1960s, the growing counterculture movement continued to use marijuana in large quantities despite the threat of jail time. Ironically, the drug's widespread use gave researchers the data they needed to disprove the prevailing notions about marijuana's influence on crime and mental health. The information gathered largely debunked the stigma surrounding the drug, as criminal behavior and instances of mental illness could not be linked to marijuana use. This was verified in multiple studies, including those conducted by the administrations of Presidents John F. Kennedy, Lyndon B. Johnson, and Richard Nixon. As the federal government consolidated its various antidrug agencies to formulate a unified approach to combating drug use (in 1968, the Bureau of Narcotics and Dangerous Drugs was established but later merged with other agencies to create the Drug Enforcement Agency in 1973), marijuana was increasingly given separate attention from opiates and hallucinogens. Since law enforcement did not view marijuana as an immediate threat to society, state governments began pulling back on sentencing laws and instead issued modest fines for possession of certain amounts.

In the late 1960s, the prohibitive tax applied to marijuana use was also called into question. Academic and activist Timothy Leary and his family were detained at the United States–Mexico border after marijuana was found in their car. As Leary was not registered as a tax stamp holder under the Marihuana Tax Act, he was charged for illegal possession of the drug. Leary challenged the law in court, however, maintaining that, by registering under the law, his Fifth Amendment constitutional rights against self-recrimination were being violated. Leary took his battle to the Supreme Court. In 1969, the US Supreme Court weighed in, unanimously deciding in *Leary v. United States* that the act would indeed place tax stamp registrants under a criminal microscope. The marijuana tax system was subsequently repealed.

Leary v. United States did not, however, halt interest in combating marijuana use. Immediately following the law's repeal, Congress passed the Controlled Substances Act (1970). This law eschewed the prohibitive tax approach and instead created a set of schedules for controlled substances based on whether the drugs in question had the potential for abuse and whether they had medicinal value. Marijuana was designated a Schedule I substance, which meant that, according to the law, it had no medicinal use and was likely to be abused by users. Meanwhile, the political landscape regarding marijuana changed significantly, as Nixon declared "war" on drugs, including marijuana, and groups like the National Organization for the Reform of Marijuana Laws (NORML) pressed for legalization of the drug.

Outside this War on Drugs, however, attitudes viewing marijuana as a danger to public health and safety were not as prevalent. Given the growing prison population and budget limitations common to the 1970s, arresting, prosecuting, and jailing marijuana users was not seen in many states as a worthwhile pursuit. A growing number of state and local law enforcement entities therefore opted to issue fines and decriminalize marijuana offenses.

This attitude changed in the 1980s. A large number of conservative organizations pressed for a return to criminal sentences for marijuana charges. Populist Republican President Ronald Reagan heard the cry and signed into law the Anti-Drug

Abuse Act, which placed mandatory sentences on marijuana possession and dealing that put the drug on the same criminal level as heroin. With the war on drugs back in full force, the notion of taxing marijuana was shelved.

Although the effort for decriminalizing or fully legalizing recreational marijuana use was stymied in the 1980s, use of the drug for purely medicinal purposes opened a new window. A wide range of studies were conducted in the late 1980s and 1990s to explore whether the active ingredient of marijuana, tetrahydrocannabinol (THC), possesses properties of value to treating painful and degenerative diseases. There were claims that the THC in marijuana helped reduce the pressure on blood vessels in the eye and therefore mitigated the effects of glaucoma. Other claims suggested that THC somehow offset the wasting effects of diseases like AIDS (which had by this time taken center stage in America's public health dialogue) and that it stimulates appetite. In light of the intense nausea and loss of appetite associated with cancer and AIDS treatment, this latter property has long been a lynchpin of the pro–medical marijuana argument. In 1996, the state of California took the bold step of embracing the idea of medical marijuana and passed Proposition 215, which allowed for the sale and use of marijuana purely for medicinal purposes.

Despite the fact that Prop 215 directly violated the federal law banning marijuana distribution and use, the law opened a floodgate of similar, state-level laws allowing for medicinal marijuana dispensaries. Between 1998 and 2014, twenty-three states and the District of Columbia passed medical marijuana laws, each of which contain rules for governing production, allowable quantities, dispensary licensure, and applicable fees and taxes. For example, in some states, patients must pay between $25 and $100 per year to register as qualifying patients, while dispensaries sometimes pay as much as $30,000 per year for their licenses. In California, medical marijuana is subject to state and local sales taxes, which range between 7.5 and 10 percent.

The tax revenues generated by medical marijuana are significant. In California, the Board of Equalization estimates that the state brings in between $58 and $105 million annually in revenue from the sales tax on medical marijuana. In Colorado, medical marijuana generated $5.4 million in sales tax revenue alone in 2012. With registry and license fees included, the state brought in more than $20 million. Many of these state programs began with little to no funding for the establishment of dispensaries and related infrastructure. After the first year or two of implementation, however, a large number of state medical marijuana laws became self-sustaining, with taxes and fees more than covering the costs of the programs.

In 2012, the marijuana game was officially changed. Colorado voters passed a ballot initiative to amend the state constitution to legalize both medicinal and recreational marijuana use. Under the law, which went into effect in December 2012—though the first recreational dispensaries did not open until January 2014—Colorado marijuana retailers are charged a 15 percent excise tax, and buyers must pay a 10 percent marijuana sales tax as well as the standard 2.9 percent sales tax. For the first five months of the law's existence, the state reported about $12 million in revenues from retail marijuana sales.

The new Colorado law is not, however, without its problems. When the law was initially passed, supporters argued that tax receipts for legalized recreational marijuana would generate about $33.5 million. The difference between the anticipated and actual revenue figures, analysts say, is due to the fact that, while tourists flooded to Colorado when the law was passed, they brought with them more marijuana than they purchased at stores. Additionally, the fact that Colorado's medical marijuana tax is much less than the recreational tax meant that more Colorado residents were purchasing their marijuana through medicinal marijuana dispensaries at a substantially reduced cost. Colorado, therefore, saw a much smaller revenue figure than they anticipated. Revenue leaders have since significantly modified their projected annual revenue figures.

Colorado's example has inspired many other states to explore legalization. In 2012, Washington State passed a similar law by ballot initiative, but left its already operational medical marijuana program largely unregulated. Local lawmakers, however, have introduced legislation that would level the playing field between medicinal and recreational in an effort to keep Washington residents from taking advantage of the medical system at the state's expense. Advocates argue that such issues can be effectively addressed, while the potential revenues from sales will bolster state and local budget coffers.

Legalized marijuana and the potentially significant tax revenues it could generate are on the minds of voters across the country. In November 2014, Oregon, Alaska, and the District of Columbia will vote on full legalization. During the 2016 presidential election, California, Nevada, and Vermont are also expected to go before the voters with legalization proposals. These states do not necessarily amount to a dramatic shift in government's attitudes toward marijuana—each of the states considering or that have already passed legalization measures are largely politically liberal states. There are many others who oppose legalized marijuana and are morally opposed to the idea of profiting (through taxation) from an illicit activity. This discussion will likely continue as more states take up their own ballot initiatives in the near future.

—Michael P. Auerbach

Bibliography

Chandler, Jamie P., and Palmer Gibbs. "Legalizing Marijuana for Profit is a Bad Idea." *Politix*. Topix, 2014. Web. 19 Aug. 2014.

Deitch, Robert. *Hemp: America's History Revisited: The Plant with a Divided History.* New York: Algora, 2003. Print.

Downes, Lawrence. "The Great Colorado Weed Experiment." *New York Times*. New York Times, 2 Aug. 2014. Web. 19 Aug. 2014.

Garvey, Todd, and Brian T. Yeh. "State Legalization of Recreational Marijuana: Selected Legal Issues". *Fas.org*. Congressional Research Service, 13 Jan. 2014. Web. 19 Aug. 2014

Gittens, Hasani. "High Times: The Next Five States to Tackle Pot Laws". *NBC News*. NBC, 2014. Web. 19 Aug. 2014.

Hartnett, Edmund. "Drug Legalization: Why It Wouldn't Work in the United States." *Police Chief*. Intl. Assoc. of Chiefs of Police, 2005. Web. 19 Aug. 2014.

Ingold, John. "Colorado Lawmaker Seeks Marijuana Tax Review Amid Disappointing Sales." *Denver Post*. Denver Post, 12 Aug. 2014. Web. 19 Aug. 2014.

Kriho, Laura. "Marihuana Act of 1937 Rises from the Dead." *Boulder Weekly*. Boulderweekly.com, 31 Oct. 2013. Web. 19 Aug. 2014.

Lee, Martin A. "Let a Thousand Flowers Bloom." *Nation* 18 Nov. 2013: 23–28. Print.

"Medical Marijuana Policy in the United States." *Huntington's Outreach Project for Education at Stanford (HOPES)*. Stanford, 2014. Web. 19 Aug. 2014.

Rotblat, Cameron, and Zak Newman. "Marijuana and Federalism: An Entwined History." *Yale Undergraduate Law Review*. Yale, 9 July 2012. Web. 19 Aug. 2014.

Stein, Joel, et al. "The New Politics of Pot." *Time* 4 Nov. 2002: 55. Print.

Marijuana Is Legal.
Time to Regulate and Tax It.

By Joni Balter
Bloomberg View, January 8, 2014

Calling all pot-o-preneurs: In Washington state, where recreational marijuana is now legal for adults, political leaders are urging participants in this emerging industry to join the Rotary. Go mainstream. Be part of the business community.

We are just starting to see the first, hard details in the tricky balancing act of transforming an illegal business into a legal one, in Washington as well as in Colorado. With numerous state regulations and considerable watchdogging by the federal government, which still considers marijuana illegal, the big deal about legalization is that it may not be such a big deal. At least not right away.

In Washington, it now seems that tax revenue won't be as plentiful as expected a little more than a year ago, when voters approved legalizing recreational marijuana. Seattle won't be Amsterdam, with pot smoke wafting out of coffee shops. (No smoking in public, no selling in coffee shops.) Pot stores won't be omnipresent.

In Seattle, starting in May or June, consumers will have almost two dozen retail outlets where they can find their herb of choice, with dozens more in surrounding suburbs. There will be up to 334 stores statewide. Even if that sounds like a lot (there are almost 700 Starbucks coffeehouses in Washington and they seem ubiquitous), some rural towns and counties might have only one or two pot shops.

"I think the hype about cannabis being legalized is huge, but the impact on society is not going to be as big," said Randy Simmons, deputy director of the state Liquor Control Board. The pot law follows old liquor laws, which limited the number of stores and prohibited people under age 21 from buying in those stores. "There is a control factor that will take away from the image of a store on every corner and large pot parties in the park every day," he said.

Hundreds of people showed up online on Nov. 18, the first day applications were accepted for licenses. They were Microsoft Corp. veterans, construction workers, farmers, pastry chefs, all hoping to grow or process or to open one of the private retail outlets that will operate a bit like—and, one hopes, not be as ugly as—those boxy, old-fashioned state liquor stores. And, according to the rules, no free samples allowed.

Washington will slap an excise tax of about 44 percent on pot by the time the consumer buys it in a retail store. But the state isn't anticipating meaningful revenue from marijuana for a few years.

"We have to emphatically temper expectations of tax revenues," said Reuven Carlyle, a Democrat who is chairman of the Finance Committee in the state House of Representatives. "This is completely art, not science."

Colorado, which also legalized recreational marijuana in 2012, may get more tax revenue more quickly. Stores there opened on Jan. 1, and existing medical marijuana outlets are allowed to convert to selling recreational pot. Taxes will vary from jurisdiction to jurisdiction. In the Denver area, levies on the final product will be about 30 percent to 35 percent.

In Washington, experts conservatively estimate that the new recreational marijuana outlets, which have to start from scratch, will reach only 13 percent of the market in June, 25 percent a year later and 80 percent in five years. State-regulated stores have to compete with medical marijuana and black markets.

Washington-grown retail giants such as Costco Wholesale Corp. and Starbucks Corp. won't be part of the party. The regulations don't permit marijuana to be sold in stores that sell things other than pot edibles, liquids and paraphernalia.

Jamen Shively, a former Microsoft manager who made a splash announcing a plan for a national brand of marijuana, won't get far here. For one thing, the rules limit the number of licenses investors can acquire.

The state of Washington won't set prices for marijuana, with its many mellifluous and colorful strains. The legalization initiative didn't provide for that.

The market will set the price. Marijuana that costs, say, $10 to $12 a gram on the street today could cost $14 to $18 in a pot store, counting taxes, security and other costs. Or prices could be about the same. It depends on whom you talk to. Over time, legal pot should become cheaper and more desirable.

"There is enormous value in being able to walk safely into a store and know you are purchasing a high-quality, safe product that previously carried big risk," Carlyle said.

Moving people from the illicit marketplace to the legal one is a challenge. Safety is a selling point: State-approved products will be screened for pesticides, mold and bugs. (That black-market stuff has spider mites and chemicals you might not want to know the names of.)

Perhaps the most acrobatic balancing act is between taxation and price. Tax legal marijuana too much, and fewer people will buy it. Tax it too little and public support could wane if minors get a hold of it or if it slips across state lines.

The Department of Justice announced late last summer that it wouldn't interfere with legalized recreational marijuana in Washington and Colorado with several big ifs—if it stays out of the hands of minors, if it doesn't migrate across state borders, and if the states manage drugged driving.

Some experts say law enforcement should ramp up and push illegal purveyors out of the market more rapidly. Local communities might not be able to afford to redirect law-enforcement resources in this way.

"This is the birth of a new industry," Simmons said. "People want this thing to be born as a fully grown adult. But it's still a baby, and we have to nurture it and protect it and help it grow."

Washington and Colorado are the pioneers, adventuring, or lurching, forward; others will follow. Social attitudes toward legal marijuana for adults are changing quickly.

The rollout of recreational pot will hit many bumps along the way. Yet if these states and the new entrepreneurs manage the controlled experiment competently, they will become the model for the rest of the U.S. and for other countries—which are already calling for advice.

Why Legalizing Marijuana
Is a Smart Fiscal Move

By Bruce Bartlett
The Fiscal Times, January 3, 2014

On January 1, sales and use of recreational marijuana became legal in the state of Colorado. Washington State and the nation of Uruguay will follow later this year. Other states such as Oregon and California have ballot initiatives scheduled that may legalize marijuana there as well. It is a virtual certainty that if these initial experiments work out, as was previously the case with casino gambling, it will spread rapidly to other states.

Several factors appear to be at work in the drive to legalize recreational marijuana. First is the abject failure of the war on marijuana, which, surprisingly, began right at the moment when prohibition of alcohol was ending.

Polls are unanimous in showing rising support for marijuana legalization, especially among younger Americans. Opponents are gradually dying off, literally, according to an April 2013 Pew poll.

In October, Gallup found that support among all Americans for legalization exceeded maintenance of the status quo for the first time since it began asking the question in 1969.

Importantly, support for marijuana legalization is not driven mainly by those who use it now or would like to; that is, it's not just an issue of self-interest. Rather, it is because non-users no longer see marijuana as a gateway drug that automatically leads to the use of more serious drugs, according to a December Associated Press/Gfk poll. In fact, a rising percentage of people believe that legalization of marijuana will actually curb the use of harder drugs—17 percent now from 10 percent in 2010.

Perhaps the dominant factor driving marijuana legalization is the desperate search for new revenue by cash-strapped state governments. The opportunity to tax marijuana is potentially a significant source of new revenue, as well as a way of cutting spending on prisons and law enforcement. The California Secretary of State's office, for example, estimates savings in the hundreds of millions of dollars from both factors. The following summary is from a proposed state ballot initiative in California (No. 1617).

Summary of estimate by Legislative Analyst and Director of Finance of fiscal impact on state and local government: Reduced costs in the low hundreds of millions of dollars annually to state and local governments related to enforcing certain marijuana-related offenses, handling the related criminal cases in the court system, and incarcerating and supervising certain marijuana offenders. Potential net additional tax revenues in the low hundreds of millions of dollars annually related to the production and sale of marijuana, a portion of which is required to be spent on education, health care, public safety, drug abuse education and treatment, and the regulation of commercial marijuana activities.

Interestingly, anti-tax crusader Grover Norquist has given his blessing to taxes on marijuana, since it is an extension of existing taxes on cigarettes and liquor applied to a comparable commodity, rather than a new tax per se.

The potential revenue obviously depends a lot on details that are presently unknown—the ultimate price of legal marijuana, which could be substantially lower than the present price in illegal markets; the tax rate; the elasticity of demand for marijuana; and the extent to which states and the federal government permit a legal marijuana market to function without crippling regulation.

A 2010 Rand Corporation report found that many financial estimates of marijuana legalization are simply unknowable since existing research is limited by the availability of data for a market that has long been illegal. A new Rand report on marijuana use in the state of Washington now estimates that usage may be 2 to 3 times greater than previously estimated.

It is not surprising that revenue considerations should be critical in the marijuana legalization movement. That was previously the reason why cigarettes were not banned until the 1920s despite a strong nationwide movement to do so. In the wake of Prohibition, governments simply needed cigarette tax revenue too badly. And when Prohibition ended, the need for new revenue after the Great Depression decimated government budgets was a driving force.

Indeed, according to author Daniel Okrent, expectations of the revenue from taxing legal liquor were so great in 1932 that some people thought it might permit the repeal of income taxes. It's worth remembering that in 1900, taxes on alcohol and cigarettes constituted half of all federal revenues. Indeed, the only reason Prohibition was possible in the first place was that the income tax established in 1913, which was greatly expanded by World War I, would replace the revenue lost from the liquor tax after Prohibition.

The principal opponents of marijuana legalization are industries that presently benefit from it being illegal. For example, it is reported that the beer industry invested heavily against a 2010 marijuana legalization initiative in California that ultimately failed. Other vested interests that currently benefit from the outlawing of marijuana include police unions, the private prison industry, prison guard unions, and pharmaceutical companies fearing that low-cost legal marijuana might replace profitable high-cost prescription drugs such as Vicodin.

I don't have the data to prove it, but I have long suspected that virtually every economist favors the legalization of marijuana and probably most hard drugs as well—regulated as has long been the case with alcohol and, increasingly, tobacco. The famous economists Milton Friedman, Gary Becker and Robert Barro have written many columns advocating legalization, and I am not aware of a single economic analysis in opposition to legalization. I think most economists believe it's just a repetition of the mistake of Prohibition.

I am doubtful that the legalization of marijuana or any other currently prohibited drug is likely at the federal level any time soon. There is no movement in Congress to do so and politicians such as former New Mexico governor Gary Johnson and Baltimore mayor Kurt Schmoke who supported the idea got nowhere. It will happen at the grass roots level in states that permit voters to propose initiatives and at the federal level only after we have enough years of experience to have a good understanding of the consequences. It may take another 20 years, but eventually it will happen.

Economic Benefits of
Marijuana Legalization

By Abbas P. Grammy[1]
Premier Thoughts: The CSUB Business Blog, March 26, 2012

Marijuana prohibition is so controversial that it has become a source of humor in comedy clubs. My favorite comic, Ahmed Ahmed, has made his case for marijuana legalization:

> I dated a girl for six months. She broke up with me over smoking pot. She said, "I don't date people who do drugs; so you have to make your mind. It is me or the pot. Which one is it?" Well, that is not brain surgery! Let's stop fighting sweetie and you tell me where you hide the . . . Doritos. Thank you! (crunch . . . crunch . . . crunch). I will miss you!

> Listen, I am not advocating it; I am not promoting it. Marijuana is a plant. It grows from the ground. Our good Lord put it here. We didn't put the . . . here. She wasn't hearing me though. So, I sat her down one night for three hours and explained to her the story of Moses and the burning bush. She didn't know the . . . story. They said God spoke to Moses through a burning bush. Helloooooo! That is what it says in the book. I believe the bush was burning. Perhaps, it was burning because Moses was smoking it! They say he came down the mountain with a glazed look on his face! No wonder he was lost in the desert for forty years! I can't even go to the store high without getting lost![2]

Fair enough, Mr. Ahmed! Let me now make a *"dismal science"* case for legalization.

A critical aspect of marijuana legalization is its effect on the demand and supply. Prohibition imposes a risk on marijuana production and consumption. Legalization removes this risk. The supply is going to increase as more growers switch to the crop. However, the government can control the supply increase by imposing a sizable production tax, which would cause the cost to growers to rise. In the short-run, the demand is going to skyrocket as marijuana becomes easily available and more people feel like trying it. Though, the long-term effect of legalization on the demand is hard to predict. Consumer taste may gradually shift away from marijuana, as some recreational users choose not to take it, just like many people today abstain from alcohol and tobacco use.

Referring to a study by Jeffrey Miron (2005)[3], more than 500 economists, led by Nobel laureates Milton Friedman, George Akerlof, and Vernon Smith, supported marijuana legalization.[4] They agreed that, like alcohol and tobacco, marijuana legalization generates substantial tax revenues and create considerable public savings for the federal government and state and local governments.

Miron illustrates that the government can generate revenues from replacing prohibition with a regime in which marijuana is legal, but taxed and regulated like other goods. He estimates that legalization generates $6.2 billion annually if it were taxed like alcohol and tobacco. When I adjust this amount for inflation, the annual tax revenues balloon to $8.9 billion in 2011 prices.[5]

Estimated Benefits of Marijuana Legalization (2011 Prices)		
	United States	**California**
Tax Revenues	$8,928,000,000	$151,776,000
Public Savings	$11,088,000,000	$1,414,080,000
Police Protection	$2,550,240,000	$328,320,000
Judicial and Legal	$7,761,600,000	$982,080,000
Corrections	$776,160,000	$103,680,000
Total Benefits	$20,016,000,000	$1,565,856,000

Additionally, Miron argues that prohibition requires direct enforcement costs. If marijuana were legal, government expenditure declines in the area of law enforcement, including police protection, judicial and legal systems, and corrections. He estimates that legalizing marijuana saves $7.7 billion per year in government expenditure to enforce prohibition. Once again, when I adjust this amount for inflation, the annual public savings expand to $11.1 billion in 2011 prices. This benefit is distributed to $2.6 billion for police protection, $7.7 billion for judicial and legal systems, and $813 million for corrections. Of the total public savings of $11.1 billion, $7.6 billion accrue to state and local governments and $3.5 billion accrue to the federal government.

Adding the inflation-adjusted estimates of $8.9 billion in tax revenues to $11.1 billion in public savings results in total benefits of $20 billion annually from marijuana legalization for the United States economy.

Likewise, Miron estimates that California's share from marijuana legalization would be $105 million in tax revenues and $982 million in public savings per year. California's total benefits add to $1.1 billion annually. Adjusting for inflation, California gains nearly $1.6 billion in 2011 prices, including $152 million in tax revenues and $1.4 billion in public savings.[6]

No worries, Mr. Ahmed! Prohibition will eventually end as it did for alcohol in the 1930s. Like alcohol and tobacco use, parents, schools, governments, and the media must educate the youth about the health effects of smoking pot. Education is the best vehicle to control the demand.

Notes

1. Professor of Economics, California State University, Bakersfield, agrammy@csub.edu
2. http://www.youtube.com/watch?v=LfR42upb3KQ&feature=fvsr
3. Miron, J., "The Budgetary Implication of Marijuana Prohibition," 2005, http://www.prohibitioncosts.org/mironreport.html
4. Moffatt, M., "Time to Legalize Marijuana? – 500+ Economists Endorse Marijuana Legalization," About.com, http://economics.about.com/od/incometaxestaxcuts/a/legalize_pot.htm
5. To make the adjustment, I used the average values of the Consumer Price Index for alcoholic beverages and tobacco products for 2005 and 2011.
6. Miron's estimates are consistent with the study by Gieringer, who calculates the total benefit of legalization to California between $1.5 and $2.5 billion annually. See Gieringer, D., "Benefits of Marijuana Legalization in California," California NORML Report, 2009.

Marijuana Legalization Could Be a Tax Windfall for States

By Associated Press
Associated Press, September 19, 2012

A catchy pro-marijuana jingle for Colorado voters considering legalizing the drug goes like this: "Jobs for our people. Money for schools. Who could ask for more?"

It's a bit more complicated than that in the three states—Colorado, Oregon and Washington—that could become the first to legalize marijuana this fall.

The debate over how much tax money recreational marijuana laws could produce is playing an outsize role in the campaigns for and against legalization—and both sides concede they're not really sure what would happen.

At one extreme, pro-pot campaigners say it could prove a windfall for cash-strapped states with new taxes on pot and reduced criminal justice costs.

At the other, state government skeptics warn legalization would lead to costly legal battles and expensive new bureaucracies to regulate marijuana.

In all three states asking voters to decide whether residents can smoke pot, the proponents promise big rewards, though estimates of tax revenue vary widely:

- Colorado's campaign touts money for school construction. Ads promote the measure with the tag line, "Strict Regulation. Fund Education." State analysts project somewhere between $5 million and $22 million a year. An economist whose study was funded by a pro-pot group projects a $60 million boost by 2017.

- Washington's campaign promises to devote more than half of marijuana taxes to substance-abuse prevention, research, education and health care. Washington state analysts have produced the most generous estimate of how much tax revenue legal pot could produce, at nearly $2 billion over five years.

- Oregon's measure, known as the Cannabis Tax Act, would devote 90 percent of recreational marijuana proceeds to the state's general fund. Oregon's fiscal analysts haven't even guessed at the total revenue, citing the many uncertainties inherent in a new marijuana market. They have projected prison savings between $1.4 million and $2.4 million a year if marijuana use was legal without a doctor's recommendation.

"We all know there's a market for marijuana, but right now the profits are all going to drug cartels or underground," said Brian Vicente, a lawyer working for Colorado's Campaign To Regulate Marijuana Like Alcohol.

But there are numerous questions about the projections, and since no state has legalized marijuana for anything but medical purposes, the actual result is anyone's guess.

Among the problems: No one knows for certain how many people are buying black-market weed. No one knows how demand would change if marijuana were legal. No one knows how much prices would drop, or even what black-market pot smokers are paying now, though economists generally use a national estimate of $225 an ounce based on self-reported prices compiled online.

"It's difficult to size up a market even if it's legal, certainly if it's illegal," said Jeffrey Miron, a Harvard University economist who has studied the national tax implications of the legalization of several drugs.

In Colorado, the $60 million figure comes from Christopher Stiffler, an economist for the nonpartisan Colorado Center on Law & Policy. He looked at the state's potential marijuana market in a study funded by the pro-legalization Drug Policy Alliance. The figure comes from a combination of state and local taxes and projected savings to law enforcement.

Marijuana smokers and dealers, he argued, pay a premium now because the drug is illegal, and if government can find a way to capture that excess, tax collections should rise.

"You can basically take advantage of economies of scale, and the price of marijuana will go down and government can come in and capture the difference," Stiffler said.

The biggest unknown: Would the federal government allow marijuana markets to materialize?

When California voters considered marijuana legalization in 2010, U.S. Attorney General Eric Holder warned that the federal government would not look the other way and allow a state marijuana market in defiance of federal drug law. Holder vowed a month before the election to "vigorously enforce" federal marijuana prohibition. Voters rejected the measure.

Holder hasn't been as vocal this year, but that could change. In early September, nine former heads of the U.S. Drug Enforcement Administration called on Holder to issue similar warnings to Colorado, Oregon and Washington.

That political uncertainty could translate into states spending thousands of dollars to defend the laws, critics say.

"I think it's important that this ballot lay out for the voters how much litigation is going to result from this," said Colorado assistant Attorney General Michael Dougherty, a critic of the legislation.

Legalization proponents counter that some of the 17 medical-marijuana states already collect pot taxes in violation of federal law, which does not condone medical use of the drug. Colorado collects several million dollars a year in pot-related taxes, including sales taxes, licensing fees and fees paid by patients to acquire the drug. Oregon last year doubled the cost of a medical marijuana card to raise money for things like clean water and school health programs.

"Marijuana can be regulated, can be taxed, can be sold. We're doing it now, just currently to sick people," said Vicente, the lawyer working on the Colorado legalization campaign.

Backers concede there are big questions about how marijuana would be taxed and regulated, but they are hoping to sell voters on taking the chance.

"We're like *Star Trek*. We're heading into a new world," said Art Way of the Drug Policy Alliance, answering tax questions recently posed by law students gathered at the University of Denver to learn about Colorado's initiative.

In the end, voters deciding the marijuana questions won't be making up their minds based on the impact on taxes, said Miron, the Harvard economist.

"It's small potatoes," Miron said of marijuana's tax implications. "I'm as firmly in the pro-legalization camp as anybody in the world, but it's because I think smoking marijuana is not the government's business.

"That is the question—not whether it will produce revenue, but whether these drugs should be legal."

Marijuana Tax Touted as Budgetary Benefit to US and States. Really?

By Allison Terry

The Christian Science Monitor, March 29, 2013

A federal marijuana tax could potentially pump millions of dollars into struggling state economies, say two US congressmen who have introduced legislation that would create such a tax and also protect state regulation policies.

Representative Jared Polis (D) of Colorado, who introduced the Ending Federal Marijuana Prohibition Act last month, told *Politico* Thursday that his state could see as much as $100 million a year from a federal marijuana tax, which could make a "substantial dent in needed school improvements, particularly in poorer districts."

Representative Polis joins fellow Democratic Representative Earl Blumenauer of Oregon, who has introduced the Marijuana Tax Equity Act, which would create a $50 excise tax on each ounce of marijuana sold.

The two bills would help balance the federal and state budgets, the congressmen say, by reducing how much the Drug Enforcement Agency spends on fighting the war on drugs and also adding revenue that would help reduce the budget deficit.

"It is billions of dollars we spend to arrest [660,000] people a year for something that half of Americans think should be legal," Representative Blumenauer told Fox News last month. He said the legislation would result in about $100 billion in savings and new revenue over the next decade.

But there's disagreement among policymakers and economists about just how much revenue a federal marijuana tax would raise.

If marijuana were taxed in the same way as alcohol and tobacco, estimates for new tax revenue would be closer to $6.4 billion—$4.3 billion for federal coffers and $2.1 billion for the states—not the hundreds of millions others have estimated, Harvard economics professor Jeffrey Miron, a scholar at the libertarian Cato Institute, told *Politico* Thursday.

"This is not a cash cow that can solve anyone's fiscal problems," Mr. Miron said. "There is a lot of exaggeration about how big the revenue can be."

Another factor is that nationwide legalization would reduce the cost of marijuana, noted Rosalie Liccardo Pacula of the RAND Drug Policy Research Center, according to the *Politico* report. She expects prices in Colorado and Washington, where voters last fall opted to legalize possession, to drop by 70 to 85 percent—and thus the value of any taxes levied on marijuana consumption would also drop.

Claims that legalizing marijuana would benefit states and the US economy are not new.

In 1994, Dale Gieringer, then coordinator of California's chapter of the National Organization for the Reform of Marijuana Laws, produced a study looking at the economic impact of a marijuana tax on California. He estimated that a $50 tax per ounce of marijuana, which then cost between $280 and $420, would raise $1.2 billion a year for the state. Plus, legalization would generate $12 billion to $18 billion in other economic activity, his study said.

The inherent problem in calculating how much revenue a tax would raise is that it is all conjecture, Ms. Liccardo Pacula told *Politico*. "You have to know more about the structure of the demand curve, which we don't have any data on because this is black-market," she said.

Polis said he understood the potential risk of taxing marijuana too much: It could drive buyers to the illegal market if the legal price is too expensive.

"You want to make sure the black market doesn't have an advantage over the regulated market because if it does, then the whole concept fails and people will continue to buy marijuana illegally—so there has to be a price advance for the legal market," Polis told *Politico*.

The marijuana tax legislation is unlikely to get far in Congress, but out in the states interest is keener. Colorado and Washington are now debating how to structure their regulatory and tax systems, and other states appear poised to join the discussion. On Thursday, Maine legislators announced details for a bill that would legalize and tax marijuana. According to the Marijuana Policy Project, a legalization advocacy group, similar bills have been introduced in Hawaii, Maryland, Massachusetts, and New Hampshire. Pennsylvania and Vermont are expected to consider similar legislation this year.

Ultimately, Polis said, states should be able to choose how they will regulate the murky system of marijuana production and sales—particularly without fear that the federal government will come in and shut down the new distribution businesses.

"Congress should simply allow states to regulate marijuana as they see fit and stop wasting federal tax dollars on the failed drug war," he said in a statement last month when introducing his bill.

Both Polis and Blumenauer see this as an "inevitable transition of marijuana policy," according to a report they co-authored, "The Path Forward: Rethinking Federal Marijuana Policy."

"Public attitude, state law, and established practices are all creating irreconcilable difficulties for public officials at every level of government," Blumenauer said in a statement last month. "We want the federal government to be a responsible partner with the rest of the universe of marijuana interests while we address what federal policy should be regarding drug taxation, classification, and legality."

Legalizing Marijuana for Profit Is a Bad Idea

It Flies in the Face of Social Responsibility

By Jamie P. Chandler and Palmer Gibbs
Politix, April 25, 2013

The push to legalize Marijuana is going Gangnam style. In the past several months, 55 percent of voters in Colorado and Washington approved a ballot measure making it legal for medical and nonmedical uses, and a slew of polls indicate that a majority of Americans now support making Marijuana as legal as cigarettes and alcohol.

Changing public attitudes is a big reason why the drive to let people legally "toke" up is gaining traction. But the question on the minds of politicians and business leaders is how much money can be made from this new industry?

Earlier this month *Fortune* magazine ran an unusual cover story attempting to answer this question. The article featured a group of West Coast cannabis entrepreneurs who are seeking investments from prominent venture capital firms. These entrepreneurs want to produce and market products that will make smoking pot easy, sexy, and appealing. What's their selling point? Cannabis could represent a $47 billion industry opportunity.

A broader selling point is that legalizing marijuana could help state governments cut their enforcement budgets and generate tax revenue. Since 1970, state and federal authorities have spent billions enforcing marijuana laws, but pot continues to be ubiquitous. Police have not reduced production, and laws are applied inconsistently across the spectrum of socioeconomic and minority populations.

The economic argument carries great weight for proponents. As revelers lit up last weekend to mark 4-20, the annual celebration of all-things weed, it's tough to argue that consumer demand isn't there. Legalizing an already booming black-market industry means the potential for job creation and a fresh source of income for state treasuries scrambling in the age of the sequesters.

However, once you clean the bong, this line of thinking goes up in smoke.

First, just because public opinion and economic arguments indicate otherwise, Congress must ask some hard questions before it changes 50-years of national drug policy. Questions like: why has marijuana enforcement failed? Is the Controlled Substances Act of 1970 fundamentally flawed? And if so, what can be done to reform it?

Finding the answers to these questions is not at the top of the political agenda. Attorney General Eric Holder testified recently about federal policies in relation to the newly passed Colorado and Washington initiatives, and Senate Judiciary Committee Chairman Patrick Leahy (D-Vt.) promised that the panel would discuss federal policies in light of the country's patchwork of state marijuana laws. But there has been no concerted push for broad scale reform similar to the activities associated with the Affordable Care and Patient Protection Act of 2009 or the Tax Reform Act of 1986.

Second, legalizing cannabis for profit is simply a bad idea. It flies in the face of social responsibility. The acquisition of profit is driven by self-interest, not the common good. Business decisions are made based on how the outcome will improve the bottom line.

It wouldn't be long before marijuana companies—likely backed by big tobacco, with its in-place marketing and distribution teams—started aggressive efforts to win consumers. They'll develop attractive packaging, new and interesting flavors and strains, optimal paper to enhance the smoking effect, and compelling advertising campaigns all designed to get consumers hooked.

There will be messages appealing to long-time pot smokers and new pot smokers. There will be brands for youths, college kids, minorities, the poor, women, and urbanites. Smokers will come to believe they can't live without their daily "wake & bake" just as they believe they can't live without their Smartphones or iPads. The mass-market consumption of marijuana will bring with it the same negative and ubiquitous effects we've seen with alcohol and cigarettes: health problems, driving under the influence, and addiction.

Once the industry gets rolling, those celebrated tax revenues will probably evaporate. Just in the last few days, Colorado State University released a study indicating that the tax revenues expected from the Centennial State's newly legal industry will not pay for its regulation. Nor will it bring in a windfall of money proponents promised would pay for new school construction and other social benefits.

Even if the tax projections do pan out, as the industry grows in size and influence, lobbyists will exert pressure on politicians to lower taxes and loosen regulations, just as the tobacco industry has done in the past, to maximize profitability. This is the nature of the interplay of business and politics; for the most part, business has the upper hand.

Other advocates point to the potential of a diminished drug trade—growers, particularly Mexican drug gangs, will no longer have as lucrative a demand for their wares, and dealers won't be engaging in criminal activity because their sales have dried up. But this too doesn't factor in the flip side of business: where one market opportunity ends, another one begins. Drug lords may see a short-term curtailment of their revenue upon legalization, but they'll branch out to sell other illegal substances, like some new designer drug or some drug that has been out of vogue.

Legalizing marijuana isn't a simple, creative way to fill up the government's depleted bank account or strike it rich in a new industry. It will only add to the cacophony of big businesses jockeying for your dollar and competing for politicians' favor. The public needs to take a long-pause before it starts clamoring for the legal right to buy marijuana at the local 7-Eleven. Social responsibility dictates caution.

Colorado's Marijuana Debate Heats up as Activists Argue against Heavy Taxation

By Kristen Wyatt
Associated Press, October 3, 2013

Marijuana sellers and growers in Colorado joke that it's rare for an industry to seek a tax on its own product—in their case, a 25 percent tax rate that goes before voters next month. Republicans, Democrats and large dispensary owners agree the taxes will boost state revenues and pay for the nation's first intense state oversight of the recreational pot business.

But not everyone is happy about the proposed sales and excise taxes, which, if approved, would go into effect when sales begin on Jan. 1.

A few dozen marijuana activists have banded together to oppose the tax rates, saying they're too high and will keep people in the black market. They've organized three joint giveaways, events that don't violate state law as long as the joints are free and recipients are over 21.

Their protests have been spirited. At a Denver joint giveaway this week, activists jeered dispensary owners who support the tax and even Democratic Governor John Hickenlooper, who attended a $1,000-a-person fundraiser to support the tax campaign.

"If we overtax it, just watch. The whole thing's going to collapse and the black market isn't going anywhere," said Larisa Bolivar, a former dispensary owner in Denver and executive director of the campaign against the tax measure.

If approved, Colorado pot taxes would be lower than taxes on tobacco but more than taxes on alcohol. Tobacco has a 34 percent excise tax. Colorado excise taxes for alcohol are 8 cents per gallon for beer, 7.33 cents per liter for wine, and 60 cents per liter for liquor.

The Nov. 5 ballot measure includes a 15 percent excise tax and an initial 10 percent sales tax. State enforcement has been estimated to cost about $7 million.

Still, all sides agree that there's no way to know what the marijuana tax rate should be. Economists can only guess what pot users are paying now and how much they'd pay to shop in a regulated store, not grow their own or shop on the black market.

Economists at Colorado State University have warned the taxes may not raise enough money to pay for the state's proposed enforcement scheme.

In an April report, Colorado State's Colorado Futures Center predicted the rates won't make a big difference in the state budget. The forecasters used a higher rate than the one proposed to voters—a 30 percent combined sales and excise tax—and put the post-legalization price at $185 an ounce, including taxes.

They said that marijuana demand may not spike just because it's legal, depressing a possible tax windfall.

"Revenue from marijuana taxes will contribute little or nothing to the state's general fund," the report concluded. "There are likely to be offsetting effects of those attracted to marijuana or inclined to consume larger quantities because it is now legal and those who lose interest in marijuana now that the 'forbidden fruit' aspect of marijuana use is eliminated."

Washington state, the only other place in the U.S. that has legalized recreational pot, will tax retail pot at 75 percent. That rate was included in the ballot measure voters there approved last year.

Colorado's rate requires separate voter approval because of state tax law. Up to $40 million in excise tax is designated for school construction, with the rest designated for marijuana enforcement.

The architects of Colorado's marijuana amendment insist the taxes are fair. They pointed to a recent U.S. Department of Justice memo that makes clear states need vigorous pot enforcement to avoid federal intervention.

"The country is looking at us, and we have an obligation to create the greatest regulatory scheme we can," said Rick Ridder, a political consultant who attended this week's fundraiser.

They also point out that most folks don't use marijuana, so voters need an incentive to approve the drug that doesn't relate to their personal use.

"It's one of the primary reasons people support marijuana, to get the tax revenue to take this product out of the hands of cartels," said Brian Vicente, a lawyer who helped write the legalization measure.

Some lawmakers this spring feared that Coloradans would reject a tax measure, leaving the state with a hefty tab for enforcing pot sales but little cash to pay for it.

Despite the debate, the campaigns for and against taxes won't be too visible to most. Campaign finance reports filed with the state show the pro-tax side with just about $10,000 raised by the end of September. Those numbers don't include the recent fundraiser but likely won't allow television advertising, campaign managers said.

Pot tax opponents had less than $2,000 by the end of last month. That figure doesn't include an important "in-kind" donation—hundreds of free joints protesters say have been donated by an anonymous supporter. Protesters plan to keep handing out the joints until the vote Nov. 5.

"The $100 Million Question": What to Do with All That Marijuana Tax Money?

By Bente Birkeland
KUNC 91.5, February 26, 2014

The market for legal recreational marijuana in Colorado is booming, and the state is expecting millions of dollars more in tax revenues than initially projected. That has lawmakers grappling with the best way to spend all of that additional cash.

It could be as much as $100 million and there's no shortage of ideas.

While he didn't support the underlying amendment to legalize marijuana, Governor John Hickenlooper clearly has his own ideas on how to spend the money.

"Governor Hickenlooper is very concerned about some of the evidence that points to permanent memory loss for underage use," said Henry Sobanet, Director of the Governor's Office of State Planning and Budgeting. "He believes that an impact like that can affect their whole life for some fleeting moments of enjoyment."

To that end the Governor wants to put nearly $45 million into youth prevention programs. For instance a statewide campaign focusing on the dangers of marijuana, putting more health and substance abuse specialists in public schools, and additional money for addiction treatment and programs.

"I think the question we have, the $100 million question we have in the legislature is are those monies going to the programs that will make the most effective use of those funds?" said Representative Dan Pabon (D-Denver).

He's working on a bill to create a task force to study a long-term solution to the question of how best to spend the money.

"We're seeing a potential projection of a billion dollars in sales for the first two years. I think we're going to have law enforcement issues, diversion issues," said Pabon. "The Governor's budget is a good starting point. You're going zero to 60 on a lot of these so we need to make sure they're ready to implement and use the resources wisely."

It's up to state lawmakers to approve the budget for legalized marijuana–related expenses from education, to public health and law enforcement. Republican representative Cheri Gerou sits on the joint budget committee and wants more details on the Governor's proposal.

"[Be]cause $45 million is a lot of money," said Gerou. "I've never seen a marketing or educational campaign at the state level that entailed that much money. I'm trying not to judge it."

But others are judging it, and harshly.

A leading player in the effort to legalize marijuana, Mason Tevert with the Marijuana Policy Project worries that Colorado will go overboard on its education campaign and end up demonizing marijuana for everyone.

"If funds are going to be spent on marijuana related prevention and education that discussion needs to include alcohol and prescription drugs," said Tevert. "There's no reason to flush money down the toilet to tell adults it's bad to use marijuana."

Budget director Henry Sobanet says there may be some crossovers to other drugs, but says the point is to treat marijuana first.

"We're trying to get in front of the issue by finding the right messaging, explaining what the impacts are," said Sobanet. "I don't see anything we've said that's unfair or contrary to the amendment in the constitution which limits the use to adults, I assume there was a reason for that."

Others worry there's too much money slated for addiction treatment and drug counseling altogether, and say there's a risk in speaking out too strongly against marijuana.

"I think too many times we've overstated the harms and that's what led to youth use," said Representative Jonathan Singer (D-Longmont). "They experiment and then they see it's not as bad as it was actually projected, but then they get caught up in a substance that's not meant for kids."

The Colorado Department of Revenue will release the first round of sales tax figures in early March. Pueblo County is the first county to release their marijuana tax figures, collecting $56,000 in local sales taxes on nearly $1 million in sales.

Once figures are fully available, lawmakers will then begin to move measures through the statehouse, and debate in earnest what to do with it all.

Anti-Pot Group Complains That Coloradans Are Not Buying Enough Pot

By Jacob Sullum
Reason, March 12, 2014

Numbers released by the Colorado Department of Revenue this week indicate that the marijuana industry added $3.5 million to state coffers in January. That includes about $1.3 million from the standard 2.9 percent sales tax, $1.4 million from a special 10 percent sales tax, and $200,000 from a 15 percent marijuana excise tax, plus about $600,000 in license and application fees. Of that total, about $2 million comes from the newly legal recreational segment; the rest comes from medical marijuana, which is subject to the standard sales tax (and the fees) but not the other levies. Recreational sales totaled $14 million in January, the first month in which it was legal to sell cannabis for general consumption.

That's not nearly enough, according to the anti-pot group Project SAM. "It appears that Colorado is falling well short of the state's revenue projection from marijuana sales," say Patrick Kennedy, the group's chairman, and Kevin Sabet, its executive director, in a press release. A measly $2 million per month, they complain, is "far below estimates claimed by both the Governor and legalization advocates." Last month Governor John Hickenlooper proposed a spending plan based on recreational marijuana revenue of $118 million next fiscal year, more than twice as high as projected before voters approved legalization in 2012. If revenue continues trickling in at a rate of just $2 million or so a month, it will fall far short of both projections. But how likely is that?

Before we consider that question, let us pause to savor the irony of pot prohibitionists complaining that people are not buying enough pot. If the first month's tax revenue were a lot higher, of course, Project SAM would still have complained, citing the number as evidence that legalization is transforming Colorado into a state of stoned zombies. Either way, the prohibitionists can't lose: No matter what happens in Colorado, it will show legalization is a disaster.

But is Project SAM right to suggest that annual tax revenue from the recreational marijuana business will be more like $24 million than $118 million next fiscal year? Probably not. Here are a few reasons to think Hickenlooper's projection is more accurate than Project SAM's:

1. A relative handful of recreational pot stores opened for business in January.

2. Thanks to various artificial restrictions on supply, shortages were common.

---

3. After the first harvests of marijuana from plants grown especially for the recreational market, legal cannabis will be more plentiful.

4. Current cannabis consumers who were repelled by lines, shortages, and high prices will start switching from black-market dealers to legal outlets as the supply expands and prices fall.

5. After the initial adjustment period, new consumers will start venturing into the state-licensed pot shops.

Let's try a (very) rough calculation. A RAND Corporation estimate put total marijuana consumption in Washington at something like 175 metric tons in 2013. Colorado's population is three-quarters the size of Washington's, so let's say Colorado's 2013 consumption was in the neighborhood of 130 metric tons. Assuming that the price of recreational marijuana drops toward the price currently charged for medical marijuana as supply expands, it might go for $10 per gram. To hit a target of $10 million in revenue per month, as projected by Hickenlooper, you'd need about $70 million in sales, or $840 million for the whole year. At $10 a gram, that's 84 million grams, or 84 metric tons, which is 65 percent of 130 metric tons, the total pre-legalization market. Since the market is apt to expand as a result of legalization, if state-licensed stores manage to attract half of it next fiscal year, Hickenlooper's projection looks pretty plausible. More plausible, anyway, than $24 million in annual revenue, which means $168 million in sales—in this scenario, about 17 metric tons, or 13 percent of the pre-legalization market.

I've never been a big fan of tax revenue as an argument for marijuana legalization. But it seems to me that prohibitionists cannot have it both ways. If legalization leads to a huge increase in consumption, as they predict, it will generate substantial tax revenue. Whether that counts as a benefit or a cost of legalization is another question.

Appendix

❖

Cannabis Legislation in the United States	
Alaska	Medical and Decriminalization Laws
Arizona	Legal Medical Cannabis
California	Medical and Decriminalization Laws
Colorado	Legalized Cannabis Use
Connecticut	Medical and Decriminalization Laws
Delaware	Legal Medical Cannabis
District of Columbia	Decriminalized Cannabis Possession
Hawaii	Legal Medical Cannabis
Illinois	Legal Medical Cannabis
Maine	Medical and Decriminalization Laws
Maryland	Medical and Decriminalization Laws
Massachusetts	Medical and Decriminalization Laws
Michigan	Legal Medical Cannabis
Minnesota	Medical and Decriminalization Laws
Mississippi	Decriminalized Cannabis Possession
Montana	Legal Medical Cannabis
Nebraska	Decriminalized Cannabis Possession
Nevada	Medical and Decriminalization Laws
New Hampshire	Legal Medical Cannabis
New Jersey	Legal Medical Cannabis
New Mexico	Legal Medical Cannabis
New York	Medical and Decriminalization Laws
North Carolina	Decriminalized Cannabis Possession
Ohio	Decriminalized Cannabis Possession
Oregon	Medical and Decriminalization Laws
Rhode Island	Medical and Decriminalization Laws
Vermont	Medical and Decriminalization Laws
Washington	Legalized Cannabis Use

Bibliography

❖

Backes, Michael. *Cannabis Pharmacy: The Practical Guide to Medicinal Marijuana*. New York: Black Dog, 2013. Print.

Boffey, Philip M. "What Science Says About Marijuana." *New York Times*. New York Times, 7 July 2014. Web. 31 July 2015.

Caulkins, Jonathan P, Angela Hawken, Beau Kilmer, and Mark Kleiman. *Marijuana Legalization: What Everyone Needs to Know*. New York: Oxford UP, 2012. Print.

Cermak, Timmen L. *Marijuana: What's a Parent to Believe?* Center City: Hazelden, 2003. Print.

Chapkis, W, and Richard J. Webb. *Dying to Get High: Marijuana as Medicine*. New York: New York UP, 2008. Print.

Fox, Steve, Paul Armentano, and Mason Tvert. *Marijuana Is Safer: So Why Are We Driving People to Drink?* White River Junction,: Chelsea Green, 2013. Print.

Gerber, Rudolph J. *Legalizing Marijuana: Drug Policy Reform and Prohibition Politics*. Westport: Praeger, 2004. Print.

Hecht, Peter. *Weed Land: Inside America's Marijuana Epicenter and How Pot Went Legit*. Berkeley: U of California P, 2014. Print.

Lee, Martin A. *Smoke Signals: A Social History of Marijuana: Medical, Recreational, and Scientific*. New York: Scribner, 2012. Print.

Martin, Alyson, and Nushin Rashidian. *A New Leaf: The End of Cannabis Prohibition*. New York: New York, 2014. Print.

McKeganey, Neil P. *Controversies in Drugs Policy and Practice*. Houndmills: Palgrave, 2011. Print.

Mosher, Clayton J, Scott Akins, and Taj A. Mahon-Haft. *Drugs and Drug Policy*. Los Angeles: Sage, 2013. Print.

Newton, David E. *Marijuana: A Reference Handbook*. Santa Barbara: ABC-CLIO, 2013. Print.

Parks, Peggy. *Drug Legalization: Current Issues*. San Diego: Referencepoint, 2008. Print.

Payan, Tony, Kathleen A. Staudt, and Z A. Kruszewski. *A War That Can't Be Won: Binational Perspectives on the War on Drugs*. Tucson: U of Arizona P, 2013. Print.

Walker, Jon. *After Legalization: Understanding the Future of Marijuana Policy*. Washington: FDL Writers Foundation, 2014. Print.

Websites

❖

Americans for Safe Access (ASA)
www.safeaccessnow.org

The organization Americans for Safe Access focuses on the legalization of marijuana for medical purposes and research. The organization works to provide training and resources for both patients and medical professionals alike. Reports, booklets, newsletters, and legal-aid manuals highlight the available materials on the website.

Drug Policy Alliance
www.drugpolicy.org

The nonprofit Drug Policy Alliance aims to reform American drug policy—mainly by targeting the highly controversial War on Drugs and advocating decriminalization—and works to promote harm reduction and other treatment policies as opposed to more strident responses to drug abuse and misuse. The website offers numerous publications and resources, from general fact sheets on drug use and abuse, to national and state reports on drug policy initiatives and issues. Unique resources include a marijuana-related stock photo library for media use and a downloadable activist toolkit.

Law Enforcement Against Prohibition (LEAP)
www.lcap.cc

Professionals in the field of criminal justice who aim to reform marijuana laws have banded together to form the nonprofit Law Enforcement Against Prohibition. With a "frontline" knowledge of the War on Drugs, LEAP formed in opposition to the campaign and works to educate the public and lawmakers alike on what they perceive to be the failure of drug policy in America. Numerous videos of current or retired law enforcement professionals speaking out against prohibition are offered on the organization's website, along with publications, press kits, and other resources and materials.

Marijuana Policy Project (MPP)
www.mpp.org

The Marijuana Policy Project, founded in 1995, is listed as the "largest organization working solely on marijuana policy reform" in America. Online, the organization offers numerous studies and reports on issues related to marijuana reform, including drug testing and employment, teen use of marijuana, medical marijuana economics, search and seizure, and recriminalization. Popular brochures and other materials are readily accessible for downloading.

Monitoring the Future (MTF)
monitoringthefuture.org

This website serves as the home portal for the Monitoring the Future study. First implemented in 1975, the study is designed to monitor annually trends among American youth, particularly concerning drug use and abuse. Other topics surveyed for social research in the study include gender roles, educational experiences, media attitudes, and other relevant issues. An extensive list of related publications is available through the website, including relevant press releases, key findings overviews, and journal articles and books.

National Organization for the Reform of Marijuana Laws (NORML)
norml.org

NORML is a nonprofit organization that has worked to reform marijuana laws in the United States since 1970. Specifically stated, their summarized mission statement is to "move public opinion sufficiently to legalize the responsible use of marijuana by adults." In regard to research and advocacy, the organization's website is extensive—health reports, congressional testimony, public opinion surveys, arrest reports, and economic studies are just a sampling of the wealth of marijuana-related information offered by the group online. The website also features a state-by-state directory of laws, chapters, lawyers, and other related data and tools.

Smart Approaches to Marijuana (SAM)
learnaboutsam.com

SAM is a nonprofit, antimarijuana reform and legalization group that advocates for a "third-way policy" that does not include either legalization or incarceration. Two primary goals of the organization are to educate the public about the growing concerns of marijuana usage and to promote a more scientific approach to cannabis-based medicine that does not compromise health. Materials available through the organization's website include downloadable toolkits and PowerPoint presentations, as well as fact sheets and studies regarding a range of related issues, such as marijuana and driving and marijuana and public health.

Index

❖